AFRICA'S
WARS
and
PROSPECTS
for
PEACE

AFRICA'S WARS and PROSPECTS for PEACE

Raymond W. Copson

M.E. Sharpe
Armonk, New York
London, England

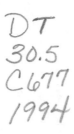

Library of Congress Cataloging-in-Publication Data

Copson, Raymond W.
Africa's wars and prospects for peace / Raymond W. Copson
p. cm.

Includes bibliographical references and index.
ISBN 1–56324–300–8. — ISBN 1–56324–301–6 (pbk.)
1. Africa—Politics and government—1960–
2. Insurgency—Africa—History—20th century.
3. Africa—History, Military.
4. World politics—1985–1995. I. Title.
[DT30.5.C677 1994 [ ] 93-28928]
[960.3′28—dc20 [ ] CIP]

Printed in the United States of America

The paper used in this publication meets the minimum requirements of
American National Standard for Information Sciences—
Permanence of Paper for Printed Library Materials,
ANSI Z 39.48-1984.

BM (c) 10   9   8   7   6   5   4   3   2   1
BM (p) 10   9   8   7   6   5   4   3   2   1

To Donna, Marjorie, and Elizabeth

CONTENTS

TABLES AND MAPS

Tables

Maps

ABBREVIATIONS

ANC—African National Congress (South Africa)
ECOMOG—ECOWAS Monitoring Group (Liberia)
ECOWAS—Economic Community of the West African States
ELF—Eritrean Liberation Front
EPDM—Ethiopian People's Democratic Movement
EPLF—Eritrean People's Liberation Front
EPRDF—Ethiopian People's Revolutionary Democratic Front
FAPLA—Popular Armed Forces for the Liberation of Angola
FRELIMO—Front for the Liberation of Mozambique
IGNU—Interim Government of National Unity (Liberia)
INFPL—Independent National Patriotic Front of Liberia
MPLA—Popular Movement for the Liberation of Angola
MINU RSO—United Nations Mission for the Referendum in Western
    Sahara
NRA—National Resistance Army (Uganda)
NPFL—National Patriotic Front of Liberia
NRM—National Resistance Movement (Uganda)
OAU—Organization of African Unity
OLF—Oromo Liberation Front (Ethiopia)
POLISARIO—Popular Front for the Liberation of Saquiet el Hamra
    and Rio de Oro (Western Sahara)
RENAMO—Mozambique National Resistance
RPA—Rwanda Patriotic Army
RPF—Rwanda Patriotic Front
SPLA—Sudan People's Liberation Army

SPLM—Sudan People's Liberation Movement
SPM—Somali Patriotic Movement
SNA—Somali National Alliance
SNM—Somali National Movement
SSDF—Somali Salvation Democratic Front
SWAPO—Southwest African People's Organization (Namibia)
TPLF—Tigray People's Liberation Front (Ethiopia)
UNHCR—United Nations High Commissioner for Refugees
UNICEF—United Nations Children's Fund
UNITA—National Union for the Total Independence of Angola
UNOMOZ—United Nations Operation in Mozambique
UNOSOM—United Nations Operation in Somalia
UNTAG—United Nations Transitional Advisory Group (Namibia)
UPA—Ugandan People's Army
USC—United Somali Congress
WSLF—Western Somali Liberation Front (Ethiopia)
ZANU—Zimbabwe African National Union

ACKNOWLEDGMENTS

The author wishes to thank the United States Institute of Peace, which provided a grant to fund the research leading to this book. He also wishes to thank the National Defense University, which provided research facilities, advice, and other invaluable assistance through its Senior Research Fellow program. The author is, in addition, extremely grateful to his employer, the Congressional Research Service of the Library of Congress, which offered many forms of support and encouragement. The author is, of course, entirely responsible for the text and any errors or omissions. The views and opinions expressed therein are attributable solely to the author and not to the Institute of Peace, the National Defense University, the Congressional Research Service, or the Library of Congress. Finally, the author thanks Robert B. Shepard, Robert G. Sutter, Donald Rothchild, and others who read and commented on the manuscript in whole or in part.

INTRODUCTION

Africa, throughout the post-independence period, has been afflicted by war. In the 1960s, major conflicts took place in the Congo, now Zaire; Nigeria; and Sudan. Estimates of the number killed in Nigeria alone run as high as one million. The 1970s saw war come to Ethiopia, to colonial Angola and Mozambique, to white-ruled Rhodesia, and to Western Sahara. In 1979, Tanzanian troops and exiled Ugandan opposition forces invaded Uganda to bring an end to the brutal dictatorship of Idi Amin.

The 1980s, a principal focus of this book, were a decade of war over much of Africa. Seven independent countries, including some of Africa's largest nations with the greatest development potential, were seriously affected by war for years—in some cases the entire decade. These included four countries that were already at war as the decade opened: Angola, Ethiopia, Mozambique, and Chad; and two—Sudan and Uganda—that fell into renewed violence as the decade advanced. A festering conflict also began in Somalia and worsened as the decade came to an end. Wars also continued in the non-independent territories of Western Sahara and Namibia.

The 1990s opened amid hopes for a more peaceful era in Africa. The successful implementation of a 1988 regional peace accord in southwestern Africa, the 1991 Angolan internal settlement, the nearly simultaneous rebel victory in Ethiopia, and evident progress in negotiations in other conflicts encouraged these hopes. The Mozambican war finally came to an end with the signing of a peace accord in October 1992.

Yet war remained a major affliction around the continent. Liberia joined the ranks of the war-torn countries as the decade opened, and Rwanda suffered an invasion by exiles that turned into a prolonged struggle. The Somali conflict developed into a humanitarian disaster that eventually compelled large-scale international intervention; and Angola fell into renewed war in the last months of 1992. Rising social tensions in several countries, reflecting political, economic, and ethnic grievances, suggested that new outbreaks remained possible.

This book examines the problem of war in Africa. It opens with a review of the costs that war has imposed on Africa and its people. The second chapter provides a brief descriptive survey of each of Africa's wars, with emphasis on the period since 1980, as a means of providing basic information to the general reader. The next two chapters are devoted to explaining Africa's wars, with Chapter 3 concentrating on domestic factors and Chapter 4 on the international dimension. The fifth chapter attempts to weigh the prospects for peace and war in Africa over the next few years, particularly in light of major changes now affecting African countries and the international system. Finally, the last chapter suggests ways in which the international community might try to influence Africa in the direction of greater peace—despite likely constraints on the resources available for exerting such influence.

AFRICA'S
WARS
and
PROSPECTS
for
PEACE

1 THE COSTS OF AFRICA'S WARS

The costs of war for Africa's people, its cultures and societies, and its economies have been immense. Indeed, measured in terms of deaths, refugees and displaced persons, and lost economic opportunities, African war is one of the great calamities of our era. It is also a calamity in dimensions that are more difficult to measure, including the anguish and suffering of millions, and the destruction of traditional ways of life, perhaps forever.

The extent of the disaster may never be fully grasped, both for technical and emotional reasons. Data on fatalities, coming from remote regions of remote countries, are highly uncertain. Available information must be treated with caution since both governments and non-governmental organizations may have an interest in over- or under-reporting casualty figures. Refugee figures are more reliable, since counts, however rough, can be made in camps outside the war zones; but in most conflicts it has been impossible for outside observers to obtain an accurate picture of the number of internally displaced persons. What may be happening to traditional human societies and to wildlife in the war zones is largely a matter of speculation. And we have no way to gauge the psychic pain of the homeless, the orphans, and the destitute. In short, in attempting to measure the costs of Africa's wars, we must work with inadequate statistics, with dry data divorced from the reality of suffering, with anecdotal information, and with conjecture.

This introduction can only review the available information, reporting ranges of published figures and noting shortcomings where appropriate. Costs can be examined by reviewing the effects of war at three levels: people, cultures and societies, and economies. The materials used in this assessment are primarily the reports and studies that have been produced by academics, international relief organizations, humanitarian groups, and journalists. Despite their inevitable limitations, these materials yield a startling and depressing picture of the ravages of war.

Effects on People

Mortality

Data on mortality in each of Africa's wars will be presented in the next chapter. Overall, they suggest that from 2 million to upwards of 4 million people have died as the direct or indirect result of war since 1980. Just where the true figure might lie is difficult to say, but it seems likely to be in the upper end of the range for two reasons. First, the death toll in recent fighting in some countries—particularly Sudan and Angola—is highly uncertain and could eventually add large numbers to the total. Second, studies completed by UNICEF for Angola and Mozambique,[1] which compare child mortality in the afflicted countries with child mortality in similar but peaceful countries, give much larger fatality estimates than those ordinarily published. If such studies were completed and accepted for the other wars, the mortality estimate for the continent as a whole could be multiplied more than twice.

For the sake of analysis, however, let us say provisionally that 3 million people have died in Africa as a result of war since 1980. According to one study, worldwide war-related deaths, civilian and military, totaled 141.9 million for the period 1500–1990.[2] Deaths in Africa's wars just since 1980 may thus approximate 2 percent of all deaths in wars in the entire modern era—surely a large enough proportion to qualify these wars as a global disaster.

War and Famine

The role of war in promoting famine was a major factor contributing to the high mortality in Africa. Africa's food producers, including settled agriculturists and nomadic herders, were often the primary victims of war, and this reality struck a major blow at food output. The farmers and herders of southern Sudan gave up their normal activities over wide areas and crowded into towns, where they waited for unreliable deliveries of food aid. In Eritrea, vegetable gardening became a dangerous activity, best done at night when the Ethiopian air force was off duty. In Mozambique, the productive Zambezi valley was rendered highly insecure by war, and thousands of Mozambican farmers became refugees or displaced persons, dependent on food aid.

In ordinary times, Africa's food shortages could be made up by food aid or by transferring food from productive areas to areas of shortage. The great drought that struck wide areas of the continent in 1982–1984 disrupted farming in many countries, but most food shortages were dealt with by food relief and the workings of the local economy. The countries that suffered actual famine were all victims of war: Sudan, Ethiopia, Mozambique, and Angola.[3] Similarly, in 1992, drought again struck several countries in southern Africa and the Horn, but it was only war-torn Somalia that suffered hundreds of thousands of famine deaths. There was also widespread hunger during this drought in southern Sudan and Mozambique, but war in these countries made it impossible for the world's media to penetrate remote areas and report on the extent of suffering.

In countries undergoing both war and drought, roads are typically cut by combatants, while relief trucks and planes become subject to attack. Relief workers fall under suspicion of helping one side or another, and both governments and guerrillas interfere with their activities. What should have been fairly ordinary relief operations in Sudan in 1988, for example, became matters of heroism and daring, as pilots spiraled their Hercules transports down into Juba and other towns. Truck drivers from Kenya and Uganda gave their lives in the relief operations in southern Sudan, while to the north other drivers working for relief agencies were undertaking hazardous journeys by night across the Sudanese border into Ethiopia to bring food to the civilian victims of another war. In April 1988, as 3 million people in northern Ethiopia were facing severe food shortages, President Mengistu Haile Mariam expelled most foreign relief workers from the region. Meanwhile, the Ethiopian government was giving priority at its ports and airfields to military cargoes, hampering famine relief deliveries.

In short, there was a synergism between war and drought in precipitating famine. In northern Ethiopia particularly, recurrent drought combined with the disruptions of war to create major hunger crises. This happened in late 1984, 1987, 1988, and again in late 1989. Drought was often a factor in other hunger situations, but it was war that turned drought into famine. War alone, however, could cause hunger and starvation, as was amply demonstrated as hunger deaths continued in southern Sudan, even after the return of good rains, because farmers and herders could not return to their work. Indeed, war could at times work synergistically with good weather to add to Africa's food production problems. The locust swarms that attacked crops over wide areas of Sahelian Africa in 1988 got their start, at least in part, when rain returned in 1986 and 1987 to areas of Chad, Sudan, and Ethiopia, whose locust control programs had broken down because of war.[4]

Injuries

Data on injuries in Africa's wars are almost wholly lacking, but it must be presumed that many countries will bear a heavy burden in caring for the wounded and lame for years to come. Some will be unable to care for them, and their misery, as a result, will be very great indeed.

Injuries to civilians caused by land mines in Angola did receive some attention and were numbered at above 10,000 by the U.S. Department of State in 1987.[5] Other estimates, in 1989, were running at between 20,000 and 50,000.[6] Many of the victims were productive farmers who suddenly became burdens on their communities after encountering mines in their fields or on rural paths. A report from southern Sudan late in the decade spoke of an increase in injuries from hyena attacks on living humans.[7] The hyenas had evidently developed a taste for human flesh after eating corpses on the battlefield. Many of those attacked did not live because of a shortage of antibiotics under wartime conditions.

Refugees and Displaced Persons

The toll of war on Africa's people is revealed in part in the statistics on refugees and displaced persons. These are people who have been forced to leave their farms and villages, as well as their homes and most of their possessions, and trek long distances in search of safety.

Table 1.1

Africa's Wars as Sources of Refugees and Internally Displaced Persons, 1992

War	Refugees	Displaced persons
Mozambique	1,725,000[a]	3,500,000
Somalia	864,800[a]	2,000,000
Ethiopia and Eritrea	834,800	600,000
Liberia	599,200[a]	600,000
Angola	404,200	900,000
Sudan	263,000	5,000,000
Rwanda	201,500[a]	350,000
Sierra Leone (de-stabilized by Liberia conflict)	200,000[a]	200,000
Western Sahara	165,000[b]	-
Chad	24,000[a]	-
Totals	**5,281,500**	**13,150,000**

Source: U.S Committee for Refugees, *World Refugee Survey*, 1993 (Washington, D.C.: U.S. Committee for Refugees, 1993), 52.
[a]Indicates that sources may vary significantly in number reported (*World Refugee Survey*).
[b]This is the number given by the Algerian government and used by relief agencies. The U.S. government estimate has been 50,000.

The pictures of these emaciated, destitute, and often nearly naked people have formed an indelible impression on minds and hearts in the developed nations.

The number of African refugees, that is, people who have left their country and fled across an international boundary, grew steadily through the 1980s, reaching 3.6 million in 1988. By the end of 1990, more than 5.2 million refugees were being reported, and there were still 5 million at the end of 1992 (see Table 1.1). The slight drop came about in part because the end of the war in Ethiopia allowed some Ethiopian refugees to return home. At the same time, the new regime in Ethiopia was unsympathetic to the Sudanese refugees taking shelter in southwestern Ethiopia, and many thousands were forced back into Sudan prematurely to face famine and continuing civil war.

Some of Africa's refugee populations were more fortunate than other victims of war. After their flight had ended, they found their way to camps where they received relief assistance provided by the host country, private agencies, and international donors. Over time, and with the help the UN High Commissioner for Refugees (UNHCR) as well as other refugee relief organizations, they could resume lives that were reasonably stable and secure. Western Sahara refugees in Algeria, for example, have been dependent on outside aid for years, but at least they are living in organized settlements with schools, farms, and health centers.

Toward the end of the 1980s, however, relief workers began to report a deterioration in many of Africa's refugee camps due to over-crowding and limited international resources for responding to the growing need. The problem was most serious in the Horn of Africa, where feeding and education programs for refugees in Ethiopia and Sudan deteriorated sharply. The health of northern Somali refugees, many of them town dwellers who had been well nourished and had some personal resources, reportedly declined in the Ethiopian refugee camps where they had taken shelter in 1988. At the same time, 20,000 southern Sudanese boys were crowded into Fugnido Camp, Ethiopia, in 1988, where food, soap, and medicines were in short supply and little education was taking place.[8] These boys were expelled from Ethiopia in 1991 to become hapless wanderers in the marshes of southern Sudan. Threatened by a government offensive in 1992, they trekked on to another camp in northern Kenya, suffering hunger, dehydration, and sometimes death along the way. Overall, some 250,000 refugees from Ethiopia, Somalia, and Sudan flooded into ill-prepared camps in northern Kenya in 1991 and 1992, creating a crisis in sanitation and health care.

Ethiopian refugees in camps in northern Somalia became caught up in the Somali war at the end of the 1980s. Many were conscripted into the Somali army, and the camps themselves came under guerrilla attack.[9] These refugees were southern Somali by ethnic origin and had fled Somali-inhabited parts of Ethiopia. Their presence in the north was resented by northerners, who regarded them as part of a southern plan to colonize the area.

Displaced persons, or "internal refugees," who have abandoned their homes but remained within their own countries, typically suffered even more severely than Africa's refugees. These people often escaped the notice of the outside world to live for years in misery. In Mozambique, for example, there were nearly 2 million displaced persons by 1991, and many were taking shelter in makeshift camps, abandoned railroad cars, and shacks in contested areas that were often as dangerous as those they had left. In Sudan, a million to a million and a half southern refugees were living in slums around the capital at Khartoum at the end of the 1980s. Some were encamped on garbage dumps, and all were subject to repeated harassment by the Sudanese authorities. In 1991, the government launched a new effort to force these internal refugees away from the capital to remote locations where they would be hard-pressed to survive. In the south itself, many tens of thousands of other displaced civilians remain trapped in the region's towns by the fighting.

Determining the number of internal refugees is a difficult task, and estimates are usually published only as broad ranges. Governments do not encourage efforts to count the displaced, since doing so would expose official failures in dealing with the human consequences of war. In any event, most live in war zones, remote rural areas, and urban slums where conditions do not permit a count. The U.S. Committee for Refugees, however, estimates that roughly 13 million were displaced by Africa's wars at the end of 1992 (Table 1.1), a number that, when added to the 5 million refugees, reveals the magnitude of Africa's suffering. These 18 million refugees and displaced persons exceeded the population of Ghana and approximated the combined populations of New York City, Los Angeles, and Chicago.

Children

The harm being done to large numbers of children by African war has been a special source of concern, both from a humanitarian point of view and because of its implications for Africa's future. The death of many thousands of children is itself a dispiriting aspect of Africa's wars. UNICEF estimates that in Angola and Mozambique, 850,000 children who would otherwise have lived, died because of war between 1980 and 1988.[10] Comparable data have not appeared for other wars, but since the wars in Ethiopia, Sudan, and Uganda were roughly comparable in scale to those in Angola and Mozambique, the toll among children must have been staggering. In Somalia, the death toll among children evidently reached unprecedented levels in 1992— in the town of Bardera, for example, some 62 percent of children under age five died between April and December 1992, according to relief workers.[11]

For those who lived, the lack of proper schooling, nutrition, or health care was certain to blight their lives—and the lives of their nations—even if the wars that had taken away their childhoods came to an end. In Mozambique, 36 percent of the schools operating in 1981 were closed by 1987.[12] Primary school enrollment in Angola fell from 66 percent in 1982 to 50 percent at the end of the decade.[13] While guerrilla movements often make a point of their efforts to promote literacy and primary education, it must be assumed that little genuine education took place over much of northern Ethiopia, southern Sudan, and rural Angola in the 1980s. In Somalia, all schools, from primary through university level, were closed down as fighting intensified at the beginning of the 1990s.[14]

Numerous instances in which children saw their parents killed and their villages burned were reported from Uganda, Mozambique, and Sudan,[15] and no doubt occurred elsewhere. Some southern Sudanese families reportedly pawned their children to others, into a sort of slavery, in order to help the children survive. The long-term psychological consequences of this alienation and exposure to violence are likely to be severe. A study of compositions by school children between the ages of thirteen and fifteen in Kampala, Uganda, in 1985 found that 49 percent had been exposed to shooting and 33 percent to looting during the fighting there, while 43 percent had been forced to flee their homes at one time or another.[16] High levels of aggression and desire for revenge were manifested in the essays. Many children reported having seen police and soldiers—summoned to protect against violence— engage in violence and looting themselves. As a result of such experiences, the children could not discriminate between legitimate forces of authority and outlaws; their sense of justice and ability to differentiate right and wrong were blurred.[17] The ability of children who have suffered in this way to realize their own potential, or to contribute fully in a peacetime civil society, is in question.

Resistance armies, and in some instances government armies, were reliably reported to have recruited boys as soldiers during the 1980s, and this too seemed certain to lead to problems for the individual and society. RENAMO (Mozambique National Resistance) guerrillas in Mozambique, in training kidnapped boys to be child soldiers, reportedly made it a policy to beat and humiliate them, to make them watch violent punishments and executions, and to require some to kill captives.[18] The risk of future violent behavior by children who have already killed is probably high. Moreover, children who have grown used to holding the power of life and death over adults are likely to have difficulty in resuming a subordinate role if peace should ever come.[19]

Human Rights

A consistent pattern of human rights violations is a typical feature of war, and Africa's wars have not been an exception. In addition to violations of civil liberties as both sides try to strengthen their grip on the population, war has brought deprivation of life and liberty on a massive scale, as well as widespread violations of personal security and integrity. The mortality and refugee statistics make this clear.

Reports based on interviews with refugees from the wars in Angola and Mozambique appeared at the end of the 1980s and described extensive human rights violations in those conflicts.[20] According to the Mozambique study, which was prepared by a consultant and published by the U.S. Department of State in 1988, the RENAMO resistance forces had engaged in a pattern of atrocities against civilians, "including summary executions, mass kidnappings, forced labor, rapes, robbery, mass murders, mutilations, and torture."[21] The U.S. Department of State affirmed in 1989 that "[a]trocities by RENAMO against defenseless civilians have been well documented from a number of governmental and nongovernmental sources, including missionaries, international organizations, and emergency relief workers."[22] The Mozambican government was also held responsible for serious human rights violations, but over time, the regime took steps to improve its performance. Expropriated church property was returned, for example, and many people detained under security laws were pardoned.[23]

A report on the situation in Angola published in 1989 by Africa Watch, a private human rights monitoring group, was critical of both sides in the conflict. The study reported indiscriminate use of land mines, the taking of hostages and other captives and prisoners of war, targeted killings and indiscriminate attacks, and attacks on possessions indispensable for the survival of the civilian population. It concluded that "UNITA [the anti-government resistance] and Angolan government forces (FAPLA) have engaged in gross violations of the laws of war causing deaths, injuries, and great hardships to the civilian population."[24] As the 1980s drew to a close, a vicious controversy began to swirl around UNITA leader Jonas Savimbi after allegations surfaced in London concerning murder, torture, and witchcraft within the movement.[25] Indeed, by 1992, after a new wave of allegations, U.S. secretary of state James Baker felt constrained to write to Savimbi seeking clarification of the charges. Allegations that Savimbi had ordered the death of a close associate and his entire family, including children, were particularly damaging to UNITA. Savimbi finally acknowledged rights abuses in the movement but blamed them on others.[26]

In Namibia, South Africa ruled with a heavy hand during long years of war, and there were numerous allegations of human rights abuses on the part of South African troops and their local allies. Human rights abuses by the Southwest African People's Organization (SWAPO) had been reported for some years prior to the 1988 settlement[27] and began to be documented as refugees returned for the 1989 voting.[28] Detentions, beatings, and executions appear to have occurred in SWAPO camps. In Sudan, the arming of southern militias by the government received outside condemnation because of the attacks on civilians, primarily Dinka, and even slave-trading that ensued.[29] Groups supported by the Sudan People's Liberation Army (SPLA) were accused of similar crimes.[30] Despite denials, it is clear that both sides had interfered with the delivery of food to starving civilians in the south.[31]

In Ethiopia, where the government's human rights record was regarded as "deplorable"[32] throughout the 1980s, indiscriminate attacks on civilian targets in the north, torture of suspected guerrilla sympathizers, and forcible recruitment—among other abuses—were widely reported.[33] Allegations of human rights violations were also made against the guerrillas, and it is at least clear that they engaged in forcible recruitment, sometimes killing those who stood in their way. The U.S. Department of State reported a 1988 incident in which one resistance group may have killed up to 100 civilians who were trying to block the recruitment of young Afar tribesmen.[34] Foreign aid and relief workers were also kidnapped by guerrillas from time to time.

In Somalia, the violent government response to opposition in the north in the late 1980s became a special focus of human rights advocacy groups.[35] During the fighting in Chad, government, guerrilla, and Libyan violence against civilians, as well as extra-judicial executions, were an ongoing problem.[36] In Western Sahara, which had been essentially stabilized by decade's end, civilians continued to be more closely monitored by security forces than in Morocco proper, and those suspected of sympathies with the Popular Front for the Liberation of Saquiet el Hamra and Rio de Oro (POLISARIO) were harshly treated.[37]

Effects on Cultures and Societies

The long-term effect of Africa's wars on the continent's cultures and societies is a largely unresearched field, but one of great significance. Whether cultures can survive such massive disruptions is an important issue in itself, at least for those who would preserve cultural diversity among the world's peoples. Moreover, severe cultural damage, to the degree that it has occurred, will surely hamper efforts to restore peace and normal ways of life when political settlements are arranged. Unfortunately, most of the information available on these subjects is anecdotal or speculative.

Large-scale killing, the breakup of communities, and the exodus of refugees must have had serious consequences for rural cultural practices and artistic expression during the 1980s. Many thousands of Africa's rural orphans must never have seen a traditional dance or heard the stories of their ancestors because of the disruptions caused by war. Ceremonies marking critical stages in the passage of life must not have been observed in hundreds of villages over wide stretches of territory in Sudan and Mozambique, and could well be forgotten.

The suffering, death, and dislocation among the Dinka in southern Sudan make it difficult to imagine how their traditional way of life, based on cattle herding, can be restored. In Uganda, disruptions in the life of the Karamojang, and their herding/rustling culture, have been documented. Automatic weapons, which became available because of war, made traditional rustling—formerly conducted with knives, sticks, and primitive guns—suddenly more deadly. Some groups were left destitute, and government efforts to control the violence displaced most of the population in southern Karamoja in 1984.[38] Meanwhile, the rustling and raiding spilled over into neighboring Kenya, provoking counter-raids and incidents between the armed forces of the two countries.

Cultural damage may not have been so great among refugees who found their way into camps—or at least into those camps that received adequate support from donors. The enforced idleness of camp life, however, must be destructive of traditional ways of earning a livelihood. Should the Western Saharan refugees return from Morocco, for example, would they wish to resume a nomadic way of life, or be able to do so, after years of dwelling in tent towns and living on donated food and crops grown in internationally funded irrigated agriculture projects? Nomads survive through their intimate knowledge of the land and rainfall patterns. With the passage of time and the deaths of the senior members of the community, this knowledge may have been lost. Thus, it may well be that when there is finally a settlement in Western Sahara, the culture of its traditional peoples will have profoundly changed.

Economic Effects

Africa's wars have had serious economic consequences for the countries concerned and for their regions. Governments, of course, have had to face the day-to-day costs of running a war, which in some instances have been crippling. Disruptions to agriculture, transportation, mining, and industry have further drained national economies. To these burdens must be added the lost opportunities for growth and development. Vast development projects have been stalled, investors deterred, and foreign aid either lost or diverted to relief. Indeed, there could be no serious thought of development in the countries undergoing major wars, and even the lesser wars have severely dimmed development prospects.

The immediate budgetary consequences of war for governments are difficult to measure. It is hard to determine how much of a government's defense budget is attributable to a war, as opposed to the ordinary costs of maintaining an army. Moreover, it is difficult to know how much a country is paying for the means to wage war. The weapons used in Africa during the 1980s were typically First World surplus, often provided at low cost, or at no cost, by a friendly foreign supplier. Soldiers, drawn from the ranks of the unemployed, were paid very little, although information on exactly how much or how often is difficult to obtain. Journalists, no doubt basing their estimates on conversations with officials and diplomats, coincidentally came up with the figure of $1 million per day each for the wars in Sudan, Namibia, and Western Sahara when these conflicts were at their height.[39] The coincidence itself suggests that the figure must be a very rough estimate indeed. If roughly accurate, however, a cost of this magnitude multiplied out over several years represents a substantial burden for less developed countries.

Yet a $1 million per day figure may well be too low for some wars. President Mengistu, addressing the November 1988 party congress in Ethiopia, stated that defense expenditure had grown to half the national budget because of the war, and some observers believed that the true figure was higher. Rough calculations based on the unsatisfactory available data suggest that this would place the cost of the war to the government at between $750 million and $1 billion annually. One billion dollars was more than the development assistance, food aid, and emergency relief given by the United States in all of sub-Saharan Africa in 1987,[40] and it is an amount that would have contributed significantly to Ethiopia's development if it had been spent for development purposes. Sudan's massive debts by the end of the 1980s, which at $12.1 billion (plus $3 billion in arrears[41]) were the highest in Africa among the non–oil producers, hint at the substantial budgetary consequences that war can have.

War struck at production and transport facilities in Africa during the 1980s, closing them down or necessitating government expenditure to keep them open. A list of major facilities that were closed by war included the Benguela railway, which once brought the minerals of southern Zaire and Zambia to the Angolan port at Lobito; the Nacala railway, which connected landlocked Malawi to a Mozambican port on the Indian Ocean; the Cabora Bassa hydroelectric project in southern Mozambique; and the Nile in southern Sudan. The Beira corridor in Mozambique was kept open only at great cost to Zimbabwe, which provided troops as guards until 1993, when the task was taken over by United Nations peacekeepers.

Normal transportation on Mozambique's other railways could not be restored during the war, despite assistance from Zimbabwe and external donors, and road travel was highly unsafe. An estimated 1,300 trucks, buses, and tractors had been destroyed, and much of the modern agricultural system was in ruins. As a result, the economy had con-

tracted by one-third between 1981 and 1987, and export earnings had
fallen to 35 percent of their 1981 level.[42] While war damaged ongoing
economic activities, it also clamped a lid on hopes for development.
Construction on a major oil pipeline project at Sudan's oil fields at
Bentiu, and on the vast Jonglei canal scheme, came to a halt because of
war, disappointing those who had thought in the 1970s that the country
was on the verge of takeoff as the "breadbasket" of the Middle East.[43]
In Ethiopia, the Italian government sharply scaled back its Tana-Beles
project, which was to bring water from Lake Tana to a potentially
fertile valley, after five Italian nationals were captured by guerrillas in
the area in 1987 and 1988.

As a general rule, donors and investors are not likely to be very
interested in major projects while a war is under way. Substantial
foreign funds may come in, but they are likely to go for relief or for
projects that are not optimal from an economic point of view. In Mozambique, donors helped establish "green zones" around Maputo and
Beira, for example, in order to supply fresh vegetables while the war
continued. If it were not for the war, Mozambique would have been
growing plenty of vegetables without foreign aid and using its development assistance funds in projects giving higher returns.

Effects on Wildlife

War is highly destructive of wildlife, one of Africa's great natural
resources. In Kenya and Zimbabwe, wildlife makes an important contribution to the economy because of the tourists it draws, and the
potential for wildlife-centered tourism exists in several of the countries
suffering from war. Wildlife products, moreover, can be significant
and reliable foreign exchange earners if they are harvested in carefully
monitored conservation programs. But the potential for preserving
wildlife in the countries affected by war was severely damaged during
the 1980s.

Wildlife was harmed in various ways, including direct attacks by
armed forces. One elephant expert who visited war-torn Chad in the
mid-1980s reported "eyewitness accounts of complete herds being
eliminated using helicopters and anti-aircraft guns mounted on vehicles," and "descriptions of large military trucks loaded with ivory"
destined for Libya.[44] Such attacks were sometimes wanton slaughters,
as happened in Uganda in the previous decade, but contending forces

also killed wildlife in order to raise funds through the sale of ivory and other trophies. Reported illegal ivory exports from southern Sudan[45] may have fallen into this category, and there were repeated allegations of exports of ivory harvested by UNITA and RENAMO through South Africa.[46] Savimbi himself acknowledged selling ivory to South Africa to pay for arms.[47] A Cuban commander, General Arnaldo Ochoa Sánchez, was accused, after returning home from duty in Angola, of ivory smuggling for private gain, and this was one of the charges that led to his execution. The charges against Ochoa may have been trumped up as part of a political intrigue, but they at least suggest that the idea of ivory smuggling occurred to more than one participant in the Angolan war.

A French expert and founder of an "Amnesty for the Elephants" campaign noted in 1988 that Kalashnikov (AK–47) automatic rifles, flooding into Africa from the eastern bloc countries via Libya, Ethiopia, Sudan, and Angola, had become the weapon of choice for poachers. They were now able to kill in one day as many elephants as it had formerly taken them a year to hunt down—leaving far too many carcasses for the lions, jackals, and hyenas to consume.[48] Poachers in Kenya and Malawi were probably using AK–47s that had spilled over from nearby wars. In Zimbabwe's Zambezi valley, poachers were reported to be using AK–47s and employing sophisticated tactics, including anti-tracking, fire and movement drill, and coordinated operations along the river's shore.[49] These tactics certainly suggest a military background acquired in one of the region's wars—although in this case it may have been the Zimbabwe struggle of the previous decade.

War also tended to close large areas to conservation authorities and to reduce the funds available for local conservation programs. As authority broke down in Chad, poachers from Kenya, the Central African Republic, Sudan, and Eritrea evidently gained a free hand.[50] Tanzanian authorities seized 127 tusks on the Mozambican border in 1989,[51] suggesting that the insecurity in northern Mozambique was having consequences for wildlife there.

Overall Economic Assessments

Academic economists, led by Reginald Green and working with the Southern African Development Coordination Conference (SADCC), put considerable effort into estimating the overall costs of the warfare in southern Africa during the 1980s,[52] and their work gives a basis for grappling with the magnitude of these costs around the continent. Those engaged in this research, it should be noted, had their own point of view—one of great sympathy for the governments of Angola and Mozambique, which were members of SADCC, and considerable hostility toward South Africa, which they exclusively blamed for the fighting. Nonetheless, it is also worth noting that their work clearly attempts a thorough accounting of the costs of war; that it factors in information from the United Nations Economic Commission for Africa (UNECA) and the World Bank, and that it has been endorsed and extended by UNICEF.[53]

Examining such factors as direct war damage, extra defense spending, higher transport and energy costs, smuggling and looting, costs associated with refugees and displaced persons, loss of existing production, and lost economic growth, SADCC studies conclude that from 1980 through 1988, the wars in Angola and Mozambique cost these states and their regions between $44 and $47 billion. This is a sizable sum, even allowing for possible overstatement. Indeed, let us assume what seems unlikely—that this estimate exaggerates the true cost by a factor of two. Let us further assume that the very destructive wars in Sudan and Ethiopia cost roughly the same amount as the wars in Angola and Mozambique, and that the war in Uganda, a smaller and more isolated country, cost half as much. These assumptions would yield a total cost for Africa's five largest wars of around $100 billion, or slightly less than the gross national product of Sweden in the mid-1980s. If wealth of this magnitude had been made available to these five countries and their affected neighbors as foreign aid—and had been well spent—development prospects in the continent as a whole would have been considerably brighter.

Benefits of War?

The costs of war are great and multi-faceted. Nonetheless, historians and others have noted that war sometimes has benefits, direct and indirect, as well. War can liberate oppressed peoples; it can force governments to reform and rationalize their behavior; and it can drive industrial and technological progress.[54]

Could Africa's destructive conflicts have had any benefits that need to be weighed against their costs? Such benefits seem unlikely in Africa, where war's devastation has been so overwhelming and where even the small arms used to wage war were nearly always developed and manufactured elsewhere. There was one case, however—the victory of Yoweri Museveni's National Resistance Army (NRA) in Uganda— where war clearly brought an evil and highly destructive political situation to an end. There may have been similar political benefits in some other wars, although they were usually highly ambiguous and subject to conflicting interpretations. Economic benefits were nil.

Political Benefits

For all its costs, war can have political benefits for a country and its people. In the most straightforward sense, a war may be beneficial if it succeeds in ousting a bad government—a government that is repressive, unrepresentative, or corrupt—and bringing a better one to power. If there had been no alternative to war for achieving such a change, if the ousted regime had been particularly violent or repressive, and if the costs of war were proportionate to the evils inflicted by the regime, then many would judge the war as just and worthwhile.

A war might also be judged beneficial if it compels governments to reform in important ways. Major reforms can ease the grievances that led to war, producing a regime that is more responsive to the needs of its people and better able to govern over the long term. Finally, war can be a trial by fire that hardens and unifies a country, forcing elites to streamline and rationalize government in order to survive while building a sense of nationalism and duty among the people.

Signs of these benefits could be detected in some of Africa's wars during the 1980s, but their significance in most instances was quite limited. In all but a few instances, it was clear that the negative consequences of war far outweighed any conceivable benefits.

Overthrowing Bad Governments

The issues surrounding the costs and benefits of the use of force to overthrow a government have not arisen often in Africa, since internal resistance forces have rarely won outright victories. The Ugandan war, however, did result in a decisive victory for the resistance, and there is no doubt that the Museveni regime, whatever its shortcomings, was far better for the Ugandan people than its predecessors. One might wish that alternative means for restoring a measure of stability and reason in Uganda had been available. But the conceivable alternatives, such as a multi-national peacekeeping force or intervention by Britain, the former colonial power, were not viable for one reason or another. Nor does it seem likely that a campaign of passive resistance or peaceful political activity would have made much headway against the increasingly violent rule of President Milton Obote or the divided junta that briefly replaced him.

It is too soon to say whether the long war in Ethiopia, which finally ousted the Mengistu regime in May 1991, will be judged beneficial, on balance, for the Ethiopian people. Certainly it led to the ouster of an evil regime, but it brought devastation and human trauma on such a scale as to leave Ethiopia's future very much in doubt. Eritrea appears permanently lost, leaving the remainder of Ethiopia landlocked and creating some potential for future conflict. Meanwhile, ethnic tensions within Ethiopia remain high, and potential combatants have ready access to arms. Chad is another instance in which guerrillas won—in this case repeatedly. No one could judge the endless war among competing factions in this impoverished country as beneficial.

In Namibia, as the 1990s began, SWAPO took power as a result of the international negotiations on Angola and Namibia, to which it had not been a party. Indeed, to some degree, SWAPO's victory must be seen as a side effect of negotiations on Angola, although it is true that the costs of the Namibian war were a factor in South Africa's decision to disengage from both countries. In any event, Namibia's march to independence won wide approval in the international community because it marked a final stage of the decolonization process that began after World War II. In that sense, SWAPO's struggle has been vindicated and few will question the benefit of the war, particularly if—in fulfillment of the highest hopes for self-determination—the new government turns out to be genuinely representative and tolerant over the long term.

Promoting Reform

In some instances, African wars pushed governments toward pragmatic policy reforms, and on that ground might be judged beneficial.

Mozambique's move away from doctrinaire socialism beginning in 1983, and its eventual acceptance of multiple political parties, were in part intended to reduce grievances within Mozambique and bring the war to an end. They also reflected international pressures for peace and economic reforms that would allow international assistance to resume. In Angola, the government also adopted somewhat more pragmatic economic policies as the 1980s progressed. In the 1991 peace accord, it accepted democratic principles and agreed to free elections. Clearly, the regimes in both countries were pushed toward these reforms in order to win peace; but it is entirely possible that reforms would have come eventually even without war. Elsewhere in Africa, regimes that had not been at war were accepting similar reforms in the face of economic necessity, popular demand, and international pressure.

Some regimes seemed to be made intransigent by war and less open to reforms than regimes at peace. Certainly this was the case with the regime of General Mohammed Bashir in Sudan, and of Mengistu in Ethiopia. Mengistu claimed to be reforming his regime at the last, but he never really gave up his determination to hold onto power by force. Thus it cannot be asserted, as a general principle, that war was a reliable force for reform in Africa.

Hardening Effects

During the 1980s, African countries and their governments showed little evidence of the hardening effects that war can have. This, indeed, was one of the reasons why Africa's wars went on for so long. Several governments, particularly in Angola, Mozambique, Sudan, and Ethiopia, continued to wage war in the same inefficient and unproductive way throughout the decade—understandably without military result. There was little evidence that war was strengthening nationhood, and much evidence that it was deepening divisions within nations.

With the changes that came in some wars at the beginning of the 1990s, it was possible that some hardening effects of war might become evident, but the emerging picture is still unclear. In Angola, where a transition to peace was attempted after May 1991, civilian and military officials on both sides of the conflict had undergone a prolonged learning experience in management, politics, and diplomacy as a result of war. There were hopes that as a result, a peacetime Angola would be governed by seasoned leaders exercising judgment and prudence in policymaking—hopes that were dashed when Savimbi shattered the peace accord and returned to armed struggle in late 1992. Nonetheless, there is a core of potential statesmen in Angola, including some recent defectors from top UNITA positions, and it may yet be that Angola will find its way to peace and good government. Many observers also have high hopes for post-war Eritrea because of the sense of national solidarity forged in the long struggle and the management skills developed by the EPLF (Eritrean People's Liberation Front) over the years. These hopes may also be realized over the long term, but in the immediate aftermath of the conflict, the EPLF was showing authoritarian tendencies and an inclination toward a single-party system. Should the regime continue along these lines, Eritrea could fall prey to the economic and political deterioration that has afflicted authoritarian, single-party states elsewhere in Africa. Meanwhile, ethnic divisions remained strong in the rest of Ethiopia, and it was far from certain that President Meles Zenawi would be able to create a regime that could govern Ethiopia as a whole. Further fragmentation seemed equally possible.

Economic Benefits

Only a creative imagination could discern significant economic benefits resulting from Africa's wars. Some individuals may have made money trading in arms or ivory, and South Africa's arms industry was further enriched by that country's participation in the wars in Angola and Namibia. Even South Africa, however, judged the net economic costs of war to outweigh the benefits, and this calculation sped its exit from the conflicts in Angola and Namibia. Eritrea's underground factories won much admiration during the war, and might conceivably spin off some benefits in terms of knowledge, skills, and technologies, but the evidence on this possibility is not yet in. Elsewhere, no new industries were created, nor new technological capabilities developed, in response to war. The arms used in these conflicts came from outside the continent, and—where they were not given for free—their acquisition was a drain on Africa's resources.

Notes

1. United Nations Children's Fund (UNICEF), *Children on the Front Line,* 3d ed. (New York: UNICEF, 1989). This study is discussed further below.

2. Ruth Leger Sivard, *World Military and Social Expenditures, 1991*, 14th ed. (Washington, D.C.: World Priorities, 1991), 25.

3. Michael Glantz, "Drought in Africa," *Scientific American* 256 (June 1987): 40.

4. The problems of war and locust plagues came together again, tragically, in December 1988, when an American locust-spraying plane, under contract to the Agency for International Development, was downed by a POLISARIO missile while flying from Senegal to Morocco. The five crew members were killed.

5. U.S. Congress, House, Committee on Foreign Affairs, and Senate, Committee on Foreign Relations, *Country Reports on Human Rights Practices for 1987*, 100th Cong., 2d sess., 1988, report submitted by the Department of State (Washington, D.C.: U.S. Government Printing Office, 1988), 9 (hereafter cited as Department of State, *Country Reports on Human Rights*).

6. Africa Watch, *Angola: Violations of the Laws of War by Both Sides* (London, April 1989), 1.

7. Mary Battiata, "Hyena's Are War's Camp Followers," *Washington Post*, 30 June 1989.

8. Jane Perlez, "For Sudanese Youths Seared by War and Starvation, a Refuge in Ethiopia," *New York Times*, 18 December 1988.

9. Robert Gersony, *Why Somalis Flee: Synthesis of Accounts of Conflict Experience in Northern Somalia by Somali Refugees, Displaced Persons and Others* (Washington, D.C.: Department of State, 1989), 63–64. Gersony was a consultant for the State Department's Bureau for Refugee Programs.

10. UNICEF, *Children on the Front Line*, 11. The authors obtained this figure by comparing child mortality in these countries with that pertaining in Tanzania, which was similar in many aspects was but at peace. Ibid., 24–25.

11. Diana Jean Schemo, "As Hunger Ebbs, Somalia Faces Need to Rebuild," *New York Times*, 7 February 1993.

12. Tony Hodges, "Mozambique Emergency Plan Highlights Rehabilitation," *Africa Recovery* (UN Development Program United Nations, June 1988): 7.

13. UNICEF, *Children on the Front Line*, 16.

14. *Africa Recovery* (15 January 1993): 11.

15. See, for example, Neil Boothby, Abubacar Sultan, and Peter Upton, *Children of Mozambique: The Cost of Survival* (Washington, D.C.: U.S. Committee for Refugees, 1991). Also, Jane Perlez, "For Sudanese Youths Seared by War," and her "Child Victims of War Tax Mozambique," *New York Times*, 1 March 1989.

16. Magne Raundalen et al., "Four Investigations on Stress among Children in Uganda," in *War, Violence, and Children in Uganda*, ed. Cole P. Dodge and Magne Ruandalen (Oslo: Norwegian University Press, 1987), 86.

17. Ibid., 92.

18. Boothby, Sultan, and Upton, *Children of Mozambique*, 20–23.

19. Pamela Reynolds, "Healing Children's Trauma after War," in UNICEF, *Children on the Front Line*, 26–28.

20. Each of these reports had its critics, who argued, among other points, that refugees were likely to tell an interviewer what he or she wanted to hear. Interviews with internal refugees in Mozambique, moreover, were criticized on the grounds that the subjects may have been trying to win favor from the government

—or escape punishment. The authors, however, cited the many safeguards they had taken against bias in their reports, which in any event were supported by information available from other sources.

21. The quotation is from Department of State, *Country Reports on Human Rights Practices for 1988.* The report itself was entitled *Summary of Mozambican Refugee Accounts of Principally Conflict-Related Experience in Mozambique,* submitted by Robert Gersony, consultant to the Bureau for Refugee Programs.

22. Department of State, *Country Reports on Human Rights Practices for 1988,* 228.

23. Ibid.

24. Africa Watch, *Angola: Violations of the Laws of War by Both Sides,* 6.

25. These allegations were aired by Fred Bridgland, Savimbi's hitherto laudatory biographer, while Amnesty International said that it had received similar reports which it had been unable to confirm. The charges were denounced by UNITA's supporters overseas as disinformation. See Craig Whitney and Jill Joliffe, "Ex-Allies Say Angola Rebels Torture and Slay Dissenters," *New York Times,* 11 March 1989; Amnesty International press release, 24 March 1989; and E.A. Wayne, "Congress Keeps Wary Eye on Angola," *Christian Science Monitor,* 20 April 1989.

26. David Ottaway, "UNITA Admits Rights Abuses, Blames Ex-Officials," *Washington Post,* 26 March 1992.

27. Amnesty International became concerned about this problem in 1986. Amnesty International, *Amnesty International Report, 1987* (London, Amnesty International Publications: 1987). 80. See also "Namibia: Inside SWAPO," *Africa Confidential,* London: 16 December 1988, 1–3.

28. "Namibia Prisoners Report Brutality," *New York Times,* 5 July 1989.

29. Douglas H. Johnson, *The Southern Sudan,* Minority Rights Group report no. 78 (London, 1988), 10. Africa Watch has also been outspoken. See the prepared statement of Holly Burkhalter of Africa Watch and Human Rights Watch in U.S. Congress, House Select Committee on Hunger and House Committee on Foreign Affairs, *Human Rights in Sudan,* Joint Hearing, 101st Cong., 1st sess., 2 March (Washington, D.C.: U.S. Government Printing Office, 1989), 70–86.

30. Department of State, *Country Reports on Human Rights Practices for 1988,* 346.

31. See the statement of Julia Vadala Taft, director of the U.S. Agency for International Development's Office of Foreign Disaster Assistance, in U.S. Congress, House Select Committee on Hunger and House Foreign Affairs Subcommittee on Africa, *Politics of Hunger in Sudan,* Hearing, 101st Cong., 2d sess., 2 March (Washington, D.C.: U.S. Government Printing Office, 1989): 101–17.

32. A term used by the Department of State in its *Country Reports on Human Rights Practices.*

33. See, for example, Amnesty International's report, *Ethiopia: Political Imprisonment and Torture* (New York, June 1986).

34. Department of State, *Country Reports on Human Rights Practices for 1988,* 109.

35. See the following Amnesty International reports: *Somalia: A Long-Term Human Rights Crisis* (London, 1988); *Somalia: Detention without Trial* (New York, August 1988); and *Somalia: Torture* (New York, June 1988).

36. Department of State, *Country Reports on Human Rights Practices,* various years.

37. Department of State, *Country Reports on Human Rights Practices for 1988,* 1444.

38. Dodge and Raundalen, eds., *War, Violence, and Children in Uganda,* 43.

39. For Sudan, see Dalia Baligh, "Economic, Political Pressures Mount on Government to Make Peace," Associated Press, 10 December 1988; for Namibia, "Why South Africa Holds On in Namibia," *The Economist,* 13 June 1987; and for Morocco, Jonathan C. Randal, "Hassan Awaits More than Kind Words from U.S," *International Herald Tribune,* 13 January 1987.

40. U.S. Agency for International Development, *Congressional Presentation, FY 1988,* main volume (Washington, D.C.: USAID 1987), 887.

41. Charles Gordon, "Debt Burden Aggravates Crisis," *Africa Recovery* (December 1988): 5.

42. "Mozambique Emergency Plan Highlights Rehabilitation," *Africa Recovery* (June 1988): 7.

43. See Jack G. Kaikati, "The Economy of Sudan: A Potential Breadbasket of the Arab World?" *International Journal of Middle East Studies* 11 (February 1980): 99–123; Peter Oesterdiekhoff and Karl Wohlmuth, "The 'Breadbasket' is Empty: The Options of Sudanese Development Policy," *Canadian Journal of African Studies* 17 (1983): 35–67.

44. R.B. Martin, *Establishment of African Ivory Export Quotas and Associated Control Procedures,* report to the CITES (Convention on International Trade in Endangered Species of Wild Fauna and Flora) Secretariat (Lausanne, 1 March 1985; revised 1 August 1985), 4, 85.

45. Ibid., 82.

46. These allegations were denied by the South African government. Eddie Koch, "Did 100,000 Elephants Die to Pay for the War in Angola?" *Weekly Mail* (Johannesburg), 2–8 September 1988. See also, "Paratroop Commander Confirms: Savimbi's Men Shot Thousands of Elephants," *Weekly Mail,* 1–7 December 1989.

47. "Jonas Savimbi: comment j'ai vaincu les Russes d'Angola," *Paris Match* (18 March 1988), 86.

48. "La dernière chance des éléphants," *Paris Match* (5 August 1988).

49. Glenn Tatham, "Rhino Poaching in the Zambezi Valley," *Pachyderm* 7 (December 1986): 3.

50. Martin, *Establishment of African Ivory Export Quotas,* 85.

51. Associated Press, 25 April 1989.

52. See Reginald H. Green and Carol B. Thompson, "Political Economies in Conflict: SADCC, South Africa, and Sanctions," in *Destructive Engagement: Southern Africa at War,* ed. Phyllis Johnson and David Martin (Harare: Zimbabwe Publishing House for the Southern African Research and Documentation Centre, 1986), 271–76.

53. UNICEF, *Children on the Front Line.* See especially Annex A, "Economic Costs of Destabilization and Warfare, 1980–1988: A Note," 35–40.

54. William H. McNeill, *The Pursuit of Power: Technology, Armed Force, and Society since A.D. 1000* (Chicago: University of Chicago Press, 1982.) See also Jeffrey Herbst, "War and the State in Africa," *International Security* 14 (Spring 1990): 117–39.

2 AFRICA'S WARS SINCE 1980: A SURVEY

Every region of Africa has been severely affected by war in the years that are the focus of this book. North Africa, the Horn, East Africa, and southern Africa saw war in the 1980s. West Africa was spared until the final days of the decade, when, in December 1989, a small rebel band invaded Liberia and swiftly gained wide support. In 1990, war came to Central Africa, as Rwanda was invaded by a dissident force drawn from Rwandan refugees in the Ugandan army.

This chapter has three purposes: to identify Africa's wars active since 1980, giving a rough indication of their comparative gravity; to outline their main trends and events; and to distinguish between Africa's wars and related conflict situations that have not, at least to date, led to war. As a survey, the chapter provides only the most basic information on particular wars as background to subsequent chapters. Experts on individual countries will no doubt feel that the summaries of main trends and events are too brief and fail to do justice to complex situations. Readers who are already familiar with African events over the past fifteen years or so may wish to skim the next pages and move on to Chapter 3. Those seeking in-depth studies of particular wars are referred to the bibliography appearing at the end of the book.

Identifying Africa's Wars

Africa's eleven wars since 1980, approximately ranked according to available mortality data, occurred in Sudan, Ethiopia, Mozambique, Angola, Uganda, Somalia, Liberia, Namibia, Western Sahara, Chad, and Rwanda (see Map 1). While these wars all had an international dimension, each was waged largely or entirely within the country or territory concerned.

Each conflict can be termed a "war" since each involved fighting on a substantial scale between troops of the regime and the armed forces of one or more internal resistance movements. These movements, at some stage of the fighting, controlled territory inside the country where the war was taking place or conducted operations over large areas. The available information is sketchy on some of the groups operating in Ethiopia, Uganda, Somalia, and Chad. But in many instances, the opposition forces participating in Africa's wars took on the characteristics of armies, with command structures, military units, and—as far as possible—uniforms.

In addition to these wars, there was a brief border clash between Mali and Burkina Faso in December 1985. It arose over a long-standing claim on Mali's part to the Agacher strip, a band of territory along the border that is thought to be rich in minerals, and was the only instance during the 1980s of armed conflict arising solely from an international dispute. Some journalists referred to this conflict as a war, but it hardly merited the name since combat ended in days and casualties were light. The two sides clearly had no real desire to become involved in prolonged hostilities, and they swiftly acceded to the wishes of their neighbors for a cease-fire. In December 1986, the International Court of Justice ruled that the boundary should be adjusted, giving each country an approximately equal share, and there was no further armed conflict on the issue.

Major Wars: Main Trends and Events

The wars in Sudan, Ethiopia, Mozambique, Uganda, Angola, and Somalia (Table 2.1) were far greater than the others in the scale of fighting and the toll they exacted. In each of these conflicts, large anti-government armies came to dominate broad stretches of territory. Deaths ranged from at least 100,000 upward, and refugees as well as displaced persons were counted in the hundreds of thousands or millions. Indeed, these six wars together were responsible for all but a fraction of the deaths resulting from war in Africa since 1980, and they accounted for more than 80 percent of Africa's refugees.[1] Vast regions

Map 1

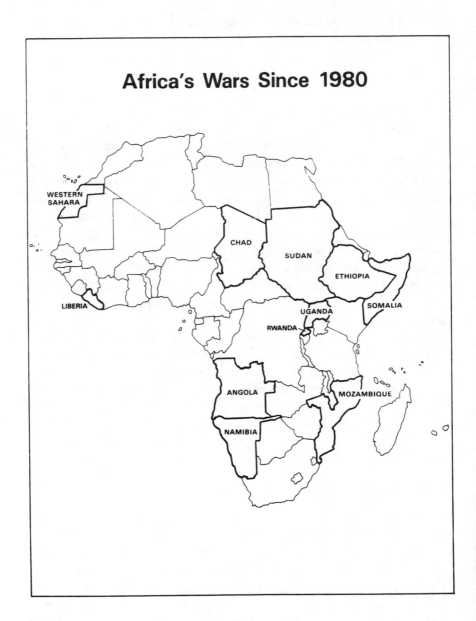

Africa's Wars Since 1980

Table 2.1

Africa's Largest Wars since 1980

Country	Population	Approximate Size	Regions Affected	Duration	Mortality Estimates
Sudan	28 million	one-third U.S.	south	1983-	500,000- one million
Ethiopia	54 million	twice Texas	north moving to center	1970- 1991	450,000- one million
Mozambique	15 million	twice California	rural areas nationwide	1979- 1992	450,000- one million
Angola	9 million	twice Texas	southeast, east; incidents nationwide	1975- 1991; renewed in 1992	300,000- 500,000
Uganda	19 million	Oregon	south and center moving north	1980-	100,000- 500,000
Somalia	7 million	Texas	northwest, spreading nationwide	1982-	300,000- 400,000

were paralyzed by war within these countries; whole towns were emptied; roads and railways were cut; and national economies became stagnant or fell into decay. The wars in Ethiopia, Sudan, Angola, and Mozambique resulted in the collapse of food production over wide areas, and international relief operations were disrupted by the fighting, bringing untold suffering to the homeless and the hungry.

The six major wars are discussed here in order of the amount of mortality they have caused, according to the most commonly offered estimates. It must be emphasized, however, that all such estimates are very rough indeed, since they are based on events in remote regions of remote countries. In view of the poor quality of information, the available data usually do not distinguish categories of mortality. Instead, estimates of combat deaths and deaths resulting from attacks on civilians are typically mixed together with estimates of the mortality caused indirectly by war's upheavals. Moreover, widely varying estimates are available from various sources—which sometimes have an interest in exaggerating or minimizing the costs of war; and choosing the highest or lowest figure for a particular country could affect its ranking. It can be said with certainty, however, that each of these wars exacted a very heavy toll—far more than the lesser wars or any of the related conflict situations.

Sudan

The wars in Sudan, Ethiopia, and Mozambique have almost certainly been the most costly African wars since 1980 in terms of lives lost, and they are difficult to distinguish from each other on the basis of mortality estimates. The weight of available evidence, however, suggests that the conflict in southern Sudan, with ongoing fighting and repeated famine over many years, probably exacted the highest toll.[2] War-induced famine and the disruption of international relief efforts because of the war resulted in immense civilian losses, with as many as 1 million deaths by the end of the 1980s, according to some estimates.[3] Estimates of between 250,000 and 500,000 deaths in 1988 alone appeared in the press, and then U.S. Secretary of State James Baker alleged that hundreds of thousands may have starved to death in that year.[4] It is not surprising, however, that the Sudanese government has advanced considerably lower estimates, maintaining in 1989 that over the course of the entire war, 259,000 had died of starvation or disease, while battlefield fatalities, including civilians, totaled 34,090.[5]

The current war began only in 1983, but this war was essentially a revival of the 1963–1972 conflict between southern rebels and the northern-based government. Both conflicts reflected unresolved social tensions arising in part from the British colonial decision to incorporate the south, with its non-Moslem Nilotic and Bantu populations, into a single political entity with an assertive, Islamic north oriented toward the Arab world. A formula that seemed to provide for the mutual coexistence of the two regions was agreed upon in 1972, when the Sudanese government, headed then as in 1983 by President Jaafar al-Numeiry, reached an accord with the rebels after negotiations in Addis Ababa, Ethiopia. The Addis Ababa accord conceded considerable political autonomy to the south, but failed to provide the impoverished region with the means of catching up with the north in economic development. This development differential, combined with the north/south religious and cultural divide, meant that the strains between the two regions persisted.

Armed southern resistance broke out in 1983 in response to regime actions and policies that were perceived in southern society as new northern attempts to dominate, Arabize, and exploit the south. Numeiry's September 1983 announcement that the criminal code would be replaced by the *sharia,* or Islamic law, throughout the country, with no exception for the non-Islamic south, was a major precipitating factor. Southern resistance was strongest among the Dinka—at 3 million the largest ethnic group in the area. Many non-Dinka southerners felt that the Dinka had come to dominate the south after the Addis Ababa accord and became recruits for pro-government armed militias.

The southern resistance formed itself into the Sudan People's Liberation Army (SPLA) and quickly forced a halt to construction on the massive Jonglei canal project and at the Bentiu oil wells in Upper Nile province (see Map 2). Both of these projects had come to be seen as means for diverting southern resources to northern development. By 1985, the SPLA was operating widely in Bahr el-Ghazal and Upper Nile provinces, and government forces were pinned down in a few garrisons while northern Sudan fell into political crisis.

President Numeiry was overthrown in April 1985, following massive public demonstrations, for a host of reasons, including Sudan's near economic collapse and the president's inability to deal with the worsening conflict in the south. Successor regimes were no more able to end the war by military means than Numeiry had been; and a series of peace initiatives promoted by domestic groups, concerned humanitarian organizations, and foreign governments came to nothing. Hopes for a settlement were particularly high under the civilian coalition headed by Sadiq al-Mahdi, which came to power in 1986. Sadiq, the British-educated grandson of a famed nineteenth century religious and anticolonial leader, had been prime minister once before and seemd to enjoy a special legitimacy for a time in Sudan. But he was never able to make the critical concessions needed on the *sharia* because of Islamicist pressures from the opposition and among his own supporters.

A military government headed by General Omar Hassan al-Bashir seized power in Khartoum on June 30, 1989; initial signs were hopeful as Bashir announced a cease-fire and took steps to facilitate the international famine relief effort for the south. By the end of 1989, however, Bashir's regime was hardening into an entrenched dictatorship, heavily influenced by Islamic resurgence leader Hassan al-Turabi. Former President Carter attempted to promote negotiations between the

Map 2

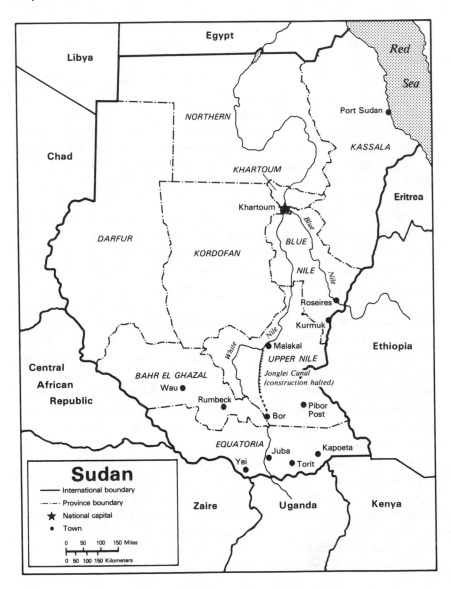

Sudan

International boundary
Province boundary
National capital
Town

0   50   100   150 Miles

0   50   100   150 Kilometers

Bashir regime and the SPLA at a meeting in Nairobi, Kenya, at the beginning of December 1989, but the talks broke down on the Islamic law issue. According to Carter, "neither side came to Nairobi prepared to take the difficult steps necessary for peace." He added, "There is no telling how many hundreds of thousands of people will die because these two sides have failed to reach an agreement."[6] In 1991, following new disruptions to the international relief effort, relief agencies were predicting that 8 to 11 million people were at risk of famine in Sudan, and it seemed certain that thousands would perish. The actual toll during this period may never be known, since vast regions of the south were virtually closed off to outside observers due to war and government-imposed restrictions.

The May 1991 victory of rebel forces in Ethiopia altered the Sudanese situation substantially, since the victorious rebels were grateful for the shelter Khartoum had offered them during long years of struggle. They moved swiftly to expel SPLA forces and southern Sudanese refugees from Ethiopian territory, creating a new humanitarian crisis for the region. At the end of 1991, Bashir forged a close relationship with Iran, and there were reports of substantial Iranian military aid beginning to arrive. Observers speculated that this aid might allow Khartoum to compensate for the loss of support it had suffered in the Arab world because of its continued friendship with Iraq after the invasion of Kuwait.

The international gains made by Khartoum in 1991 deepened existing factional divisions within the SPLA, and breakaway leaders tried unsuccessfully to oust SPLA head John Garang, whom they called a "heartless dictator" guilty of a "reign of terror."[7] Factional fighting added to the suffering of the southern civilian population, and in 1992 government forces made headway in the south, driving the SPLA from the towns it had held. Observers began to believe that the SPLA would soon be forced into an accord, but peace efforts undertaken by then Nigerian president Ibrahim Babangida, extending into 1993, failed to bear fruit.

Whether this war is at a turning point, with the Iranian-backed government on the verge of victory, is still unclear. The SPLA has demonstrated remarkable tenacity and resourcefulness over the years, and there are reports that it too has found new sources of arms. Thus it is at least possible that the apparent turning point in the war, like so many others in the past, is not a real one and that the government, the SPLA, with or without the breakaway rebel factions will struggle on—to the continuing cost of the Sudanese people.

That cost is grave indeed. In February 1993, the head of the U.S. Office of Foreign Disaster Assistance warned that a major humanitarian crisis was occurring in southern Sudan, with 1.7 million refugees in dire need of assistance and several hundred thousand people facing starvation. Many fear "another Somalia" is occurring in Southern Sudan in terms of starvation deaths among children and adults.

Ethiopia

Estimates of the death toll in Ethiopia during the 1980s are highly tentative. Some run as high as 1 million,[8] and if these are accurate, then the Ethiopian war may have been as costly as the war in Sudan. Another source puts the figure at 500,000 civilians and 70,000 soldiers from the Ethiopian revolution in 1974 through 1991.[9]

The Ethiopian fighting began in the late 1960s as a rebellion against Ethiopia's annexation of the northern province of Eritrea (see Map 3). This coastal territory had long been more exposed to outside influence —including periods of Arab, Ottoman, and Egyptian control—than the rest of Ethiopia. Under Italian rule from the 1880s through World War II, its economy began to modernize; and Eritrea experienced a period of active political life under British occupation after the Italians were ousted in 1941.

With the end of World War II, Ethiopia sought to annex Eritrea, claiming historic justification and a perceived geographic imperative to secure the Red Sea coast. Many Eritreans were insisting on a United Nations referendum on independence and were sorely disappointed in a UN decision to link the territory to Ethiopia in a federation. The federation lasted from 1952 until 1962, when Emperor Haile Selassie, who could not tolerate Eritrea's unusually open political system, manipulated the Eritrean assembly into voting for union. Eritrea's freedoms were swiftly brought to an end, and the territory was absorbed into the Ethiopian empire.

Resistance among Moslems of lowland Eritrea soon spread to urban workers and intellectuals of Christian background, and guerrilla raids from across the Sudan border began in 1970.[10] Despite bitter personal rivalries, factionalism, and internecine violence, the Eritrean resistance gained a foothold in the province, and by 1977 all but a few major towns in Eritrea were in rebel hands.

Meanwhile, the rebellion had spread to neighboring Tigray province, where the Tigray People's Liberation Front (TPLF) was organ-

Map 3

ized in 1975. The Tigray had their own long-standing grievances against Addis Ababa, which they felt had neglected and impoverished their region over many years. Many Tigray saw their own culture as superior to that of the Amhara in the capital and the true source of Ethiopian civilization. The young Marxists who led the Tigray uprising, though denying any ethnic motivation, seemed to reflect this sense of Tigrayan destiny to rule.

Trouble was also brewing in Somali-inhabited southeastern Ethiopia, a dry region known as the Ogaden, where a group calling itself the Western Somali Liberation Front (WSLF) became active. This group was closely tied to the Somali government, and when regular Somali armed forces joined in the fighting in Ethiopia in 1977, the dismemberment of Ethiopia—now under Mengistu Haile Mariam, a military dictator—began to appear possible. This was prevented only by the arrival of massive Soviet military assistance, including advisers, together with as many as 17,000 Cuban troops. The Cubans spearheaded an assault that drove the Somali forces from Ethiopia—and for a time inspired fears of a Cuban/Ethiopian takeover of Somalia. Strengthened by Soviet aid and advice, Mengistu then launched a counter-attack in Eritrea, recapturing all of its towns apart from remote Nakfa. The Eritrean Liberation Front (ELF), the main resistance movement, was badly damaged by this offensive.

The crises in Eritrea and the Ogaden coincided with upheavals in the capital as civilian revolutionaries, anti-revolutionaries, and the new leftist military government waged a bitter struggle for power. During 1977–1978, Mengistu's forces launched a Red Terror campaign against civilian Marxists opposed to military rule. Estimates of the number killed in Addis Ababa typically run to 10,000, and the killing of large numbers of young men and women left lasting hatreds.

During the 1980s, Mengistu's military position steadily deteriorated, particularly in Eritrea and Tigray. The ELF had been further damaged by fighting with its rival, the Eritrean People's Liberation Front (EPLF), and many ELF defectors crossed over to the EPLF, which now came to dominate the struggle. The EPLF threw a line of trenches across northern Eritrea and defeated a massive new Ethiopian offensive, known as Operation Red Star, in 1982. A former Ethiopian official who played a role in this campaign maintains that the Ethiopian army lost 11,000 men in the effort and badly botched an attempt to recapture Nakfa.[11]

In 1984–1985, Mengistu undertook his ill-conceived resettlement program, intended to move some 1.5 million peasant farmers from drought-prone northern areas to the southwest. Whether he also intended to weaken northern resistance by depopulating the region remains unclear, but in any event observers believe that thousands of northerners died as they were forced onto planes, trucks, and buses and taken to unprepared sites in malarial zones. Thousands more fled the country as refugees. The separation of children from their parents during resettlement was a particular tragedy. Following international criticism, the program was finally abandoned with perhaps 500,000 to 600,000 peasants moved.

Subsequent military offensives into the north met repeated failure. In March 1988, the EPLF broke through the Nakfa front and overran the Ethiopian garrison at Afabet, inflicting heavy casualties and capturing thousands of Ethiopian soldiers. This victory, which brought with it large quantities of arms, ammunition, and equipment, was the prelude to further EPLF victories in subsequent months.

The TPLF was also making remarkable new gains at decade's end, driving government troops out of Mekele, the Tigray province capital, in January 1989. The TPLF brought the smaller Ethiopian People's Democratic Movement (EPDM) into an alliance, the Ethiopian People's Revolutionary Democratic Front (EPRDF), and in this guise it made important advances in Gondar and Wello provinces. Indeed, its forces soon entered northern Shoa province, the heartland of the traditional Ethiopian empire and center of its Amhara ethnic population base. These EPRDF gains made it impossible for the government to supply its troops in Eritrea except by air. Meanwhile, Mengistu's regime faced continuing resistance from a variety of ethnically based movements, including Somali groups and the Oromo Liberation Front (OLF), strongest in western Wollega province but rooted in a widely distributed, primarily lowland people who are thought to constitute a majority of the Ethiopian population.

In the first months of 1991, the EPRDF made dramatic advances into the Amhara heartland as the Ethiopian army crumbled. Mengistu finally fled the country on May 21, opening the capital to the EPRDF. Within days, the EPLF had occupied Asmara, ancient capital of Eritrea. The country then fell into a tense, armed peace, with Tigrayan peasant soldiers patrolling the Amhara capital, Eritrea determined to go its own way, and Oromo revolutionaries beginning to assert their own demands for independence. In 1992, the OLF broke with the EPRDF alliance, and several armed clashes occurred—although the

EPRDF managed to control the outbreak by the end of the year. EPRDF leader Meles Zenawi had little choice but to concede the EPLF demand for a referendum on Eritrean independence, but Amhara university students and intellectuals in the capital were increasingly restive as the loss of Eritrea approached. Eritreans gave separation from Ethiopia nearly unanimous endorsement in the internationally monitored referendum, which took place in April 1993 and brought independence on May 24.

In Addis Ababa, Zenawi was attempting to govern through an EPRDF-dominated transitional government and a Council of Representatives, including thirty political and ethnic organizations, with the ultimate objective of creating an elected, multi-party government. His prospects for success, in view of Ethiopia's limited resources and ethnic strains, were uncertain at best.

Mozambique

The long war in Mozambique has roughly equaled the wars in Sudan and Ethiopia in terms of the toll in human life. Some sources put the toll at 1 million over the course of the war,[12] which ended in 1992, while UNICEF calculated a total of 690,000 deaths through 1988, including deaths from malnutrition and increased child mortality attributable to the war.[13] A United Nations inter-agency task force offered a figure of 900,000 deaths caused directly or indirectly by war between 1980 and 1988, including 500,000 infants and children under five.[14]

The origins of the war in Mozambique—which attained its independence from Portugal in 1975—lie partly in post-independence interference by the white regime in neighboring Rhodesia (now Zimbabwe) and partly in the early radicalism of the Mozambican regime (See Map 4). The Front for the Liberation of Mozambique (FRELIMO), the ruling party in Mozambique, had a long history of support for guerrillas in Zimbabwe, and with independence Mozambique became the base of operations for the armed wing of the Zimbabwe African National Union (ZANU), headed by Robert Mugabe, who is now Zimbabwe's president. In retaliation, white Rhodesian troops undertook a wide-ranging campaign in Mozambique, striking at transportation targets and ZANU camps, while Rhodesian intelligence operatives began to organize internal opposition to FRELIMO.[15] Mozambican dissidents apparently began to receive training in Rhodesia as the Mozambique

Map 4

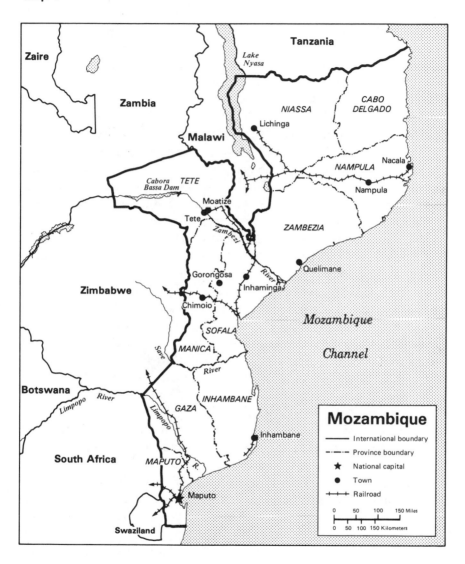

National Resistance (RENAMO) in 1976.[16] They were reportedly given additional support by wealthy Portuguese whose businesses had been confiscated in Mozambique and by individuals with ties to the colonial secret police.[17] By 1979, several hundred guerrillas had joined the resistance cause.

While the Rhodesian intelligence services were the catalyst in launching the war in Mozambique, fuel was provided by popular opposition to FRELIMO's post-revolutionary zeal. FRELIMO moved quickly to nationalize land, transportation, and industry; to abolish private education; and to establish collective farms and communal villages. Thousands of Mozambicans were imprisoned or sent to "re-education" camps,[18] and FRELIMO itself was purged to make it a vanguard movement committed to "scientific socialism." The growth of the RENAMO guerrilla movement must be attributed in part to the economic dislocation and political alienation resulting from these policies.

Zimbabwe's independence in 1980 under a ZANU government ought to have improved Mozambique's situation. But as Zimbabwe's independence approached, RENAMO's radio station and other equipment, as well as its headquarters apparatus, were transported from Zimbabwe to South Africa.[19] South African military intelligence took over RENAMO training and supply.[20] By the end of 1980, RENAMO raids were mounting, and attacks on small towns began to be reported in 1982. Cabora Bassa, a huge hydroelectric project that had been expected to earn hard currency through the sale of power to South Africa, came under RENAMO attack in 1983.

FRELIMO was backing away from its hard-line policies by 1983, taking steps to liberalize the economy and broaden its base of popular support. In 1984, Mozambique was admitted to the World Bank and the International Monetary Fund. But the reforms came too late to stop RENAMO, which had become firmly established in the countryside. The government's fortunes reached a low point in 1986, when President Samora Machel died after his plane strayed into South Africa and crashed.[21] His death coincided with a RENAMO offensive that could only be thrown back with the help of troops from Zimbabwe.

While Zimbabwe's support stabilized the military situation, FRELIMO lacked the capability to bring the war to a conclusion by military means. By the later 1980s, RENAMO was operating in all of Mozambique's ten provinces and was particularly strong in Zambezia and Nampula—home to 40 percent of Mozambique's people and the country's agricultural heartland. Of Mozambique's vital regional transport links, only the Beira corridor, which carries rail, road, and pipeline connections to Zimbabwe, was reasonably secure—and it was secure only because Zimbabwe troops were guarding it. The Mozambique government controlled the cities and towns, including the province capitals and most district capitals, but overland travel outside these centers was very risky. The short road from Maputo to South Africa was impassable to all but a few intrepid truck operators who were willing to pay bribes to RENAMO or local gangs.

Recognizing FRELIMO's limited military capabilities, President Joaquim Chissano, the former foreign minister who succeeded Machel, turned to political and economic instruments in an effort to bring the war to an end. Chissano launched an economic reform plan, approved by the International Monetary Fund, in 1987; and in 1989, FRELIMO abandoned its commitment to Marxist-Leninist principles. In 1990, Mozambique's constitution was modified to permit multiple parties and elections by secret ballot, thus meeting two important RENAMO demands. These changes brought increased Western economic aid, economic growth in secure areas, and a sharp improvement in relations with South Africa.

In 1990, there was some military progress in joint operations with Zimbabwe forces; and RENAMO was persuaded to agree, in a December 1990 accord, to refrain from further attacks on the Beira railway and on the Limpopo line running from Zimbabwe to Maputo. In exchange, Zimbabwe agreed to confine its troops to guarding these lines. There were further attacks on the rail lines in succeeding months, but mediation efforts under the auspices of an Italian church organization and Italian officials, supported by the United States and other concerned outside parties, continued.

Finally, in October 1992, Chissano and RENAMO leader Afonso Dhlakama met in Rome to sign a peace accord that called for a cease-fire and laid out a process of military demobilization and preparations for elections to take place within a year. Shortly after this accord was signed, the Angolan peace process began to come apart. Many expected that Mozambique would follow the same path as disputes arose over the pace of demobilization and the withdrawal of the Zimbabwe troops. In order to prevent this eventuality, and to prevent further embarrassment for international peacekeepers, the United Nations Security Council decided to send 7,500 peacekeeping troops, in addition to techical advisors, to Mozambique to oversee demobilization and organize the elections.[22] UN member nations were slow in designating and deploying the units that would participate in this force known as UNOMOZ (United Nations Operation in Mozambique), but peacekeepers were arriving in the first months of 1993. Meanwhile, there were repeated disagreements between RENAMO and the government over implementation of the peace accord, arrangements for disarmament, and an election law. Nonetheless, prospects for a lasting settlement in Mozambique seemed fairly bright, although the long years of warfare and progressive impoverishment continued to cast a pall over the country's future.

Angola

Few observers have ventured to guess the death toll in the war in Angola, where fighting has raged for years over vast and remote regions, but by the 1990s most available estimates ranged between 300,000 and 500,000,[23] with the renewal of warfare in 1992 certain to add thousands more. A United Nations inter-agency task force had earlier estimated 500,000 direct and indirect war deaths for the period just between 1980 and 1988,[24] while in 1989 UNICEF put the toll, including increased child mortality, at more than 430,000.[25]

The Angolan war was a continuation of the unresolved conflict between two movements that had fought to oust the Portuguese colonial government in the late 1960s and early 1970s. Most observers at the time expected Portugal to hang on to power in Angola indefinitely, but Portuguese authority began a rapid collapse with the April 1974 coup in Lisbon. The three movements that had been contesting Portuguese power in Angola met at Alvor, Portugal, in January 1975 and agreed on transitional arrangements leading to the election of a constituent assembly. The accord was a tenuous one, however, because of ideological as well as ethnic differences among the movements, and because of the personal rivalries among their leaders.

As the Alvor accord began to break down, the struggle within Angola became heavily internationalized. The Popular Movement for the Liberation of Angola (MPLA), a Marxist movement, was the beneficiary of massive assistance from the Soviet Union and Cuba, while covert U.S. aid went to the National Front for the Liberation of Angola (FNLA) and in lesser amounts to Jonas Savimbi's National Union for the Total Independence of Angola (UNITA).[26] South African troops intervened in October 1975, after a period of covert involvement, in an effort to thwart the MPLA, but the movement was able to take the reins of power at independence in November. In subsequent months, the FNLA was essentially destroyed as a fighting force, but UNITA retreated into southeastern Angola, a remote and thinly populated region, where it was able to rebuild.

UNITA began to re-emerge as a major military threat in Angola as the 1980s got under way. South Africa had begun to mount large-scale attacks into Angola in 1978, hitting principally at targets connected with the SWAPO guerrillas from Namibia but often damaging Angolan facilities. With the MPLA distracted by these attacks, UNITA, which was receiving increased South African support, was able to mount larger guerrilla raids and, from 1983, capture towns and strike at key economic targets. By mid-decade, UNITA—joined by some ex-FNLA forces—was operating guerrilla bands in the extreme north and east of Angola, striking at diamond mining towns in Lunda Norte, near the Zairean border (see Map 5).

The MPLA, initially caught off guard, began to counter-attack. In August 1985, the Angolan army, known as FAPLA (Popular Armed Forces for the Liberation of Angola), launched its first major offensive into the UNITA base area in southeastern Angola, with its "capital" at a secret location that UNITA called "Jamba." This powerful thrust was halted by UNITA, with South African help, in a major battle outside Mavinga. FAPLA pressure resumed in 1986, but UNITA counter-attacks supported by South Africa led to a major struggle around Cuito Cuanavale, the FAPLA staging area in the region. It was also in 1986 that U.S. officials publicly acknowledged launching a covert program to provide military materiel and supplies to UNITA. In September 1987, FAPLA undertook a new and larger offensive against UNITA, precipitating a regional crisis.

South Africa responded to FAPLA's offensive with air attacks, the use of powerful long-range artillery, and the intervention of combat troops, forcing FAPLA back into Cuito Cuanavale, which then fell under attack.[27] FAPLA was saved by Cuba's decision to rush additional troops to Angola and to introduce men and aircraft into combat roles in the south. With FAPLA itself benefiting from years of combat experience, replenished stocks of equipment, and a new Soviet-supplied radar system, South Africa began to lose aircraft and white conscripts —very serious losses in terms of white South African opinion and South Africa's military posture.

Map 5

This sharp escalation in the fighting evidently helped persuade the MPLA, the South African government, and Cuba to accede, at the end of 1988, to the long-standing U.S. regional peace initiative, which by this time was being actively promoted by an increasingly cost-conscious Soviet Union. South Africa had already withdrawn its troops from Angola in August 1988 in order to facilitate the peace process. The regional accord, which was concluded in New York on December 22,[28] satisfied a major South African interest in providing for a phased withdrawal of Cuban troops from Angola, to be completed in mid-1991. In exchange, South Africa agreed to allow a UN-sponsored peace process leading to independence for Namibia to go forward from April 1, 1989, with all South African troops to leave the territory by November of that year.

This agreement did not end the internal Angolan conflict between the MPLA and UNITA. Indeed, UNITA was not a party to the talks. Nonetheless, both the United States and the Soviet Union were pushing for a reconciliation in Angola, as were African leaders anxious to reduce regional tensions. In June 1989, Zaire's President Mobutu, joined by the leaders of sixteen other African states at Gbadolite, site of the Zairean presidential retreat, persuaded the MPLA and UNITA to accept a cease-fire and begin peace talks. The exact terms of the Gbadolite accord, however, soon became the subject of heated dispute. Savimbi denied that he had ever agreed to go into exile, as first reports indicated, or to accept the integration of UNITA cadres into the MPLA. By the end of 1989, heavy fighting had resumed in southeastern Angola.

FAPLA launched a final offensive into UNITA's stronghold in the southeast at the beginning of 1990—but again met with failure. Stalemate led to a new series of peace talks under the auspices of Portugal, with strong backing from U.S. and Soviet diplomats. The peace effort received a boost in December 1990, following an extraordinary meeting between Eduard Shevardnadze, then Soviet foreign minister, and Savimbi at the Soviet embassy in Washington. UNITA and MPLA representatives, as well as U.S., Soviet, and Portuguese diplomats, then held further talks at the State Department, where the two Angolan parties were presented with a set of principles, the "Washington Concepts," that might govern a settlement.

Further diplomatic jockeying took place in subsequent months, but on May 1, 1991, at Estoril, Portugal, the MPLA and UNITA finally accepted an agreement along the lines of the Washington principles. The formal signing of this accord took place in Lisbon at the end of the month at a ceremony attended by the UN secretary general, the chairman of the Organization of African Unity, the U.S. secretary of state, and the Soviet foreign minister. The accord provided for a cease-fire to be supervised by a joint military commission, including representatives from the two sides, and from the United States, Portugal, and the Soviet Union, backed up by a force of United Nations monitors. The armed forces of the two sides, under the accord, would move to assembly points where, under international supervision, most would be demobilized with the remainder combining to form an armed force of 50,000. Elections were to be held by November 1992.

The conclusion of this agreement, after sixteen years of conflict, initially seemed a milestone in the history of the region and of Africa as a whole. Its elaborate terms and the explicit role given to external monitors, in sharp contrast to the ill-defined character of the abortive Gbadolite accord, suggested that it could well endure. Angola seemed to fade from the international agenda throughout the rest of 1991 and into 1992, until the initial round of elections at the end of September 1992 ended in disaster. Savimbi rejected the outcome of the vote, which saw a decisive MPLA victory in the legislature but would have forced a runoff presidential election between himself, with 40 percent, and President Eduardo dos Santos, with just under 50 percent.

The United Nations representative in Angola declared that "there was no evidence of major, systematic, or widespread fraud" in the election, but Savimbi retreated to Huambo, in Central Angola, where his Ovimbundu people are strong, and reports began to appear of UNITA troop movements. In November, Luanda, the capital, exploded in violence between MPLA and UNITA supporters, and though it was routed in Luanda, UNITA made a series of startling military advances elsewhere that soon brought a resumption of full-scale fighting. Estimates of the number killed in this new fighting exceed 30,000, and some believe that as many as 10,000 died in fighting around Huambo and another 18,000 at Cuito Cuanavale, where UNITA forces beseiged a government garrison. The renewed war also brought famine to the Angolan interior, where thousands of displaced persons were beyond the reach of relief agencies. In retrospect, analysts recognize that the UN military and elections monitoring force, at about 700, had been far too small; and that both combatants, but particularly UNITA, had been able to evade the military demobilization requirements.

Uganda

In terms of mortality, the war in Uganda (see Map 6) may have been as destructive, or nearly so, as the fighting in Angola. The United States Committee for Refugees has estimated that between 100,000 and 300,000 civilians died in the fighting there between 1980 and 1986,[29] and some limited fighting continued through the rest of the decade. Uganda's president, Yoweri Museveni, the guerrilla commander who seized power in 1986, estimates that 500,000 died in the war[30]—a figure that rivals some of the mortality estimates for Ethiopia and Sudan.

Of Africa's five major wars during the 1980s, this one attracted perhaps the least attention in the international media. Uganda was a smaller country and less strategically located than the others; and the violence of Idi Amin's regime, which came to power in a 1971 coup, inured the outside world to Ugandan unrest while discouraging foreign observers from visiting the country. Amin, who was himself blamed by the International Commission of Jurists for the murder of at least 100,000 Ugandans,[31] was ousted by an invading army of Tanzanian troops and Ugandan opposition forces in 1979. By that time, the social and political fabric of Uganda had been destroyed, and the ensuing chaos brought death to an equal or greater number.

Uganda's first president, Milton Obote, came back into power in a widely questioned election at the end of 1980. He was perceived in the Bantu south, where perhaps two-thirds of Uganda's people live, as embodying what they saw as the corrupt and illegitimate rule of the northern minority groups that had dominated Ugandan politics since independence. These groups had been given disproportionate influence in the army by the British during the colonial period. Tensions between northern ethnic factions within the military, however, were another long-standing feature of Ugandan politics and an additional source of violence in the post-Amin period.

Under Obote's second regime, armed uprisings, brutal attempts by the regime to repress opposition, and the decay of the armed forces into "competing semi-private armies"[32] that preyed on civilians and engaged in factional fighting with one another resulted in an extraordinary death toll, and the violence continued after Obote fled in 1985.

Map 6

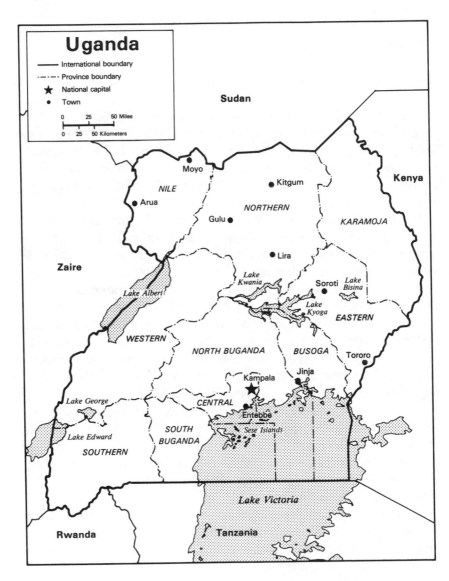

The mounting guerrilla threat after his departure and the chaos caused by a "bewildering array of armed gangs"[33] at large in the countryside brought further carnage. Finally, in the first months of 1986, the guerrillas of Yoweri Museveni's National Resistance Army (NRA) won a series of stunning victories, beginning with the takeover of the capital in January, and established a new and more orderly regime.

By the end of the decade, peace had been restored over much of the country, although lingering resistance to Museveni continued among ex-military elements in the north, particularly around Gulu, and in the east among peasants of the Acholi and Teso, where the Holy Spirit Movement (HSM) was active. The dwindling war being waged by this movement had primitive millenarian elements that were perhaps understandable in view of all that Uganda had suffered. Once commanded by Alice Lakwena, a charismatic but uneducated young woman, the movement combined the use of Christian symbols with a belief in magic and charms thought to bring invincibility. Fighting barefooted and often armed with only sticks, stones, and magical oils, thousands of Lakwena's adherents were killed during suicidal assaults on Museveni's troops in 1987.[34] At the end of that year, Lakwena fled to Kenya, but fragments of the movement continued their apparently hopeless struggle into the 1990s.

Museveni declared an amnesty to resistance fighters who surrendered, and made offers to reintegrate them into the military or civilian life. He refused, however, to grant resistance movements recognition or enter into formal peace talks. In the later 1980s and into the 1990s, poorly disciplined NRA forces in the north and east were repeatedly accused of human rights abuses, abduction, rape, and several killings of civilians.[35] The conduct of the armed forces continued to feed the lingering rebellion, particularly in the northeastern Teso area, where a group calling itself the Ugandan People's Army (UPA), headed by one Hitler Eregu, remained active.

Somalia

As conflict intensified in Somalia in the later 1980s, several thousand civilians probably died in the worst-affected areas. Twenty thousand more may have died when rebel forces struck the capital, Mogadishu (see Map 7), in December 1990.[36] The worst of the suffering, however, began only in November 1991, when factional tensions among rebel groups in Mogadishu erupted in violence. Estimates of the number killed elsewhere in southern Somalia in the subsequent months of lawlessness and famine run as high as 350,000. One-fourth of Somalia's children under age five are thought to have died during this period.

For many years, the Somali conflict was by far most intense in the north, which is home to the Issaq Somali clan. Details on the fighting in the north are murky, but an uprising in May 1988 led to heavy fighting and subsequent government retaliation against the people of the area.[37] The uprising evidently came about after a rapprochement between Ethiopia and Somalia in April persuaded followers of the Somali National Movement (SNM), who had been taking shelter in Ethiopia, that their best hope of survival lay in returning home and protecting themselves as best they could against the Siad government. According to a U.S. estimate, at least 5,000 northern Somalis were murdered by government troops in the ensuing northern Somalia violence,[38] and an estimated 300,000 to 500,000 Somalis fled the war, going to neighboring countries or elsewhere within Somalia.

In the final months of 1990, war came to the south, plunging the capital into chaos. The outbreak in the capital, beginning in December and extending into early 1991, finally forced President Siad Barre, the aging dictator, to flee.

While the worst of the violence in Somalia took place only recently, the grievances that underlay the conflict extend back to the seizure of power by Siad, as an army general, in 1969. Adopting an ideology of Marxist-Leninist "scientific socialism," ostensibly aimed at eliminating "tribalism," Siad attacked beliefs and practices that had characterized Somali society for centuries.[39] Intense propaganda aimed at overcoming resistance to these policies was backed up by the security police, and reports of the arrest and detention of political prisoners accumulated through the 1970s. Meanwhile, Siad created an inner ruling circle based on his own clan and sub-clan, adding a sub-text of self-interest and hypocrisy —perfectly evident to the Somali people—to his ideological stance.[40] Siad was also discredited in the eyes of Somalis by the loss of the war with Ethiopia in 1978 and by the infirmities that came with his advancing age.

Armed Somali opposition groups became active early in the 1980s. These groups couched their opposition to Siad in terms of human rights and political freedoms, but they tended to draw their members

Map 7

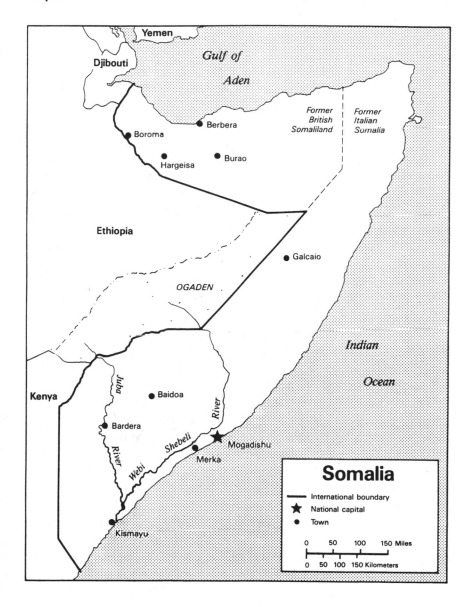

Yemen

Djibouti

Gulf of
Aden

Former
British
Somaliland

Former
Italian
Sumalia

Berbera

Boroma

Burao

Hargeisa

Ethiopia

Galcaio

OGADEN

Indian

Ocean

Kenya

Juba

Baidoa

River

Bardera

Shebeli

River

Webi

Mogadishu

Merka

Kismayu

Somalia

——— International boundary
★ National capital
● Town

0   50   100   150 Miles

0   50   100   150 Kilometers

from within particular clans—the traditional unit of social organization in Somalia. The Somali Salvation Democratic Front (SSDF), based on the southern Darod clan, was brutally suppressed, though never eliminated. In the north, however, the SNM was able to launch the May 1988 uprising, attacking Hargeisa and the port at Berbera. Siad and his supporters were shaken and their rule became increasingly uncertain and erratic. In July 1989, government troops rampaged through the capital following popular protests, and a year later they fired on a soccer stadium crowd that dared to jeer the president.

Siad tried to temporize with his domestic opposition and foreign critics, but his announcement, after the stadium shooting, of a referendum on a new constitution had no credibility. Rebel forces grew stronger as he faltered, and finally, in January 1991, Siad fled the capital in the face of an attack by combined forces of the United Somali Congress (USC), based among the Hawiye clan of central Somalia; the Somali Patriotic Movement (SPM), drawn from Ogadenis of the region straddling the border with Ethiopia; and the SSDF. The SNM did not accept the government created by these forces, and in May it announced the secession of the north. This act revived the colonial division of Somali society between British Somaliland, in the north with its capital at Hargeisa, and Italian Somaliland in the south—with other fragments in Ethiopia, Kenya, and Djibouti. However, non-Issaq groups in the North opposed the secession. Meanwhile, in Mogadishu, the USC split along sub-clan lines in November 1991. The ensuing struggle between USC leader Ali Mahdi and his erstwhile military commander, General Mohammed Farrah Aideed, divided the city and brought untold suffering to its people, who were largely cut off from the outside world. Aideed eventually founded his own Somali National Alliance (SNA).

Factional fighting in other southern Somali towns in 1992 spread the suffering to the countryside, where food production—already rendered precarious by one of Somalia's recurrent droughts—was disrupted. Despite relief efforts by the international donor community, working together with private and voluntary organizations from many countries, food could not reach the hungry because of the fighting, and widespread starvation occurred. The United States launched an airlift to towns in the interior in August 1992, but the effort was repeatedly disrupted when armed Somalis took shots at the planes. In October, relief workers fled the town of Bardere in the face of an advance by the forces of General Mohammed Hersi Morgan, Siad's son-in-law. When they returned at the end of the month, they found that 200 people a day were dying.[41] Disruptions to relief deliveries by armed gangs mounted, and on November 24, a UN ship bringing food to Mogadishu was shelled as it approached the port.

The international media, particularly television, made it impossible for the world community to ignore Somalia's suffering, and in early December the UN Security Council authorized the use of all necessary force to create a secure environment for the delivery of famine relief. This resolution had been worked out by Secretary General Boutros Boutros-Ghali in close consultation with the United States, and on December 9, U.S. armed forces launched Operation Restore Hope, which eventually brought 25,800 U.S. troops, together with 14,000 troops from other countries, to Somalia. In the first months of 1993, the U.S.-led force achieved its humanitarian objectives bringing an end to starvation and allowing near-normal life to resume. Many schools and shops reopened, Somali police were returned to the streets, and Somali political factions had reached an agreement on a transitional administration.

In June, UNOSOM II became entangled in a prolonged and damaging conflict with Aideed, who drew his support primarily from members of his own small Haber Gedir subclan living in southern Mogadishu. A former top military commander and ambassador, Aideed had aspirations to national leadership, but emerging UN plans for a political transition based on consultations among all elements of Somali society seemed certain to marginalize him. His virulent anti-UN radio broadcasts heightened tensions in the capital, and the killing of 24 Pakistani peacekeepers, evidently at the hands of Aideed supporters, brought a UN warrant for his arrest.

UNOSOM II came to rely primarily on the remaining U.S. forces for the pursuit of Aideed. The hunt proved fruitless, however, and Aideed forces were able to make the maze of streets in southern Mogadishu almost impassable to UN patrols. On October 3–4, 18 U.S. soldiers were killed in an operation aimed at arresting top Aideed lieutenants, leading President Clinton to sharply reinforce the U.S. contingent. At the same time, Clinton insisted that the United States was obliged only to give the Somali people and concerned African states a "reasonable chance" to resolve the Somali conflict. With the U.S. Congress insisting on a limit to the U.S. commitment, Clinton slated a March 31, 1994, withdrawal for American troops.

Table 2.2

Five Lesser Wars since 1980

Country	Population	Approximate Size	Regions Affected	Duration	Mortality Estimates
Liberia	2.5 million	Tennessee	north, spreading nationwide	1989-	10,000-13,000 or more
Namibia	1.6 million	half Alaska	northern border zone	1966- 1989	12,500
Western Sahara	201,500	Colorado	throughout, but moving to borders	1976-	16,000
Chad	5.2 million	three times California	northern half, east, capital	1968-	7,000 or more
Rwanda	8.2 million	Maryland	north, to capital	1990- 1993	hundreds or more

Whether UNOSOM II will be able to carry through with the Somali transition once American troops depart remains to be seen. Several other Western contributors to UNOSOM II are planning to withdraw their forces at about the same time, although new contributions from India, Pakistan, and several African countries may make up the shortfall. Meanwhile, the Somali factions have yet to reach an internal accord despite strenuous mediation efforts by the Ethiopian president and others. Thus a renewal of the conflict and of the associated civilian suffering is entirely possible.

Lesser Wars: Main Trends and Events

Five other wars—in Liberia, Namibia, Chad, Western Sahara, and Rwanda—were fought during the 1980s (Table 2.2). These wars occurred in countries or territories with generally small populations, and this factor tended to limit overall mortality. The wars in Namibia, Chad, and Western Sahara, moreover, were fought primarily in lightly populated regions, reducing the impact on civilian populations.

Two of these wars, in Namibia and Western Sahara, represented the last stage of the decolonization process in Africa, delayed in these instances because the original colonizers—Germany and Spain, respectively

—had been pushed aside by powerful and determined local actors. These local actors, South Africa and Morocco, were eventually able to win military control over local resistance forces, in part because the resistance in each case could draw on only a small population base and very limited local resources. Moreover, the arid and semi-arid conditions in each territory had forced the resistance to conduct operations in fairly open country against modern weapons deployed by the far richer occupying states. Neither Morocco nor South Africa, however, could bring the wars to a definitive conclusion by military means and each eventually turned to diplomatic solutions.

Liberia

Initially, the December 24, 1989, invasion of Liberia by a small band of rebels crossing into remote Nimba County from Ivory Coast seemed a quixotic affair of no lasting significance. The rebel leader, Charles Taylor, was a little-known former Liberian government official who had fled the country after being accused of corruption. While Taylor was thought to have some sort of tie to Libya, he had no known following in Liberia, and it was generally expected that the invaders would soon be repulsed. Instead, the rebel forces grew with astonishing rapidity and were entering Monrovia, the capital, within months. Estimates of the death toll in the Liberian fighting rarely appear, for it is rarely covered by the international media, but according to a 1991 U.S. government estimate, 10,000 to 13,000 had been killed at that time.[42] Some estimates run as high as 30,000.[43]

The surprising rebel gains in 1990 were testimony to the anger that had developed in Liberian society against the regime of Samuel K. Doe, a former sergeant who seized power in a bloody coup in 1980. Maladministration, corruption, and human rights violations were legendary in the Doe regime, and Doe sharply intensified ethnic tension by promoting disproportionate numbers of his own Krahn people, representing perhaps 4 percent of the population, into top offices. Doe conducted a highly suspect election in 1985, which provoked a coup attempt on the part of General Thomas Quiwonkpa in November of that year. After Quiwonkpa was apprehended and killed, his dismembered body was paraded around Monrovia, and Doe's troops carried out brutal reprisals against Quiwonkpa's Gio people in Nimba County.

In response to the rebel invasion in 1989, Krahn soldiers launched further attacks on civilians of the Gio and Mano ethnic groups in Nimba, intensifying the anger of the people of the area and adding fuel to the rebellion. Taylor's National Patriotic Front of Liberia (NPFL) then launched its own attacks against civilians of the Krahn and Mandingo ethnic groups.[44] Meanwhile, the NPFL split, as Prince Johnson, a guerrilla commander, broke away to found the Independent National Patriotic Front of Liberia (INPFL).

The Liberian war was marked in this period by widely publicized brutal incidents among the contending parties that contributed to a general sense of international revulsion toward the conflict. In July 1990, Doe's forces killed hundreds of displaced civilians seeking shelter at St. Peter's Lutheran Church in the capital. A photograph of Johnson exulting just after he had shot a Liberian relief worker, who was handcuffed to a French official of Catholic Relief Services, was published around the world in August 1990. In September, Johnson's forces hunted down Doe himself, who may have been trying to negotiate his departure with representatives of a West African peacekeeping force at the time of his capture. Doe was reportedly mutilated before his execution.[45]

The introduction of the West African peace force in August 1990 was an unusual and potentially hopeful aspect of the Liberian situation. Organized by the Economic Community of West African States (ECOWAS) and known as the ECOWAS Monitoring Group (ECOMOG), the force quickly grew to 7,000 troops after its initial smaller deployments proved inadequate, and had reached more than 11,500 by 1993. ECOWAS secured Monrovia and orchestrated the choice of Dr. Amos Sawyer, a respected political figure and long-time opponent of Doe's regime, as president of the Interim Government of National Unity (IGNU). In November 1990, after prolonged effort, ECOWAS arranged a cease-fire among the contending factions. Fighting within the country died down after this accord, although there were occasional clashes between NPFL fighters and those of the United Liberation Movement (ULIMO), largely consisting of Krahn followers of the late Doe.

Despite its successes, ECOMOG was troubled by dissent over its role among the West African states, where many have been concerned that it is furthering the interests of powerful Nigeria. The Nigerian army and its officers dominate the force. Despite the November 1990 accord, ECOMOG was unable to move decisively beyond the capital, leaving most of the country in the hands of Taylor's NPFL. Taylor resisted pressures to allow ECOMOG to disarm and encamp his forces prior to an election, as specified in the agreement. Meanwhile, he tried to intimidate ECOMOG participants into quitting the force—this at least is the interpretation given the 1991 invasion of Sierra Leone by guerrillas possibly including Sierra Leonean dissidents backed by the NPFL.

In October 1992, ECOMOG imposed a tough, new blockade on the Taylor-held zone and launched a military offensive intended to force the rebel leader to capitulate. The offensive at times seemed uncoordinated, and there were numerous reports of Nigerian jets mistakenly attacking civilian targets and humanitarian relief convoys. While ECOMOG made substantial military gains, its reputation suffered as the fighting dragged on for ten months. The West African force also drew criticism for coordinating its efforts with ULIMO, even though ECOMOG commanders argued that this cooperation was a matter of military necessity. Meanwhile, the continued participation of Nigerian troops, the backbone of ECOMOG, began to come into question as their country moved into an era of political crisis and transition.

Thus, the stage was set for a new round of negotiations. Finally, on July 17, 1983, following intensive mediation by UN Special Envoy Trevor Gordon-Somers and OAU Eminent Person Canaan Banana (former president of Zimbabwe), Sawyer's government, the NPFL, and ULIMO accepted a new accord at a Geneva peace conference. The agreement calls for an interim council of state to include NPFL and ULIMO representatives; free elections; and the disarming of the contending Liberian armed forces by ECOMOG forces under UN supervision. The ECOMOG forces that implement the disarmament are to be new troops drawn from African countries that have not yet participated.

Most observers give this accord a good chance for success in view of the war-weariness of Liberians and the role given to impartial outsiders. Many of Taylor's Liberian opponents, however, believe that the country would be more secure if he had been defeated. They worry that he will remain a disruptive force, partciularly if the elections go against him.

Namibia

The Southwest African People's Organization, the armed movement resisting South Africa's occupation of Namibia, was founded in 1960. The organization had its origins in a labor movement among the northern Ovambo people. The Ovambo, variously estimated at just above or just under half of Namibia's population, are themselves a major component of Namibian society and had long resented the low wages and poor working conditions offered by South African employers. South Africa's heavy-handed rule in Namibia, including the suppression of dissent and the denial of political rights to blacks, brought SWAPO thousands of recruits from other elements in society, including young urban blacks, who were drawn by the movement's militant stance.

There had long been opposition to South African policies in Namibia, but tensions mounted in the 1960s as the South African government moved toward imposing its system of "separate development," or apartheid, in the territory. Many saw this trend as evidence not only of increased political and economic repression to come, but also of a hidden South African plan to absorb Namibia within the white-ruled Republic of South Africa. SWAPO launched its armed struggle in 1966, after the International Court of Justice, on technical grounds, refused to hear a case charging that South Africa was violating the League of Nations mandate that gave it legal authority over the territory. Under the mandate, South Africa was obliged to promote the economic well-being of the people of the territory and work toward their eventual independence—objectives that were antithesis of apartheid and absorption.

SWAPO's tactics took the form of hit-and-run attacks and assassinations of black opponents for the first decade. But with the collapse of Portuguese rule in neighboring Angola, larger guerrilla bands began to infiltrate the territory. Power lines and roads were frequent targets, and from time to time there were attacks on military targets. South Africa responded with a variety of counter-insurgency measures, including land clearing along the border, the construction of a border security fence, and the resettlement of Ovambo away from the boundary region.

South Africa undertook an aggressive counter-insurgency program in 1978, combining this strategy with frequent ground and air attacks against SWAPO targets in Angola.[46] Large-scale thrusts across the border were accompanied by the use of small-scale, mobile counter-guerrilla operations on both sides of the frontier. Making use of fast, all-terrain armored vehicles and native trackers, South African forces moved freely back and forth across the border as they hunted down the lightly armed guerrilla bands moving on foot.[47] Increasingly, South African troops were supplemented by local forces, including the large Southwest African Territorial Force (SWATF), made up of both blacks and whites, and a special native counter-guerrilla force, Koevoet (Crowbar), noted for its brutality. South Africa's military might was disastrous for SWAPO. The organization is thought to have lost 10,000 to 12,000, killed over more than two decades of fighting, while losses on the other side, including South African troops and troops recruited within Namibia, have been estimated at around 500.[48] South African military intelligence claimed in 1987 that SWAPO's guerrilla strength had been reduced from 16,000 in 1968 to 8,700,[49] although other sources were still using an estimate of 12,000 guerrillas at decade's end. SWAPO was torn by factional strife, some of it ethnically based, some generational, and some arising from the pervasive fear of South African espionage. Questions about detentions and disappearances within SWAPO and doubts about the quality of its aging leadership cost it some foreign and domestic support.

Yet SWAPO persisted. When the South African regime finally concluded, in 1988, that it needed to disengage from the costly wars to the north and refocus its energies at home, it had to come to terms with SWAPO's demands including independence and free elections. Under the U.S.-brokered regional peace accord, the transition to independence began on April 1, 1989, with the arrival of the United Nations Transitional Advisory Group (UNTAG). UN-supervised elections to a constituent assembly, which later became the first national assembly, were held in November, and the last South African troops left at the end of the month. SWAPO had won 57 percent of the vote in the constituent assembly elections—somewhat less than expected—but Namibia became independent on March 21, 1990, under a SWAPO government headed by the SWAPO president, Sam Nujoma.

Western Sahara

The death toll in the war in lightly populated Western Sahara has been estimated at about 16,000, with all but 3,000 deaths occurring among the armed forces of the Moroccan government and those of the armed resistance.[50] Western Sahara had been a neglected colony of Spain from 1904 until 1975. Even in the late 1950s, the native inhabitants of the region remained primarily nomads, with strong tribal identities[51] and warring traditions. They are ethnically distinct from the Arab/Berber populations of Algeria and Morocco.

Opposition to Spanish rule began to appear in the 1960s, among the more modern elements of the population, including students educated outside the territory, workers on Spanish projects, and members of the security forces.[52] POLISARIO—the Popular Front for the Liberation of Saguiet el Hamra and Rio de Oro, the two Spanish administrative districts in the territory—was formed in 1973 and soon took a stance that was strongly nationalist and revolutionary.[53]

Faced with this internal pressure as well as pressure from regional states and the United Nations, Spain began to move forward with plans for a referendum expected to lead to Saharan independence and Spanish withdrawal. Morocco's King Hassan thwarted the move toward independence on November 6, 1975, when he launched the "Green March" of 350,000 unarmed Moroccan citizens across the border and into the territory. Hassan justified this action in terms of what he maintained was Morocco's historic sovereignty over the region. A large part of the population of Western Sahara, however, could not accept the prospect of Moroccan rule. Perhaps 60,000 crossed into Algeria.

Spain, in the face of the Green March, decided that it would get out quickly rather than confront a potential war with Morocco. Under a tripartite agreement with Morocco and Mauritania, Spanish troops were gone by the beginning of 1976. In April, Morocco and Mauritania partitioned the territory, with Mauritania receiving a comparatively small slice in the south. Mauritania was forced out in 1979 by POLISARIO military pressure, and Morocco took over its claim.

POLISARIO was fairly effective in the early stages of its war with Morocco and Mauritania partly because of help from Algeria, which provided shelter as well as large quantities of light arms, anti-aircraft missiles, anti-tank launchers, and land mines.[54] Moroccan commanders were floundering in an effort to find tactics that would succeed against the mobile desert guerrillas. Finally, in 1980, they hit upon the idea of a wall that could be quickly pushed up by bulldozers over vast arid stretches. As a first step, the "useful triangle"—from Smara, to Bou Craa, to el-Ayoun—was sealed off, allowing the reopening of the phosphate conveyor to the coast in 1982.[55] Then, in six stages, the wall was extended to the east and south until by 1987 it reached for some 1,500 miles, leaving only 7,500 square miles of Saharan territory unenclosed.[56] POLISARIO guerrillas could penetrate the wall between strong points, but they were likely to be detected in doing so and quickly attacked by Moroccan forces coming from support bases behind the wall. Important economic targets were now many miles from the wall itself, so that even if a small band crossed the wall and operated undetected for a time, it could do little of military consequence.

POLISARIO attacks were suspended in September 1988, and in February 1989 the movement announced a cease-fire while it pursued negotiations with King Hassan. At the beginning of 1990, the UN secretary general renewed his own efforts, first undertaken in 1988, to arrange a settlement. Progress was slow in these negotiations, and Hassan seemed tempted by stratagems that would allow him to delay the day of reckoning. From time to time, POLISARIO would launch attacks at the wall in order to maintain pressure on Hassan.

Each side had strong incentives for coming to terms, however. Despite his military successes, Hassan had been unable to eliminate POLISARIO as a fighting force. This reality meant that he could not reduce Morocco's costly deployments in Western Sahara without risking renewed attacks. Yet Hassan faced grave economic problems at home, where mounting popular frustrations broke out into violent riots in December 1990. POLISARIO, meanwhile, had no further capability for decisive military action, in view of Morocco's strong defenses, leaving a negotiated settlement as the only available means of achieving its objectives. Algeria, while it continued to shelter POLISARIO and the Western Sahara refugee population, seemed unlikely to take any action that would change this situation. Because of its own severe economic problems and Islamic fundamentalist agitation, both reflected in anti-government rioting in 1988 and again in 1991, POLISARIO's mentor had no interest in devoting resources to further tensions with Morocco.

Finally, after one last flareup of fighting in 1991, a United Nations transition team was allowed into Western Sahara. The 2,000-member United Nations Mission for the Referendum in Western Sahara (MINURSO) faced a difficult challenge in carrying out its mandate to monitor the cease-fire, certify eligible voters on the basis of a 1974 Spanish census, and perform other tasks in a harsh physical environment under tight budgetary constraints. Hassan's cooperation was reluctant at best and Morocco was retaining troops in the territory during the transition period. Over the years it has brought in some 100,000 settlers from Morocco proper who will not participate in the referendum but, like the Moroccan troops, have a strong interest in the outcome. By mid-1993, Hassan was again emphasizing Morocco's sovereignty over Western Sahara and urging POLISARIO to accept that it must return and live in a Moroccan region. Thus the stage seems set for further stalemate or a potential renewal of fighting.

Chad

Chad is a faction-ridden country of numerous tribes, clans, and subclans engaged in generations-old rivalries and intrigues. At the same time, it has been the continuous object of the attentions of Libya's leader, Muamar al-Qadhafi, who has repeatedly interfered in Chad's politics and covets the northern mineral-rich zone known as the Aouzou strip. A regime of unusual strength and finesse would have been required to win popular support and avert political violence in such a situation. Instead, Chad has had a series of weak regimes that have ruled without wide support, repeatedly resorting to repressive measures in unsuccessful attempts to maintain control.

Chad's history of conflict is difficult to recount in any reasonable space, and this overview must be confined to a few main trends and events. One key dimension of conflict in the early years was resistance among the northern Toubou people, also known as the Goranes, to incidents of repression on the part of a government based among the southern Sara. The Toubou are a proud and independent Muslim people from the Tibesti mountains, who may number about 250,000,[57] while the Sara are a Christianized group living in the capital region where higher levels of rainfall make farming possible. Northern resistance forces heavily backed by Libya managed to seize the capital in 1979. Goukouni Oueddei, son of the Derde, the traditional Toubou leader, became head of a coalition government composed of four armed factions.

With northerners in power, the focus of conflict shifted to rivalries among Toubou leaders and clans. Hissein Habré, a former partner of Goukouni's, and once described as a "Marxist-ex-lawyer turned guerrilla leader,"[58] had been included in the Goukouni regime as defense minister. Habré is also a Toubou, but from a different area and subgroup than Goukouni. The two leaders soon fell out, and Libyan troops helped Goukouni drive Habré from the capital in 1980.

Goukouni did not trust Qadhafi's intentions, however, and asked Libyan forces to leave in late 1981. He unwisely put his fate in the hands of an Organization of African Unity (OAU) peacekeeping force. In 1982, this force was outflanked by Habré's guerrillas, who had regrouped in Sudan and came in from the east. Goukouni retreated to the north, where he began to reorganize—again with Libyan help.

In an effort to repel a return of a Libyan-backed regime, France sent troops and aircraft into Chad in 1983 to establish a "Red Line" across the country at the 16th parallel. Under an agreement with Libya in late 1984, the French pulled out, only to return in 1986 after Goukouni's forces, reportedly stiffened by Libyan troops,[59] attacked south of the Red Line. The United States also flew in emergency aid in response to this renewed threat from the north. Habré was further strengthened when Goukouni and Qadhafi had a falling out in Libya, leading, in December 1986, to defections among Goukouni's guerrillas in the Tibesti mountains.

This weakness among enemy forces set the stage for Habré's remarkable offensive into the north in 1987. Making use of light overland vehicles mounted with machine guns and cannon, Habré's highly mobile columns swept into northern oases and forced the Libyans to retreat from their base at Faya Largeau by the end of March. In August 1987, the Habré forces entered Aouzou, and in September, they struck across the border at a Libyan airbase. These positions could not be sustained, however, and the two sides drew back from an escalating war to accept an OAU call for a cease-fire. Thousands of disoriented and demoralized Libyan troops, as well as large stores of equipment, including tanks and aircraft, were captured by the Habré forces in 1987. The Libyans had been trapped in defensive positions and were unable to make effective use of their Soviet-built tanks against the lightning attacks of the Chadians.

After 1987, tensions eased for a time in Chad. Qadhafi seemed to be seeking regional respectability, which required that he abstain from open interference in Chad, while French forces, though reduced, remained as a stabilizing influence. Habré scored a series of internal political successes, reconciling with his most important opponents and bringing various exiled ethnic and ideological factions home to join an umbrella political party, the Union for Independence and Reconstruction.

Yet even as outside observers were praising Habré for building a national consensus, resentment to his rule was growing among key elements of Chadian society. Complaints were heard in the capital over the "Goranization" of government by Habré's northern tribal allies. Political repression mounted, and evidence came to light after Habré's ouster of large-scale torture of political prisoners, who may have numbered in the thousands.[60] Habré turned on his tribal allies, and reports of attacks on the Zaghawa group, a branch of the Goranes, proved his undoing. Habré evidently suspected prominent Zaghawa in the government of plotting against him, and this precipitated the decision of Colonel Idris Deby, a Zaghawa, to flee with others into Sudan.[61] Deby was the tactical mastermind of the 1987 victory over Libya, and such a grave threat that Habré sent forces into Sudan in an unsuccessful effort to apprehend him. The Deby forces were widely suspected of receiving substantial Libyan support in Sudan.

Fighting within Chad began to be reported again in March 1990, and within a few months it was clear that the military threat was a serious one. France, perhaps stung by mounting charges of human rights violations against a leader it had helped to protect for years, showed no inclination to play the part of savior once again. Thus, at the beginning of December, as the world's attention was focused on the Persian Gulf crisis, Deby's forces swept in from the Sudan border and Habré fled. Soon charges of repression in southern Chad were being leveled against Deby, who appeared to be under the influence not only of Libya but also of Sudan and the Sudanese Islamic resurgence leader Hassan al-Turabi. In subsequent months, and into 1993, there were ongoing reports of outbreaks of armed resistance around Lake Chad and along the Sudanese border. It seemed certain that Chad's long history of factional strife and political violence would continue.

Rwanda

The human costs of the Rwanda war, which broke out unexpectedly in October 1990, are unclear, but it appears that hundreds have died. According to government sources, about 550,000 people have had to flee areas of fighting.[62] This conflict has its roots in the long history of conflict between the Tutsi ethnic minority and the Hutu majority. In pre-colonial times, a Tutsi elite had ruled in Rwanda through a monarchical government, a feudal economic system based on the exchange of cattle, and a highly stratified social system which placed the Hutu at the bottom of the scale. While the Tutsi remained the favored social group for most of the colonial period, the Belgian colonial authorities, as they prepared for departure, revolutionized society by putting Hutu in control. They were evidently motivated by a belief that Tutsi nationalists were too radical and a conviction that a majority-based system would be more just.

The change in Belgian policy led to rising social tensions, and hundreds, including many Tutsi chiefs and sub-chiefs, were killed in 1959. Thousands of Tutsi fled to neighboring countries, and after independence in 1961, bands of Tutsi guerrillas, calling themselves Inyenzi, or "cockroaches," began to launch armed raids back into Rwanda. After a large raid in December 1963, Hutu gangs carried out attacks on Tutsi civilians remaining in Rwanda, killing an estimated 10,000.[63] The Inyenzi raids ended after 1966, but by that time there were perhaps 150,000 Tutsi refugees in neighboring states, including 50,000 to 70,000 in Uganda.[64] The Tutsi in Rwanda may number about 10 percent of the population today, down from 14 percent in the colonial period.[65]

The Tutsi refugees in Uganda, whose numbers grew to perhaps 200,000 by natural increase, also experienced economic hardship and discrimination. A wave of violence against Rwandans in Uganda— Hutu as well as Tutsi—broke out in 1982, evidently with official encouragement.[66] Nonetheless, through hard work and with assistance from international relief agencies, some refugees managed to advance their economic status and attain modern educations. Suffering like other residents of Uganda under the rule of Amin and Obote, many joined Yoweri Museveni's NRA, and a few—including for a time Uganda's deputy defense minister—moved into top command positions.

While the Rwandans seemed increasingly integrated into Ugandan society, tensions persisted. Many refugees continued to hope for repatriation, or at least wanted the right to repatriation, in the belief, probably mistaken, that their economic opportunities might be better in their homeland. Some Rwandans, including officers in the NRA, organized the shadowy Rwanda Patriotic Front (RPF), advocating a formal program of unity, democracy, and an end to discrimination in Rwanda.[67]

At the end of September 1990, officers and soldiers of Rwandan origin in the NRA began to desert their posts and move toward the border. They crossed on October 1 and, declaring themselves the Rwanda Patriotic Army (RPA), advanced rapidly toward the capital until troops from Belgium and France arrived, ostensibly to protect foreign nationals, and the situation stabilized. An unknown number of Tutsi villagers, probably in the hundreds, were killed within Rwanda in Hutu revenge attacks after the initial invasion, but fears of killings on the scale of 1959 did not materialize. Estimates of the RPA's size range up to 7,000 men, and the group—despite its initial defeat—continued to launch raids from forest shelters in 1991.

In November 1991, the RPF was able to launch a new offensive, killing a number of Rwandan soldiers. Violent clashes continued in 1992, and at the beginning of 1993, there was bitter fighting at Ruhengeri, forty miles northwest of the capital. International mediators continued to push for a negotiated settlement, and the OAU sent a military monitoring group to Rwanda in an effort to stabilize the situation. An accord calling for an all-party government and the deployment of a small international peacekeeping force was finally signed on August 4, 1993. However, the willingness of the international community to bear the risks and costs of a peacekeeping operation in Rwanda remained unclear. In the absence of a substantial international commitment, outbreaks of Tutsi/Hutu fighting might well recur.

Whether President Museveni had foreknowledge of the initial RPA invasion is a topic of hot debate in East Africa. His critics say that he must have known about the plans and activities of such a large part of his military and they accuse him of planning to set up a satellite state in Rwanda.[68] Defenders note that Museveni has been a pragmatic leader since coming to power, and not given to this sort of grandiose scheme, which would have been more characteristic of Amin or Obote.

Related Internal Conflict Situations

Africa has experienced much internal conflict, including coups, strikes, riots, and student demonstrations over the years that have not resembled war and had little potential for evolving into war. However, many conflict situations have resembled Africa's wars in certain ways. Table 2.3 lists a number of these situations occurring since 1980. Some were marked by a particularly high death toll. For example, the unsuccessful Hutu uprising against the dominant but minority Tutsi in Burundi in 1988 had a level of mortality higher than that in some of the lesser

Table 2.3

Related Conflict Situations since 1980

Country	Situation/ Location	Date	Mortality Estimates
Burundi	Hutu protest in north	1988	7,000-13,000
	ethnic violence surrounding attempted coup by Hutu military elements	1993	uncertain, probably thousands
Djibouti	armed Afar resistance to Issa-dominated regime	1991-	probably low hundreds
Kenya	Somali unrest, poaching in north and east	1964-	probably less than 100 in the 1980s
	tribally based cattle rustling in northwest	1964-	possibly hundreds in the 1980s
	political opposition groups in urban areas; political/ethnic violence in western Kenya and Rift Valley	escalating since mid-1980s	some deaths among political prisoners and demonstrators; deaths in recent ethnic clashes nearing 1,000
Lesotho	armed opposition along borders and in capital	1970-1986	probably less than 100 during 1980s
Malawi	exiled opposition groups, alleged secessionism in north	1981-	few
Mali, Niger, Algeria	Tuareg unrest	1990-	perhaps 100 or more
Mauritania	black African opposition in the south and capital	1987-	200 or more

Table 2.3 *(continued)*

Niger	Hausa/Peul fighting over cattle grazing rights	1991-	100
Senegal	separatist movement in south	1982-	low hundreds
	violence against Mauritanians	1989	60
South Africa	armed opposition groups, urban and external	1961-	low hundreds during 1980s
	urban political violence	1913-	several thousand in 1980s, 6,000 since 1990
Tunisia	raids by Libyan-backed opposition at Gafsha	1980	25 - 300
Zaire	diverse dissident groups in several regions, urban protests	continuous	uncertain
Zimbabwe	Ndebele dissidents in southwest	1982-1988	2,000-2500

wars. The religious strife in northern Nigeria, stemming partly from the activities of the pseudo-Islamic Maitatsine sect and partly from Islamist opposition to a secular regime, had a nearly comparable toll. Some of these conflicts also involved armed dissident movements, which nearly acquired the capability of confronting the armed forces of regimes in war.

The South African conflict in particular has been regarded by many analysts as essentially a civil war—particularly from 1976, after the ranks of the exiled African National Congress (ANC) were swelled by volunteers for guerrilla warfare following the Soweto uprising, until 1990, when the ANC was legalized and negotiations began.[69] The military wing of the ANC, Umkhonto we Sizwe, came to command thousands of troops, many with foreign training; to possess large quantities of modern weapons; and to control external military bases. But if the confrontation was a war, it was a different sort of war than the others discussed in this book. South Africa's military and security apparatus proved fully capable of keeping the great bulk of the ANC's military forces at bay outside South Africa, preventing the movement from controlling territory within the country. Only small numbers of guerrillas were successfully infiltrated. ANC military operations consisted largely of symbolic attacks intended to inspire popular resistance rather than accomplish military objectives.[70] Combat casualties, which occurred primarily when South African forces intercepted infiltrators, were limited.

The large majority of deaths in South Africa's racial strife during the 1980s occurred not in these clashes but in political violence, in the African townships and as a result of the "excessive use of force by police"[71] against civilians. Clearly they were not the indirect result of guerrilla action in the way that civilian deaths in southern Sudan or Mozambique were. Thus, the situation in South Africa in the 1980s was unlike the wars occurring elsewhere in Africa in many important ways.

During the 1980s and early 1990s, in short, none of these other conflict situations developed into a war involving government forces and a resistance army waging combat on a substantial scale. In rare instances, particularly in the case of the unrest in southwestern Zimbabwe, avoidance of war reflected a regime's eventual ability to come to terms with the underlying grievances that led to conflict. In other instances where war seemed possible, it was avoided simply because the regimes in question proved powerful enough, at least for the moment, to suppress the opposition. Could some of these conflict situations that were not wars develop into wars in the future? An answer to this question, which will surely vary from case to case, requires an analysis of the causes of Africa's wars, and of the contributing factors, both internal and external, that helped make them possible.

Notes

1. Based on 1989 data appearing in U.S. Committee for Refugees, *World Refugee Survey—1989 in Review* (Washington, D.C.: U.S. Committee for Refugees, 1990).

2. Sivard gives an estimate of 500,000 civilian deaths in Ethiopia from 1974 through 1990, and the same number in Sudan for the years just since 1984. Sivard reports 1 million civilian deaths and 50,000 deaths among soldiers in Mozambique due to war and famine between 1981 and 1990. Thus, according to her

data, the Mozambique war was the most serious. Ruth Leger Sivard, *World Military and Social Expenditures, 1991,* 14th ed. (Washington, D.C.: World Priorities, 1991), 25.

3. This was the estimate used by the Honorable Howard Wolpe, chairman of the House Subcommittee on Africa, in March 1989. House, *Politics of Hunger in Sudan,* Joint Hearing, 1.

4. Statement on Peace and Relief in Sudan, 8 February 1989. See also the testimony of the Hon. Frank Wolf suggesting that as many as 1 million may have died in 1988. House, *Politics of Hunger in Sudan,* Joint Hearing, 7.

5. Sudanese radio broadcast, recorded in U.S. Foreign Broadcast Information Service, *Daily Report, Sub-Saharan Africa,* 14 November 1989, 2. (Hereafter, the sub-Saharan edition will be referred to as *FBIS.)*

6. "Sudan Peace Talks Fail over Islamic Code," *New York Times,* 6 December 1989.

7. *Africa Research Bulletin,* Political Series, September 1991, 10282.

8. This is the estimate used by former President Carter for battle casualties and starvation resulting from the war in northern Ethiopia. "Carter Likes Mood of Ethiopia Talks," *New York Times,* 10 September 1989. A former official of the Ethiopian government estimates that the mortality in Eritrea included 90,000 Ethiopian soldiers, 9,000 guerrillas, and 280,000 civilians between 1975 and 1983 alone. Dawit Wolde Giorgis, *Red Tears: War, Famine, and Revolution in Ethiopia* (Trenton, N.J.: Red Sea Press, 1989), 113.

9. Sivard, *World Military and Social Expenditures, 1991,* 25.

10. Paul Henze, *Rebels and Separatists in Ethiopia: Regional Resistance to a Marxist Regime,* report prepared for the Office of the Under Secretary of Defense for Policy (Santa Monica, Calif.: Rand Corporation, December 1985), 35.

11. Wolde Giorgis, *Red Tears.*

12. As noted above, Sivard reported 1,050,000 deaths from 1981 through 1990. *World Military and Social Expenditures, 1991,* 22. After the 1992 accord was signed, the figure of 1 million dead was often cited in the press. See Jane Perlez, "A Mozambique Formally at Peace is Bled by Hunger and Brutality," *New York Times,* 13 October 1992. An estimate of 600,000 also appeared. See Trevor Rowe, "UN Force for Mozambique Sought," *Washington Post,* 8 December 1992.

13. UNICEF, *Children on the Front Line,* 3d ed. (New York: UNICEF, 1989), 24–25.

14. United Nations Inter-Agency Task Force, Africa Recovery Program/Economic Commission for Africa, *South African Destabilization: The Economic Cost of Frontline Resistance to Apartheid* (Addis Ababa and New York, October 1989), 21.

15. Barbara Cole, *The Elite: The Story of the Rhodesian Special Air Service,* 2d ed. (Amanzimtoti, South Africa: Three Knights, 1984), 244.

16. Stephen Metz, "The Mozambique National Resistance and South African Foreign Policy," *African Affairs* 85 (October 1986): 493.

17. Jack Wheeler, "RENAMO: Winning One in Africa," *Soldier of Fortune,* February 1986, 68; Allen Isaacman, "Mozambique and the Regional Conflict in Southern Africa," *Current History* (May 1987): 216.

18. Precise figures are not available, but in 1980, the State Department estimated that between 2,000 and 10,000 remained in detention. U.S. Congress, House, Committee on Foreign Affairs, and Senate, Committee on Foreign Rela-

tions, *Country Reports on Human Rights Practices, for 1981,* 100th Cong., 2d sess., 1982, report submitted by the Department of State (Washington, D.C.: U.S. Government Printing Office, 1981), 181 (hereafter cited as Department of State, *Country Reports on Human Rights).*

19. Wheeler, "RENAMO: Winning One in Africa," 118; Metz, "The Mozambique National Resistance and South African Foreign Policy," 495; and David Martin and Phyllis Johnson, "Mozambique: To Nkomati and Beyond," in Johnson and Martin, *Destructive Engagement: Southern Africa at War* (Harare: Zimbabwe Publishing House for the Southern African Research and Documentation Centre, 1986), 13–14.

20. Ken Flower, *Serving Secretly: An Intelligence Chief on Record—Rhodesia into Zimbabwe, 1964–1981* (London: John Murray, 1987), 262.

21. A South African–sponsored investigation, including British and American experts, concluded that the crash resulted from errors on the part of the crew. President Chissano, without specifically naming South Africa, claimed that Machel was murdered; Maputo radio broadcast, 17 June 1987, recorded in *FBIS,* Middle East and Africa ed., 19 June 1987, D1–D2.

22. Andrew Meldrum, "Mozambique: Lessons from Angola," *Africa Report,* January–February 1993, 22–24.

23. Sivard estimates 320,000 civilian deaths and 21,000 military deaths in the years 1975 through 1990; *World Military and Social Expenditures, 1991,* 25.

24. United Nations Inter-Agency Task Force, *South African Destabilization,* 26.

25. This includes the deaths of 330,000 infants and children as well as 100,000 war-related famine deaths at mid-decade. Combat deaths would add many more; UNICEF, *Children on the Front Line,* 24–25.

26. John Stockwell, *In Search of Enemies: A CIA Story* (New York: W.W. Norton, 1978); Wayne S. Smith, "A Trap in Angola," *Foreign Policy* (Spring 1986): 66–69.

27. Gillian Gunn, "A Guide to the Intricacies of the Angola–Namibia Negotiations," *CSIS Africa Notes* (8 September 1988): 3.

28. U.S. Department of State, Bureau of Public Affairs, *Agreements for Peace in Southwestern Africa,* Selected Documents, no. 32 (Washington, D.C.: December 1988).

29. U.S. Committee for Refugees, *Human Rights in Uganda: A Season of Hope for its Refugees and Displaced Persons,* Issue Brief (Washington, D.C.: May 1986), 3. Sivard puts the figure at 300,000 civilians and 8,000 soldiers for the period 1981–1987; *World Military and Social Expenditures, 1991,* 25.

30. Catherine Watson, "Uganda's Women: A Ray of Hope," *Africa Report,* July–August 1988, 29.

31. U.S. Department of State, Bureau of Public Affairs, *Uganda: Background Notes* (Washington, D.C.: September 1985), 4. Museveni estimates that 300,000 died under Amin. Watson, "Uganda's Women," 29.

32. Mahmood Mamdani, "Uganda in Transition: Two Years of the NRA/NRM," *Third World Quarterly* 10 (July 1988): 1159.

33. Ibid.

34. See Jonathan Wright, "The Gospel, According to Uganda's Rebel Priestess," *Kenya Daily Nation* (Nairobi), 30 October 1987; Sheila Rule, "The Rebel-

lion Withers for a Priestess in Uganda," *New York Times*, 26 December 1987; Todd J. Shields, "Priestess Loses in Uganda Long March," *Washington Post*, 23 November 1987.

35. Amnesty International, *Uganda: The Failure to Safeguard Human Rights* (London, 1992).

36. *Africa Research Bulletin*, Political Series, February 1992, 10472.

37. Amnesty International, *Somalia: A Long-Term Human Rights Crisis* (London: 1988), 7, 39.

38. Robert Gersony, *Why Somalis Flee Synthesis of Accounts of Conflict Experience in Northern Somalia by Somali Refugees, Displaced Persons and Others* (Washington, D.C.: Department of State, 1989), 61. Africa Watch places the figure at between 50,000 and 60,000; *Somalia: A Government at War with Its Own People* (New York and Washington, D.C.: January 1990), 10.

39. I.M. Lewis, "The Ogaden and the Fragility of Somali Segmentary Nationalism," *African Affairs* 88 (October 1989): 573–79.

40. Ibid.

41. U.S. Library of Congress, Congressional Research Service, *Somalia: War and Famine*, CRS Issue Brief 92112, by Theodros S. Dagne (Washington, D.C.: continuously updated).

42. U.S. Agency for International Development, Office of Foreign Disaster Assistance, *West Africa—Displaced Persons*, Situation Report no. 15, (Washington, D.C.: USAID 25 January 1991), 1.

43. Reed Kramer, "Liberians Turn Toward the Future," *Washington Post*, 10 April 1991.

44. Africa Watch, *Liberia: A Human Rights Disaster; Violations of the Laws of War by All Parties to the Conflict*, Washington, D.C.: 26 October 1990.

45. Ibid., 9.

46. Robert Jaster, *South Africa in Namibia: The Botha Strategy* (Lanham, Md.: University Press of America; Boston: Center for International Affairs, Harvard University, 1985), 20–21.

47. Jim Hooper, "COIN Operations in Namibia," *Armed Forces* 7 (May 1988): 218–22. See also Hooper, "Namibia's Bush War: Scant Success for SWAPO," *International Defense Review* 20 (1987): 1467–69.

48. Hooper, "Namibia's Bush War," gives an estimate of 12,000 killed and captured. The *Economist*, however, in "Why South Africa Holds On in Namibia", 13 June 1987, reports a South African estimate of 12,000 guerrillas killed. Another source estimates that 10,000 guerrillas had been killed over the previous decade; William Claiborne, "Namibia's Forgotten Bush War," *Washington Post*, 16 June 1987.

49. Claiborne, "Namibia's Forgotten Bush War."

50. Sivard, *World Military and Social Expenditures, 1991*, 25.

51. On Saharawi history and culture, as well as the geography and natural history of the region, see John Mercer, *Spanish Sahara* (London: George Allen and Unwin, 1976).

52. John Damis, *Conflict in Northwest Africa: The Western Sahara Dispute* (Stanford: Hoover Institution Press, 1983), 13.

53. Tony Hodges, "The Origins of Saharawi Nationalism," *Third World Quarterly* 5 (January 1983): 52–54; Damis, *Conflict in Northwest Africa*, 39–42.

54. Damis, *Conflict in Northwest Africa*, 82.

55. Ibid.

56. John Marks, "Africa's Forgotten War," *Africa Report*, September–October 1987, 18.

57. J.P. Peroncel-Hugoz, "Chad at the Risk of Peace: President Hissein Habré Will Have to Know How to Resist the Temptations of Absolute Power," *Le Monde*, 2 December 1988. Translated and reprinted in *FBIS*, 5 January 1989, 2.

58. Samuel DeCalo, "Chad: the Roots of Center–Periphery Strife," *African Affairs* 79 (October 1980): 503.

59. French officials and Habré reportedly gave an estimate of 5,000 Libyan troops in Chad at this time; Judith Miller, "Libya Continues to Deny It Fights for the Rebels in Chad," *New York Times*, 21 February 1986.

60. British Broadcasting Corporation, BBC Focus on Africa, 6 December 1990; recorded in *FBIS*, 7 December 1990. Kenneth B Noble, "Torture is Linked to Chad Ex Chief," *New York Times*, 7 December 1990.

61. "Chad: The Threat from Darfur," *Africa Confidential*, 15 December 1989.

62. Reuters, 12 February 1993.

63. U.S. Committee for Refugees, *Exile from Rwanda: Background to an Invasion*, prepared by Catherine Watson (Washington, D.C.: February 1991).

64. Ibid., 6.

65. Ibid., 6. This source notes that some observers believe the true figure to be somewhat higher.

66. Ibid., 10.

67. Ibid., 14.

68. "Rwandan Debacle: Museveni's Failed Gamble," *New African*, December 1990.

69. Stephen M. Davis, in an authoritative study, uses the terms "armed insurgency" and "civil war"; *Apartheid's Rebels: Inside South Africa's Hidden War* (New Haven: Yale University Press, 1987), 21, 35.

70. Ibid., 120.

71. U.S. Congress, House, Committee on Foreign Affairs, and Senate, Committee on Foreign Relations, *Country Reports on Human Rights Practices, for 1987*, 100th Cong., 2d sess., 1988, report submitted by the Department of State (Washington, D.C.: U.S. Government Printing Office, 1987), 272.

3 DOMESTIC CAUSES AND CONTRIBUTING FACTORS

The roots of Africa's wars lie in what many scholars now acknowledge to be a "problem with the African state":[1] its failure to respond to Africa's "heterogeneous social reality."[2] In the era when most African states were coming to independence, outside observers and African political leaders had high expectations of the African state. Many thought that it would be able to "mobilize" African populations, extract an economic surplus, and "modernize" African societies. Some saw this modernization as leading Africa toward political and economic systems modeled on those of the West, with a strong private sector, political checks and balances, and protection of basic human rights. Others expected Africa to move in a socialist direction, with a leading economic role for the state and guarantees of economic justice.

With the passage of time, these high expectations were disappointed. Efforts to mobilize African societies seemed to lose energy, and some of the governments that had most actively sought such mobilization, as in Ghana, evolved into personalist forms of rule. Within a few years of independence, bloody military coups began to occur and high levels of political corruption in many countries became impossible to deny. Africa's economic decline in the 1970s, worsening problems in governance around the continent, and the widening scale of Africa's wars led to a shift in scholarly attention away from the capabilities of the African state to its "incapabilities."[3] Far from being able to transform and modernize African societies, some states were, by the early 1980s, seen as so weak that they owed their existence primarily to the international recognition they happened to enjoy.[4] Others were able to extract substantial economic resources from society, but spent those resources primarily on a small ruling clique, the police, and the military—while failing to deliver basic services or foster economic development.[5] A new vocabulary, including such terms as the "soft state,"[6] "lame Leviathans,"[7] and "pathological patrimonialism,"[8] was developed to describe the essential nature of the contemporary African state.

Many observers of African affairs have now concluded that the underlying reason for the weakness of African states was the widening gap after independence between African states and African societies. After independence, around the continent, opportunities for political participation—including opportunities to oppose, compete, and dissent —steadily eroded[9] as African leaders sought to hold on to power and promote their own interests and those of their immediate supporters.[10] Patrimonial or "prebendal"[11] forms of government became widespread, as "the distinction between public trust and private gain"[12] fell into disuse. Mistakenly, leaders believed that they could undermine opportunities for participation without encountering significant opposition from within the societies they governed. It turned out, however, that many states were far weaker than their leaders realized, and that in many societies there were sources of opposition with a strong indigenous base. These included factions with a political, ethnic, or clan origin; regionally based opposition forces; religious movements; and local leaders and strongmen.[13]

In most African countries, for a variety of reasons, the widening gap between state and society did not lead to war. Some states, though increasingly authoritarian over time, remained capable of some adjustment to social reality. These included several states with what one leading text describes as "administrative-hegemonial" regimes,[14] as in Kenya, Zambia, Malawi, and Zaire. In these states, rulers sought to marginalize and exclude their most articulate and effective opponents, often making use of repressive tactics. In doing so they sometimes encountered resistance, such as student strikes and urban demonstrations. But they were pragmatic enough to make concessions and provide benefits to the principal ethnic, regional, religious, and other groups in society—and to include their representatives in the government. Often, they were assisted in this careful balancing act by large infusions of foreign aid.[15] As a result, some administrative-hegemonial regimes managed to hold on to power for years, although mounting opposition from within society, together with donor pressure for economic and political reforms, now appears to be bringing most of them to an end.

One regime, that of South Africa, had instruments of coercion at its disposal sufficient to prevent internal war despite the denial of participation to vast dissenting groups within society. But there too, societal and international pressures are at last bringing regime change. A few states, such as Botswana and Senegal, have allowed fairly broad participation and some expression of dissent through multi-party systems, so that major groupings within society have not had reason to resort to war.

In the countries that fell victim to war, governments refused to permit broad participation in the state even though they lacked instruments of coercion that remotely approached those available to the South African regime. They were too weak to impose their policy decisions on reluctant ethnic, regional, religious, or other groups within society or to force them to forever tolerate repressive, corrupt, or arbitrary behavior. This fundamental error often led to war, particularly when contributing factors, such as access to weapons, an external sponsor, and the availability of remote areas for organizing resistance, were present.

Errors of Policy and Conduct

Each of Africa's wars has been preceded by grave errors of policy and conduct on the part of the regime. Major policy decisions were sometimes taken suddenly with little or no attempt at consultation with affected groups and no genuine effort to accommodate their interests or obtain their consent. Opportunities for these groups to complain and seek redress after the fact were limited, and expressions of dissent were likely to be punished. Resistance was the inevitable outcome, and when governments proved unable to control that resistance, war followed.

Even the war in Mozambique, which is often attributed solely to outside interference from Rhodesia and South Africa, shows evidence of this pattern. In the aftermath of revolution, an exuberant FRELIMO attempted to revolutionize Mozambican society. Decisions that required major changes in education, religious life, the economy, and peasant farming were taken by an inner group within an elite party at the 1977 party congress, at a time when many rural Mozambicans were still only dimly aware that a revolution had taken place. FRELIMO was a small, primarily urban-based Marxist party that had no mandate for this sort of change—either from the rural population of northern Mozambique, where it had operated during the revolution, or from the south, where it had hardly any presence before independence. Consequently, when the party tried to impose its revolution on society, consigning dissenters and those suspected of dissent to re-education camps, imprisonment, or worse,[16] elements of Mozambican society became alienated from the state. It was this alienation that enabled Rhodesian intelligence to foster armed resistance to the regime. FRELIMO finally moderated its policies and tried to broaden its base of popular support, but with external help RENAMO had by then established itself in the rural areas and could not be eradicated.

The renewal of the war in southern Sudan reflected a similar pattern. President Numeiry, as an Arab, a Moslem, and a northerner, was perhaps even more divorced from the society of southern Sudan than was FRELIMO from Mozambican society. Northern political elites had always had limited knowledge of the south, even though they felt a call to reshape the region's society along the lines of northern Arab-Islamic culture.[17] The dangers of this attitude had already been made fully clear in the first southern war, and Numeiry's drastic decision to redivide the south and impose Islamic law in 1983 inevitably brought new armed resistance.

King Hassan's decision to launch the Green March into Western Sahara was the same sort of dramatic initiative, launched without reference to the affected society, and it also provoked a war. The decision may have been popular in Morocco itself at the time, but it showed a contempt for views and opinions within the very distinct society of Western Sahara. Haile Selassie attempted to clothe his annexation of Eritrea in an aura of legitimacy by winning approval from the Eritrean assembly. But Eritrean society had developed its own separate identity, and within that society it was widely accepted that the assembly had been intimidated and subverted. Mengistu persisted in attempting to force the government's will on Eritrea and on the other resistant elements of the Ethiopian population—a policy error that eventually brought his overthrow at the hands of a rebel army.

In some instances, it has not so much been policy that provoked societal resistance but repressive, corrupt, and abusive behavior on the part of the regime. This sort of conduct was of course a factor in the resistance to Mengistu in Ethiopia, and it undermined the willingness of Ethiopian soldiers to die for his regime. The brutal excesses of the Doe regime in Liberia, particularly in the wake of the 1985 Quiwonkpa affair, were directly related to the swift collapse of government authority in the Gio and Mano inhabited areas after Taylor's invasion. In Uganda, President Obote's grab for power in the disputed 1980 election was too much for key elements in society to accept. Major political opponents and a large part of the Baganda and other Bantu ethnic groups could not tolerate the prospect of a return to the corruption and repression of the first Obote regime. Many feared that Obote would perpetuate the domination of the Bantu south by a capricious northern military that had backed Amin. In Somalia, meanwhile, Siad Barre brought on a war through human rights abuses and the repression of dissent aimed at excluding major clans—the essential elements of Somali society—from power.

More prudent governments would have taken care to build consensus among key elements in society before launching major policy initiatives; and they would have sought to avoid shocking abuses of power that could alienate them from those key elements. More capable governments, with ample resources at their command, might have had some hope of forcing the affected elements in society to accept unpopular policies and actions—but most of the governments that fell victim to war had very limited capabilities. The Moroccan regime did over time build up a powerful and efficient army that belatedly acquired the ability to put down armed opposition inside Western Sahara. South Africa nearly succeeded in achieving a military solution in Namibia. But even these regimes could not achieve a final resolution of the underlying conflicts by force alone. Less capable governments had little hope of forcing their errors of policy and conduct on resistant societies.

Sources of Societal Resistance

When African governments committed errors of policy and conduct, they ran up against opposition forces that articulated their grievances in terms of modern political ideas, including Western ideals of human rights and democracy, and Marxist concepts of class struggle. Those advocating these positions, however, were typically based in a major ethnic group within society or in a region that had developed some sense of distinctness over time. In this sense, Africa's resistance leaders were often closer to society—or to important elements in society—than were the leaders of government. It is the strength of such ethnic and regional forces that has proved so surprising to those who thought the post-independence period in Africa would be an era of "state building."

Ethnic and Regional Factors

Africa's wars are often thought of as essentially tribal wars—wars of one tribe, which happens to control the government, against some excluded tribe, which may be in the majority and seeking to take over the government, or a minority aiming at secession. The reality of Africa is never this simple. None of the major rebel movements active during the 1980s justified its stance in terms of tribal ambitions. Most insisted that they were fighting not for tribal hegemony or secession but for broader human rights and political change in society as a whole. Most movements included at least some representatives of diverse tribal or ethnic backgrounds, and they typically denounced any suggestion that they were essentially tribal groups.

Nonetheless, the fact that most African resistance movements had a base in a major ethnic group or region, or sometimes both, can hardly be denied. Such ties are sometimes referred to as "primordial" in the sense that they preceded the creation of the independent state—although scholars note that the emergence of an ethnic or regional awareness is often quite recent.[18] British colonial policy, for example, helped to solidify the concept of shared society in southern Sudan,[19] just as the Italian colonizers helped to create the idea of "Eritrea." In the post-independence period, as the gap between state and society has widened, these "primordial" allegiances have often deepened.

The Tigray People's Liberation Front offers one example of resistance leaders who are firmly based in an ethnic group advocating modern political concepts. Until its moderation at the end of the 1980s, the TPLF ideology had been a strident, Marxist call to revolution and not an assertion of ethnic objectives. It was devised by an educated leadership, many of whom had left the Addis Ababa university during the chaos of the 1970s. But these leaders were Tigrayan, and their movement thrived because of a sense of solidarity among the people of Tigray, who nurture historic grievances against the Amhara. A

Tigrayan rebellion had broken out against the Ethiopian government as recently as 1943.[20] Many Tigrayans, moreover, regard their culture not only as ancestral to the Amhara culture of Addis Ababa, but also superior to it. Primordial loyalties may also have affected government behavior in the Ethiopian war, as in other wars. Many believe that Mengistu perceived himself as heir to the line of Amhara warrior-emperors, expanding the empire and pacifying the fractious provinces. Clearly, large numbers of Amhara objected to Mengistu's policies and conduct, but many gave grudging assent to his rule in the hope that he could hold Ethiopia together—or at the end, in the disappointed hope that he could protect them from a Tigray takeover.

POLISARIO, to take another case, represents itself as a nationalist movement, with a complete political and economic program, rising above the tribes and factions that have historically disputed the Western Saharan region. But the peoples of Western Sahara, though diverse, are ethnically separate from the Arab/Berber societies of Algeria and Morocco. They have a sense of unity as the "people of the Sahel," with a common language and an economy based historically on commerce, nomadism, and raiding.[21] POLISARIO leaders were rooted in this culture, and cultivated the ancient sense of Saharan solidarity in winning recruits and gaining popular support. The motivations of King Hassan, attempting to annex a vast territory—which, though poor, would go some way toward fulfilling his hope of restoring the patrimony of the Moroccan sultanate—were also at least partly primordial.

These examples indicate that the primordial element in Africa's internal wars cannot simply be called "tribal," since that word carries connotations of primitive organization, purpose, and belief that were not generally a factor.[22] Rather, the primordial ethnic or regional loyalty represented a social identity that people turned to as they defined themselves in the struggle against policy errors and misconduct of regimes. The belief that a region or ethnic group was being unjustly oppressed or exploited by outsiders, as in Tigray or southern Sudan, and perhaps losing an advantage once enjoyed, as in the case of Eritrea or Uganda's Baganda population, was an especially powerful force.

At times the primordial force was seen in the form of affinities that were even narrower than ethnic or regional loyalties. Mozambican peasants, for example, sometimes joined or supported RENAMO in the hope that the movement would protect the freedom of their area or village from what they perceived as the arbitrary actions of a distant and alien regime. It is worth noting, moreover, that narrower primordial ties were sometimes a source of weakness for the resistance, promoting factionalism and violence within resistance movements that appeared outwardly united on ethnic grounds. This happened among resistance fighters in Chad and Namibia when individuals from differing sub-clans and locations fell into disagreement, even though they were part of the same general ethnic group.

The workings of the ethnic and regional factors in Africa's wars are complex and perhaps impossible for anyone but a participant to understand fully. The following capsule summaries indicate the main trends:

Angola. UNITA's strength is greatest among Savimbi's own Ovimbundu people, the country's largest ethnic group at about 37 percent of the population. The Ovimbundu dwell primarily in the south-central highlands. The MPLA was founded as a Marxist movement by mixed-race Angolans, a few radical Portuguese whites, and Angolan *assimilados.* Nonetheless, many MPLA leaders have roots in the Mbundu ethnic group, about 25 percent of the population, which dominates the capital and spreads westward into the hinterland.

Chad. Chad is fragmented among more than 200 ethnic groups, and it is easy to interpret the fighting there as a kaleidoscopic conflict among and within Toubou (or Goran), Sara, nomadic Arab tribes, and other groups. In the past, however, there was an overarching north–south dimension to Chad's wars, while the Habré/Goukouni struggle could be seen in part as a struggle between Toubou factions from different localities.

Ethiopia. Eritrea, with about 4 million people or 10 percent of Ethiopia's population, lacks ethnic unity. Christian highland Eritreans are ethnically tied to Tigrayans and are distinct from Moslem lowlanders. However, a regional consciousness, emerging during the colonial period, was solidified by Ethiopia's attempt at annexation. Both the EPLF and ELF were inspired by this regional solidarity, although the ELF more strongly represented the Islamic elements of the population. Elsewhere, Oromo (40 percent or more of the population), Tigray (9 percent), Afar, and Western Somali liberation fronts had an ethnic basis. Many followers of these fronts saw themselves as resisting domination by the Amhara, who number about 32 percent of the total population.

Liberia. Prior to Doe's regime, ethnic tensions did not appear to be a major source of unrest in Liberian society. There was resentment among indigenous peoples against the power and privilege enjoyed by the Americo-Liberians, but tensions among indigenous groups were not reported.[23] Doe's advancement of fellow Krahn began to raise ethnic tensions, and today, most of this tiny group of 125,000 people from Grand Gedeh County have fled the country in fear for their lives. Doe's brutal reprisals against the Gio and Mano of Nimba County in the wake of the Quiwonkpa affair set the stage for Taylor's success, although Taylor himself is reportedly from the capital area.[24] After he launched his invasion, Gio and Mano came under attack by government forces in Nimba County and in the capital.

Mozambique. RENAMO appears strongest among the Ndau sub-group of the Shona peoples in central Mozambique. Elsewhere, its support is drawn from the less modernized, rural sectors where there is strong local resistance to encroachments by the central government. The government is based in the more developed southern area. Mixed-race individuals and Mozambicans of Goan descent play a prominent role in the regime, evidently contributing to initial popular resentment.

Namibia. Members of the Ovambo group, accounting for about half of Namibia's African population, dominated SWAPO, which some perceived as essentially an Ovambo liberation front. SWAPO recruited successfully among the Nama and Herero, but factional strife generally worked to the disadvantage of non-Ovambo members. Tensions within SWAPO between members of Ovambo sub-groups were reported during the war.

Rwanda. Ethnologists tend to regard the Hutu and Tutsi not as distinct ethnic groups but rather as separate castes in traditional Rwandan society. In that society, the Tutsi were the upper caste. The distinction between the two groups intensified in the colonial period, when the Belgians favored the Tutsi, who then numbered about 14 percent of the population, and to some degree ruled through them. In 1959, following a Belgian policy shift, the Hutu gained the upper hand, and thousands of Tutsi fled. Today, they may number 10 percent of the population.[25]

Somalia. Somalia, whose people share a common language, religion, and history, was often cited in the past as Africa's one true nation-state. However, clan divisions within Somali society have now split the country. The SNM, which controls the north, is based among the Issaq clan. In announcing secession in 1991 as "Somaliland," the SNM revived the colonial division between British Somaliland in the north and the Italian south. Some cultural differences had remained from this division, although to outsiders they seemed slight. Support for the Siad Barre government came primarily from the president's own Marehan and some Majerteen; but there are splits in both clans, while the other resistance movements are also ethnically based. These are the USC (Hawiye); the SPM (Ogadeni); and the SSDF (Darod). Ali Mahdi's faction of the USC is based in the Abgal sub-clan of the Hawiye, while Aideed draws his support primarily from the Haber Gedir Hawiye sub-clan.

Sudan. The SPLA, with members from diverse southern groups, is strongest among the Dinka—at 3 million, about 12 percent of Sudan's population. Nuer, another southern group, tended to rally to Anya-Nya II, which once favored secession but then waged its own war with government aid against the SPLA. The northern, Islamic government has armed local militias including Arab Rizeigat and Fertit tribesmen against the SPLA. In Darfur, Rizeigat herders are engaged in a conflict of uncertain dimensions with the Fur, an agrarian, African group. In the Nuba mountains of south Kordofan, the native hill-dweller population is being forced out, evidently to benefit Arabized former nomads moving into the area.

Uganda. The NRA was essentially an army of Baganda peasants, although Museveni is reportedly Bahima (a small, cattle-herding group).[26] He is more often described as Banyankole, meaning he is from the Ankole region of western Uganda. Museveni's critics have sometimes tried to link him with the Banyarwanda immigrants to Uganda in an effort to excite Baganda hostility toward him,[27] but as far as is known this claim is not true. The Baganda and other groups in the south are part of the broad African Bantu grouping, setting them apart from northerners. Resistance after the NRA victory was centered among the Langi, ousted president Obote's group, and other northerners, notably the Acholi, Teso, and Karamojang.

Western Sahara. POLISARIO founder El-Ouali was born a nomad of the Reguibi, a warrior tribe that was dominant in the region.[28] Tindouf, the Algerian town where the Western Sahara refugees have settled, was historically under Reguibi control. However, an ethnic consciousness surpassing tribal divisions evidently unites the Saharan people today.

Political Belief and Ideology

While the primordial element has been so important as a basis for societal resistance in Africa, it is also true that modern political beliefs and ideology were a major motivating factor for several resistance movements. None of the resistance movements can be understood entirely in terms of stated political beliefs, but most of them, at least to some degree, were inspired by modern political ideas about the organization of the state, human rights and political freedoms, the distribution of power among groups and regions, and the mechanisms of decision making. Such ideas helped to define most resistance groups in their struggle against regimes, inciting both leaders and followers to demand participation in the state.

Most of Africa's major resistance groups adopted broad political programs rather than narrow sectarian agendas, and portrayed themselves as resisting government repression, corruption, and exploitation on behalf of higher political ideals. Each of the major resistance movements was headed by a general secretary, chairman, or president—almost never a tribal leader[29]—usually backed up by an executive committee, central committee, or politburo. Most held regular party congresses which passed resolutions and issued manifestoes, while a steady stream of press releases, pamphlets, and party magazines flowed from their information offices. Even movements that were essentially fighting organizations from their inception, notably the NRA in Uganda or the SPLA in Sudan, took care at the outset to create civilian political organizations.[30] In so doing, they tried to make it clear that they were political movements with respectable political objectives and not mere warrior bands.

The political platforms of resistance movements were authored by the leaders, who had come to maturity in a post-war, post-independence intellectual environment and perceived themselves as working on behalf of the higher ideals found in that environment. In framing their objectives, they drew from the storehouse of modern political concepts—from Western democratic principles to Marxist dreams of leading the proletariat to a classless society. Moreover, in establishing their movements, they took their cues from political and revolutionary movements elsewhere in the modern world. Some leaders, such as Garang, Museveni, or Savimbi, claimed that their ideas and their movements could transform entire nations. Even where the independence of the primordial territorial unit was the final goal, however, as in Eritrea or Western Sahara, leaders defined themselves and their movements, with some evident sincerity, in terms of universal political ideals. Followers, including the soldiers of the resistance movements, may have been less interested in these ideals, but reports suggest that leaders of UNITA, the EPLF, the TPLF, POLISARIO, the NRA, and other movements made genuine attempts to convey their view of the ideological basis for the struggle to the resistance fighters.

Modern political beliefs and ideologies have been an important source of strength to resistance movements, providing them with a conceptual framework to guide their actions and policies, while helping them to forge political and intellectual links in the wider world. Any movement that failed to develop such an orientation, such as Lakwena's Holy Spirit Movement or the Maitatsine religious movement in northern Nigeria, was not likely to thrive. Ethnic, regional, or religious groups that failed to create a modern political organization, were destined to remain politically powerless. By contrast, the major resistance movements were able to make use of organizational principles and resistance warfare tactics developed elsewhere; to enter international forums espousing ideals that already had wide support around the world; to win the sympathy of like-minded intellectuals and journalists; and to form alliances with sympathetic foreign governments and private groups.

In drawing from the storehouse of modern political ideas, most resistance movements chose beliefs or ideologies on the left of the political spectrum, running from the mildly socialist to the strongly Marxist-Leninist with heavy emphasis on class struggle. In making these choices, the resistance movements were only reflecting the predominant tendency in political thought in Africa, where teachers and intellectuals who shape political views, and sometimes join the political fray themselves, have been primarily on the left. However, a few, such as UNITA, have advanced mixed but comprehensive political and economic programs, blending socialism, reformism, the principle of the self-determination of peoples, and democratic precepts—perhaps leavened with an insistence that these ideals should be adapted to African conditions. The recent moderation in the Marxist views of the EPLF and TPLF (see below) suggests that such a blend of ideas will become more common among African opposition forces in the future. This moderation reflects a changing intellectual environment in Africa as well as the pragmatic recognition that doctrinaire Marxism has little credibility in the post–Cold War and post-Soviet world. Groups advocating strict Marxism-Leninism today would have few sympathizers and little external support.

Cynics may doubt, of course, that Africa's armed opposition movements are sincere in claiming that they are inspired by higher political purposes as opposed to ethnic and regional loyalties or the personal ambitions of their leaders. RENAMO's political positions, in particular, have been highly controversial. The movement's opponents portray its political program as part of an image-building campaign waged by non-Mozambican overseas publicists at the urging of foreign backers aware of the value of good public relations.[31] They note that the movement has not published the lengthy political tracts, characteristic of other movements, that have been hammered out by intellectuals and political leaders at party congresses.[32] For many, this means that the movement is a collection of freelance guerrillas headed by a warlord, rather than a genuine political movement.[33]

The political positions taken by other movements have also sometimes come under suspicion. The authenticity of UNITA's political program has been questioned for years by critics portraying UNITA leader Savimbi as a strongman and opportunist—an agent first of the Portuguese colonial authorities and then of South Africa.[34] In 1989, Issayas Afewerki, the EPLF leader, maintained while visiting the United States that his movement was neither Marxist nor secessionist and that accusations to the contrary were American excuses for denying his movement assistance. To some observers, this seemed to be an opportunistic shift in position that ran counter to the weight of EPLF statements and publications over many years. The mellowing of the TPLF, which became an advocate of free elections and reconciliation in the later 1980s, also aroused suspicion. Its leader, Meles Zenawi, had reportedly founded the Marxist-Leninist League of Tigray in the 1970s,[35] and the movement's publications had consistently taken hardline revolutionary stances. Observers have also argued, though with less evidence, that the Sudan People's Liberation Movement (SPLM), a political wing of the SPLA, the SNM in northern Somalia, and Uganda's National Resistance Movement (NRM), and some other movements, in their heart of hearts, are more authoritarian and farther to the left than their public stances—perhaps shaped with a view to Western opinion—would indicate.

We may never know with certainty, of course, what is in the minds and hearts of the leaders of particular resistance movements, but it is at least worth noting that after Mengistu's ouster, Zenawi and Afewerki did behave with considerable restraint rather than revolutionary fervor, suggesting that the moderation in their stated beliefs was genuine and that these reformed beliefs were a true guide to behavior. In some instances, moreover, the political views advanced by resistance leaders seemed an authentic outgrowth of their life experiences. Before Yoweri Museveni became a resistance leader, for example, he had earned a degree in political science and economics from the University of Dar es Salaam in Tanzania, participated in the anti-Amin resistance, and served briefly in post-Amin regimes. His advocacy of a mixed economy that would avoid the "overnationalization" found in some socialist countries appeared to be a genuine reflection of his experiences in socialist Tanzania, which was experiencing a prolonged economic decline. Meanwhile, his support for grass-roots democracy and an end to sectarianism and corruption in Uganda were a logical consequence of his background in Ugandan politics and the opposition. Savimbi's political platform, however, is now no longer taken very seriously by most observers. His rejection of the results of Angola's first democratic election, after years of proclaiming himself a democrat, has gravely undermined his credibility, even among former strong supporters.

Some resistance movements found themselves fighting governments that at least on paper held somewhat similar political positions, and this also raises questions about the importance of political belief as a genuine source of societal resistance to the state. The EPLF and TPLF, for example, during their most Marxist phases, were resisting a government that firmly avowed its own loyalty to Marxism. UNITA's economic program had distinct socialist elements that blurred its ideological differences with the MPLA, which itself encouraged private foreign investment and eventually won membership in Western financial institutions. There were socialist elements in the platform of the NRM, which went to war against Milton Obote, one of Africa's first socialist presidents. These apparent similarities of view, however, do not detract from the importance of political belief as a source of resistance. Marxist resistance leaders in Ethiopia devoutly insisted that Mengistu, with Soviet help, had betrayed the revolution, for example, while Obote's opponents saw his socialism as a mere sham, designed to obscure his attempt at personalist rule.

The political stances taken by Africa's resistance movements are summarized here in capsule form.

Angola. UNITA, while endorsing a generalized racial consciousness termed "negritude," advocates a political program blending democratic and socialist elements. UNITA maintains that democratic values must be adapted to African conditions by emphasizing consensus and giving proportional representation to ethnic groups, clans, and classes. It backs a comprehensive socialist economic program but insists that it would respect private property and private enterprise.[36] Party organization and military doctrine reflect the early influence of Mao Tse-tung on Savimbi. The sincerity of UNITA's commitment to these positions was increasingly questioned toward the end of the 1980s as a result of allegations of human rights abuses and authoritarian rule within the movement.

Chad. Political belief appears to have played a minor role among Chad's resistance forces, which instead have been motivated primarily by ethnic group and clan rivalries, as well as the personal ambitions of their leaders. Idris Deby, whose Popular Salvation Movement seized power in December 1990, did denounce the Habré regime for human rights violations and promised free elections.

Ethiopia. EPLF positions became elusive in the late 1980s when the organization claimed to be a mere front favoring a referendum on independence. Historically, however, it has been a cohesive revolutionary movement aiming at independence and advocating Marxist and Maoist concepts, including nationalization of industry and confiscation of land. Strong egalitarian principles characterized EPLF statements and practice,[37] drawing praise from sympathetic journalists.

TPLF literature has historically been laden with extreme Marxist terminology. "Soviet imperialism" came in for heavy criticism, and "American imperialism" was also a "fundamental enemy." The TPLF aimed not at secession but "democratic revolution" through a protracted people's war[38]—leading ultimately to voluntary national unity. TPLF stances, like those of the EPLF, appeared more moderate toward the end of the decade, as the organization began to insist that it was merely a coalition of disparate groups seeking free choice for all Ethiopians.

Some other resistance factions also had Marxist orientations. A royalist group faded, while the democratically oriented Ethiopia People's Democratic Alliance (EPDA) apparently did not field guerrillas in the 1980s.

Liberia. The Liberian armed resistance won wide domestic support because of the human rights abuses of the Doe regime. Apart from outrage over injustice, however, political belief and ideology have not been factors in inspiring support for the NPFL or the INPFL.

Mozambique. RENAMO statements and communiqués maintain that the organization is committed to democracy, constitutional government, national unity, and the free market.[39] At the same time, they demand respect for the traditions and customs of the Mozambican people. In foreign affairs, RENAMO documents take a nonaligned tone, but supporters insist that it advocates a "pro-West foreign policy."[40]

Namibia. During the long years of armed struggle, SWAPO was a revolutionary socialist movement committed to "overthrowing capitalist exploitation and construction of a socialist society."[41] As independence approached, however, statements by SWAPO leaders moderated considerably on such questions as nationalization of private property. Namibia's independence constitution, adopted by a SWAPO-dominated constituent assembly, received wide praise for its commitment to democratic principles.

Rwanda. The importance of deeply held political beliefs, apart from a desire that the human rights of Rwandans now in exile be respected, is uncertain in this struggle. The Rwanda People's Front, however, which is affiliated with the Rwanda People's Army, has advanced a political platform calling for democracy and national unity.

Somalia. Opposition to human rights violations by the Siad Barre regime was a major source of societal resistance. In May 1990, 100 prominent citizens signed a manifesto calling for an end to violence against civilians and corruption. Ali Mahdi Mohammed, the leader of the USC who became interim president after Siad's ouster, was one of the signers.[42]

SNM ideology is vague, but the organization maintains that it favors clean government and free elections in a multi-party state. Before the north seceded, the SNM supported decentralization and regional autonomy as the best means of ending corruption and the abuse of power. Nonetheless, the movement maintained that Somalia and Ethiopia, which was governed by a Marxist regime throughout the 1980s, share an "inseparable destiny," and it advocated friendship with other nations in the Horn and Red Sea area.[43] This SNM cordiality toward Mengistu's Ethiopia, a major backer, no doubt had a pragmatic basis.

Sudan. The SPLA/SPLM insists that its objectives are national, not regional; unitarian, not secessionist; socialist—in accordance with local conditions—not communist; and pragmatic rather than dogmatic. The movement continues to seek the creation of a secular state throughout Sudan, although Garang has many critics among southerners who regard this objective as unrealistic. Regional autonomy where appropriate and religious freedom are part of the movement's platform.[44]

Uganda. The NRA/NRM advocates popular and parliamentary democracy, national unity rather than sectarianism, an end to corruption, and a mixed economy with most activities carried out by the private sector while the state participates at certain fulcrums. Local resistance committees played an important role in the revolution, and in government since the takeover.

Western Sahara. POLISARIO's main thrust has been toward independence through armed struggle under the slogan "all the homeland or martyrdom." Economic principles are non-specific but emphasize development, fairness, and an end to exploitation. Internationally, the organization supports Arab unity, African liberation, and Central American revolutionaries. It opposes "plots hatched by imperialism."[45]

Contributing Factors: Aspects of Poverty

While the root cause of war in Africa lay in the gap that had emerged between African states and African societies, there were a number of additional domestic factors that contributed to outbreaks of war in Africa. All of these were related in one way or another to Africa's poverty—a condition that afflicted countries around the continent but touched the war-torn countries and territories with particular severity.

Poverty as a Source of Incapability

Most of Africa is extremely poor in global terms, but the countries afflicted by war are poor even by African standards. Average per capita income in these countries was probably about $230 annually in the later 1980s[46]—or $180 if oil-rich Angola is excluded—as against more than $600 in the remainder of the continent.[47] Gross domestic product, a rough measure of power, averaged $2.4 billion among the states suffering war within their territory proper (not including South Africa and Morocco), and this figure too was well below the $6.3 billion average for the rest of the continent. Poverty of this magnitude contributed to the emergence of war by exacerbating underlying social tensions and depriving governments of the means of ending war.

Poverty was not an immediate limiting factor in South African operations in Namibia, where South Africa's forces were backed up by a $60 billion home economy. Morocco, with its $12 billion economy, was also less constrained than some other governments in dealing with resistance forces, particularly since those forces were based on the tiny population in Western Sahara.[48] Over the long term, however, even these countries found themselves constrained by war and sought face-saving exits.

Elsewhere, national poverty had a major impact on the ability of governments to wage war against armed resistance movements. This impact was particularly evident in three of the largest wars: those in Sudan, Ethiopia, and Mozambique. The government in each of these countries was essentially out of money by the end of the decade. Each was caught in a vicious circle of war and impoverishment, with the ability neither to alleviate grievances that were contributing to the internal crisis nor to win military victories, but with war driving them ever deeper into paralyzing poverty. Mengistu's Ethiopia, ranked by the World Bank in 1985 as the world's poorest country with an average annual per capita income of $110, was trying to maintain three large armies, including a northern force of 150,000–175,000 men. The government was not meeting payments to coffee growers—the sole earners of foreign exchange—and they were responding by switching to subsistence crops, sometimes even pulling up the coffee bushes. Sudan's foreign debt was the highest of Africa's thirty-four low-income countries,[49] and Mozambique owed but could not pay an annual foreign debt service that was three times export earnings.[50]

Military training, pay, and morale could hardly be sustained in such a situation. Mengistu resorted to coercive tactics in an effort to keep his troops in the field in the north, where many had served in foxholes and trenches for years without relief or adequate provisions. After the EPLF broke through on the Nakfa front at the end of 1987, Mengistu ordered the execution of a popular general, together with a number of officers, non-commissioned officers, and troops. The rout of government forces at Afabet ensued. In an effort to continue the war as the decade drew to a close, Mengistu was forcibly recruiting thirteen- and fourteen-year-olds.

The failure of Mozambican soldiers to pursue RENAMO guerrilla bands and destroy their bases was decried by military analysts during the 1980s, but it was hardly surprising in view of the conditions the army had to endure. Soldiers were paid poorly and sporadically, and they often had to spend part of each day foraging for food. Some officers in Sudan's once-proud army reportedly became entrepreneurs in marketing pilfered food aid during the Sadiq era.[51] No wonder the

Sudanese commanders issued an ultimatum to the government at the beginning of 1989 demanding a change of course, and that they felt it necessary to affirm that:

> Our Armed Forces have carried out their duties professionally, courageously, and with sacrifice in unfavorable circumstances and with the minimum availability of the basic requirements for conducting combat operations. . . . We have lost territories not because of any shortcoming on the part of the combatants of our brave Army, but because of the scarce combat resources and shortcomings in the movement of regular reinforcements.[52]

Yet the government was reluctant to negotiate with the SPLA from a position of weakness, and the war went on. The coup that finally came in June 1989 was no surprise.

Governments with greater resources would have had a wider choice of options for ending war, if they had had the will to do so. Regional development schemes, attractive payoffs to resistance soldiers and leaders if they would stop fighting, and offers to integrate ex-combatants into an expanding post-war economy might have had some appeal to the opposition and improved prospects for a negotiated settlement. Proposals for such open-handed approaches to conflict resolution were sometimes discussed, but they could make little headway where impoverished governments had scant hope of carrying them out.

Limited Opportunities as a Source of Grievance

Africa's poverty, combined with the state-oriented economic policies so many countries have followed, means that opportunities for aspiring elites as well as ordinary citizens are limited. This problem is especially severe in the poorest countries, such as those that fell victim to war. A university or secondary school graduate in these countries might aim at a position in government or teaching at an appropriate level, but those positions have become increasingly hard to obtain as the number of graduates has grown and resource constraints have tightened. Those with less education have found that jobs in manufacturing and other parts of the modern sector are scarce and that farming is an unattractive option because of the low prices paid to producers.

This lack of opportunity can intensify the sense of grievance among social groups suffering discrimination. When opportunities generally are scarce, discrimination can take away any hope of finding employment. In tearing the last shreds of hope, it causes deep resentment and destroys any sense among its victims that they have a stake in society. In Sudan, Liberia, Uganda, and Rwanda, the denial of opportunity and impoverishment of people linked by primordial ties undoubtedly contributed to the strength of societal resistance to the state.

Participation in a resistance movement, moreover, could provide the opportunities for recognition, promotion, and material gain not available elsewhere to both leaders and followers. At the highest levels of the resistance forces, guerrilla leaders could become figures of global importance, reported upon and interviewed in the world's press, and traveling almost as heads of state. Indeed, Savimbi, who met with President Reagan in the Oval Office in 1986, was accorded welcomes in the United States and western Europe that most African heads of state could only dream of. The formerly reclusive Issayas Afewerki of Eritrea was emulating the peripatetic Savimbi at the end of the 1980s, while John Garang was traveling more often and meeting with a succession of Sudanese and foreign political figures. RENAMO's Afonso Dhlakama was less welcome in foreign capitals, but he received foreign reporters in the bush. As a result, his words and photograph appeared around the world. Meanwhile, the overseas representatives of many armed opposition movements live lives comparable to those of regular African diplomats in London, Lisbon, Washington, and New York.

This is not to say that resistance leaders took up arms in order to gain recognition and status. But they faced very limited opportunities for advancement in their societies, despite their obvious talents and in some cases their considerable attainments. The backgrounds of Museveni and Savimbi have already been noted. Garang had been educated in economics in the United States and received professional military training at Fort Benning, Georgia. Much of the leadership of resistance movements in Ethiopia and in Western Sahara had university backgrounds. If there had been genuine career opportunities that allowed such people to contribute to the peaceful development of their societies, most would surely not have been tempted by life in the bush.

The foot soldiers of Africa's wars were typically people who would otherwise have spent their lives—usually brief—in poverty and desperation. Alice Lakwena, the Ugandan peasant leader, articulated their suffering:

> I am poor and needy. I am hurt to the depths of my heart. Like an
> evening shadow, I am about to vanish. I am blown away like an insect.
> My knees are weak from lack of food.[53]

In the end, Lakwena failed to provide her followers with an alternative
way of life, but the peasant who found his way into UNITA, the EPLF,
the SPLA, or SWAPO was rewarded not only with food but also with
camaraderie and a sense of purpose. No doubt forced recruitment and
coercion of troops, as well as other human rights abuses, sometimes
occurred within such organizations; and no doubt some engaged in
practices that were destructive to the lives and cultures of other poor
people. But the ability of so many movements to sustain themselves
for long periods of time suggests that they were offering rewards to
their members that were not otherwise available in society.

The EPLF and the TPLF were particularly noted for the opportunities they made available to women. Women's emancipation was an
important part of the program of each movement, and each claimed to
have made great strides in promoting literacy and health care for
women, as well as freedom from the burdens of heavy domestic labor
and early marriage. Women fulfilled combat roles in the EPLF; however, the TPLF believed that this would "cause problems to their health
and physical condition."[54]

The rewards that leaders and followers derive from guerrilla life
probably contribute to the persistence of Africa's internal wars. Once a
leader has held a position that is like a president's, and has been a
commander-in-chief, there are few peacetime positions that are suitable for him. Museveni and Zenawi solved this problem by seizing the
capital and taking over leadership of the state; but where this is not an
immediate possibility, as in Sudan, resistance leaders may be more
likely to fight on than to accept a compromise that would reduce their
stature—as long as the battlefield situation does not compel them to do
otherwise. As for the troops, their life might be spartan, but it is a life
that has had its appeal throughout human history. A stunning defeat or
a very attractive peace offer could be required if they are to be persuaded to give it up.

Geographic Scale and Remote Regions

The limited capabilities of states tied in with another factor, the large
size of many African states and the existence of remote regions in

others, to strengthen resistance forces and worsen the problems of the regimes they confronted. At independence, many states inherited vast regions that had rarely been under effective control even in colonial times. Northern Chad, eastern and southeastern Angola, and central Mozambique, for example, were never fully tamed. Access for the forces of government, commerce, and the military was always difficult; and it became more difficult when post-colonial governments with limited capabilities took power. Even smaller states could have remote regions where security was difficult to maintain—as the Doe regime discovered with respect to the Nimba County area.

The existence of these remote and poorly controlled areas gave determined opposition forces, such as Angola's UNITA or Sudan's SPLA, ample opportunity to organize, recruit, and train while out of reach of the authorities. Willing foreign suppliers—using land vehicles, air drops, or even air strips—could easily deliver arms to guerrillas taking shelter in remote regions with little fear of detection or interdiction.

A government in a developed country can control even remote areas by making use of advanced capabilities in transport and communications while deploying, if necessary, its substantial armed forces and police. This development advantage was an element in South Africa's military success in northern Namibia. But comparable capabilities were not available to most of the African governments facing war. Sudanese authorities, who could afford no better, were attempting to control a raging rebellion in an area larger than Texas with a poorly equipped army totaling 54,000.[55] In Mozambique, a country almost twice as large as California, FRELIMO was confronting a nationwide rebellion with armed forces of less than 40,000. Mengistu had vastly larger armed forces, but they were too debilitated to control the country's large, rebellious regions. The Angolan government had generous military support from Cuba and the Soviet Union, but even with this aid it could not control the country's vast and thinly populated frontier regions, nor prevent UNITA from freely receiving aid from foreign supporters by air and land.

Access to Weapons

Easy access to arms throughout large parts of Africa is another factor enabling groups demanding participation in the state to resort to war.

Regimes in more developed countries can if they choose control the availability of arms with considerable effect, but this is a capability generally lacking in today's Africa. Arms are plentiful in Africa partly because of previous struggles that have left large quantities of weapons in the countryside. The 1963–1972 conflict in the southern Sudan, the fighting in Zaire in the 1960s, the Ethiopia/Somalia war of 1977–1978, the anti-Portuguese wars in Angola and Mozambique, and the long years of struggle in Uganda have created vast stocks of cheap and available weapons. A Ugandan educator has testified that after Amin's overthrow,

> Submachine guns could be traded for a carton of cigarettes, and a few packets of cigarettes could buy a hand gun. Ammunition was a more common commodity than many consumer goods.[56]

Even at the end of the 1980s, the visitor to Kampala could not help but notice the automatic weapons casually held in the hands of ordinary household guards, nor avoid hearing random gunfire throughout the night. In southern Sudan, a journalist commented on the anomaly of Taposa warriors who "are so unaffected by the modern world that they wear no clothes, although they do carry Kalashnikovs."[57]

Weapons were often given to resistance groups in plentiful supply by neighboring states and other foreign suppliers sympathetic to their cause—a subject discussed in the next chapter. Governments also obtained vast stocks of arms from foreign sources, and they sometimes became an unwitting channel of supply for the guerrillas. This came about in part because of the indiscipline that results in the wholesale abandonment of arms during battle. Analysts do not doubt that the EPLF, as it claimed, was armed almost entirely with tanks, artillery, and smaller weapons seized from the Ethiopian army. The EPRDF rode into Addis Ababa in 1991 on captured tanks and military vehicles.

The arming of local militias, as in Sudan, was another government conduit that channeled weapons into the countryside. Creating militias is an attractive option to impoverished regimes, since militia troops need little training and can be given surplus and obsolete weapons. But exercising this option can heighten the carnage, as when undisciplined Sudanese tribal militias attacked Dinka civilians, and it can help to arm the resistance. The Mozambican regime, for example, undertook a large-scale program to expand its People's Militia to counter

RENAMO's widening influence, but observers believe that many of the rifles going to the militia found their way into RENAMO hands through capture or barter. When Ethiopian troops were routed in Tigray in 1989, they were harassed as they withdrew by peasants firing weapons given to locals in an abortive militia program ten years before.[58]

Environmental Factors

Environmental factors arising from climate change and large-scale development projects sometimes contributed to the problem of regional development differentials, and hence to the emergence of societal resistance. Developed countries, with complex economies, would have been better able to deal with the dislocations resulting from these environmental factors, but impoverished African states had more limited options.

The problem was perhaps clearest in southern Sudan, where concern over the environmental impact of the Jonglei canal project was an important cause of the war that began in 1983. The canal, more than 200 miles long, was a massive undertaking intended to relieve the water shortages suffered by Sudan and Egypt, its joint sponsors. It was to increase the flow of the Nile, and reduce losses from evaporation, by diverting water from southern Sudanese marshes. In theory, the south was to benefit from the draining of the Sudd swamp in Upper Nile and from development projects that were to be sited along the canal. As the project went forward, however, many southerners came to believe that the canal would destroy traditional ways of life by disrupting grazing patterns and wildlife migration routes while bringing an influx of settlers from the north, and possibly even from Egypt.[59] Outsiders, from the southern perspective, would gain while the south would be exploited—reinforcing what southerners regarded as a long-standing pattern.

In Ethiopia, the underlying tensions between the Amhara and the Oromo derive from the historic pattern of Amhara migration away from the arid northern plateau toward better-watered lands in the south.[60] Meanwhile, the alienation of northern Ethiopian society was deepened by Mengistu's abortive resettlement scheme, which was portrayed as a means of dealing with the increasing aridity and recurrent drought in the area. TPLF propaganda played on popular hostility toward resettlement, calling it an attempt to destroy the social base of their movement, rather than a genuine relief program, and a scheme to provide forced labor for state farms in the south.[61] Interruptions in the delivery of famine relief were another constant source of tension—and of endless recrimination between the government and the guerrillas.

Environmental change is also playing a role in some of the conflict situations that have not yet developed into wars. In the Casamance region of Senegal, for example, the encroachments by outsiders that are causing tension result from the increasingly arid conditions farther north. In neighboring Mauritania, tensions between blacks and Moors have been heightened by competition for farmland along the Senegal River. The drier conditions in the region have led to increased interest in these lands at a time when the completion of two dams is changing settlement patterns. The Tuareg unrest in Mali has probably also been exacerbated by prolonged drought.

Conclusion

The poverty that contributes in so many ways to causing war in Africa will probably not be significantly alleviated for many years to come. However, there is reason to hope for progress with respect to democracy and governance as democratic movements, domestic and foreign human rights organizations, and the Western donor community press for political reforms around the continent. Should the reform movement continue to make headway, the domestic social and political tensions that have brought so much violence and suffering to Africa could well be eased. This is a subject discussed further in Chapter 5. Meanwhile, some favorable developments have also occurred with respect to the international dimension in Africa's wars. This dimension is the subject of Chapter 4.

Notes

1. Martin Doornbos, "The African State in Academic Debate: Retrospect and Prospect," *Journal of Modern African Studies* 28 (June 1990): 179.

2. Naomi Chazan et al., *Politics and Society in Contemporary Africa* (Boulder, Colo.: Lynne Reinner, 1988), 172.

3. Victor Azarya, "Reordering State–Society Relations: Incorporation and Disengagement," in *The Precarious Balance: State and Society in Africa,* ed. Donald Rothchild and Naomi Chazan (Boulder, Colo.: Westview Press, 1988), 3. For a useful summary of the scholarly critique of the African state, see Otwin

Marenin, "The Managerial State in Africa: A Conflict Coalition Perspective," in *The African State in Transition,* ed. Zaki Ergas (New York: St. Martin's Press, 1987), 65–69. See also Ergas's introduction to the same volume.

4. Robert Jackson and Carl G. Rosberg, "Why Africa's Weak States Persist: The Empirical and the Juridical in Statehood," *World Politics* 35 (October 1982): 1–24.

5. Michael Bratton and Donald Rothchild, "The Institutional Bases of Governance in Africa," in *Governance and Politics in Africa,* ed. Goran Hyden and Michael Bratton (Boulder, Colo.: Lynne Rienner, 1992), 263.

6. This concept was initially developed by Gunnar Myrdal with reference to states of South Asia. See Goran Hyden, "Problems and Prospects of State Coherence," in *State Versus Ethnic Claims: African Policy Dilemmas,* ed. Donald Rothchild and Victor A. Olurunsola (Boulder, Colo.: Westview Press, 1983), 73–74.

7. Thomas Callaghy, "The State as Lame Leviathan: The Patrimonial Administrative State in Africa," in Ergas, *The African State in Transition,* 87–116.

8. Ergas, *The African State in Transition,* 9.

9. Nelson Kasfir used the term "departicipation" in writing about Uganda in the 1970s; *The Shrinking Political Arena: Participation and Ethnicity in African Politics, with a Case Study of Uganda* (Berkeley: University of California Press, 1976).

10. See the discussion on the concentration and elaboration of state power during the 1960s and 1970s in Chazan et al., *Politics and Society in Contemporary Africa,* 44–61.

11. For this term, see Richard A. Joseph, *Democracy and Prebendal Politics in Nigeria: The Rise and Fall of the Second Republic* (Cambridge: Cambridge University Press, 1987).

12. Otwin, "The Managerial State in Africa," 66.

13. Joel S. Migdal writes of a "melange of social organizations" in postcolonial Africa and Asia, each advocating competing rules and norms for individual behavior in an "environment of conflict." *Strong Societies and Weak States: State–Society Relations and State Capabilities in the Third World* (Princeton: Princeton University Press, 1988), 28–29.

14. Chazan et al., *Politics and Society in Contemporary Africa,* 134.

15. Hyden, "Problems and Prospects of State Coherence," 74.

16. For one account, see Salu Daka Ndebele (with Dan Wooding), *Guerrilla for Christ* (Achimota, Ghana: African Christian Press, 1979).

17. Abdelwahab El-Affendi, ' "Discovering the South': Sudanese Dilemmas for Islam in Africa," *African Affairs* 89 (July 1990): 372–73.

18. René Lemarchand, "The State and Society in Africa: Ethnic Stratification and Restratification in Historical and Comparative Perspective," in Rothchild and Olurunsola, *State Versus Ethnic Claims,* 44–66. Lemarchand argues that in favoring or disfavoring particular groups, colonial regimes contributed to the emergence of ethnic consciousness and class conflict.

19. Kamal Osman Salih, "British Policy and the Accentuation of Inter-Ethnic Divisions: The Case of the Nuba Mountains Region of Sudan, 1920–1940," *African Affairs* 89 (July 1990): 417–36.

20. Paul Henze, *Rebels and Separatists in Ethiopia: Regional Resistance to a Marxist Regime,* report prepared for the Office of the Under Secretary for Defense Policy (Santa Monica, Calif.: Rand Corporation, December 1985), 18–25.

21. Tony Hodges, "The Origins of Saharawi Nationalism," *Third World Quarterly* 5 (January 1983): 32–33.

22. The Holy Spirit Movement in Uganda would be an exception. Witchcraft is sometimes alleged to be a factor in other internal wars, notably in Mozambique. For a fascinating discussion of these forces in the Zimbabwe revolution, see David Lan, *Guns and Rain: Guerrillas and Spirit Mediums in Zimbabwe* (London: James Curry; Berkeley: University of California Press, 1985).

23. Africa Watch, *Liberia: A Human Rights Disaster; Violations of the Laws of War by All Parties to the Conflict,* Washington, D.C., 26 October 1992, 3.

24. "Nimba Citizens Issue Statement on Crisis," *Torchlight* (Monrovia), 11 April 1991. Reprinted in U.S. Foreign Broadcast and Information Service, *Daily Report, Sub-Soharan Africa* (hereinafter, *FBIS),* 24 May 1991, 37.

25. U.S. Committee for Refugees, *Exile from Rwanda: Background to an Invasion,* prepared by Catherine Watson (Washington, D.C., February 1991) 6. As noted in Chapter 2, some believe the true figure to be somewhat higher.

26. Ibid., 10.

27. Ibid., 13.

28. See Hodges, "Origins of Saharawi Nationalism," 51; and John Mercer, *Spanish Sahara* (London: Goerge Allen and Unwin, 1976), 125–26, 132.

29. The exception here would be Chad's Goukouni Oueddei, son of a traditional Toubou leader. In Angola, Savimbi's grandfather was reportedly a "traditional chief." Fred Bridgland, *Jonas Savimbi: A Key to Africa* (London: Hodder and Stoughton, Coronet edition, 1988), 33.

30. These were the National Resistance Movement (NRM) and the Sudan People's Liberation Movement (SPLM).

31. See, for example, Kevin Lowther and C. Payne Lucas, " 'Massive Evil,' in Mozambique," *Washington Post,* 27 April 1988; Metz, "The Mozambique National Resistance and South African Foreign Policy," *African Affairs* 85 (October 1986): 497; and Robert Jaster, "The Security Outlook in Mozambique," *Survival* 27 (November–December 1985).

32. RENAMO reportedly held its first party congress in June 1989 at a location inside Mozambique.

33. RENAMO has supporters, however, who insist that the statements and communiqués issued by the movement constitute a "well thought out and documented political program" that expresses deeply held views. See Grover Norquist, *Reality in Mozambique Punctures a State Department Myth,* Executive Memorandum (Washington, D.C.: Heritage Foundation, 22 September 1987).

34. See, for example, William Minter, ed., *Operation Timber: Pages from the Savimbi Dossier* (Trenton, N.J.: Africa World Press, 1988).

35. Jane Perlez, "A Hard-Line Marxist who Mellowed," *New York Times,* 30 May 1991.

36. See W. Dohning, *UNITA* (Kwacha UNITA Press, 1984).

37. See the "National Democratic Programme of the EPLF (1977)," reprinted in *Behind the War in Eritrea,* ed. Basil Davidson, Lionel Cliffe, and Bereket Habte Selassie (Nottingham: Spokesman, 1980), 143–50.

38. See "Joint Communiqué of the Ethiopian People's Democratic Movement (EPDM) and the Tigray Peoples Liberation Front (TPLF)," *People's Voice,* Tigray People's Liberation Front, August 1988, 11–12.

39. "Mozambique National Resistance Programme," and "RENAMO's Provisional Economic Manifesto for Free Mozambique" (RENAMO publications, no date).

40. Norquist, *Reality in Mozambique*.

41. "Declaration of the Central Committee of SWAPO of Namibia Adopted at Its Second Annual Meeting Held at Gabela, People's Republic of Angola, 4–7 January 1979," reprinted in Department of Information and Publicity, SWAPO of Namibia, *To Be Born a Nation: The Liberation Struggle for Namibia* (London, Zed Press: 1981), 317.

42. Somali radio broadcast, recorded in *FBIS*, 31 January 1991, 7.

43. Somali National Movement, "Peace for the Horn of Africa in the Political Program of the SNM," paper submitted at the Fourth Annual Conference on Conditions for the Possibilities of Peace in the Horn of Africa, City College of the City University of New York, 26–28 May 1989.

44. See Mansour Khalid, ed., *John Garang Speaks* (London and New York: KPI, 1987).

45. Sahrawi Arab Democratic Republic, Mission to the United Nations and North America, *Sixth Congress of the Polisario Front, 7–10 December 1985*.

46. For the purposes of this calculation, the per capita incomes of Morocco ($500) and South Africa ($1,700) were not included, since their wars were taking place in adjacent territories. Income data for Namibia's black population and Western Sahara were not available but were assumed to be $200, the same as in Sudan and Somalia. Data were taken from U.S. Central Intelligence Agency, *The World Factbook, 1988* (Washington, D.C., 1988). Most are for 1987, although some are slightly earlier.

47. This figure does not include Libya, which is atypically wealthy.

48. This is not to say that either government was unconstrained in its operations by economic factors. Indeed, budgetary constraints were an important factor in propelling South Africa toward a Namibia/Angola settlement.

49. World Bank, *World Debt Tables: External Debt of Developing Countries, 1988–1989 ed.*, vol. 1, *Analysis and Summary Tables* (Washington, D.C., 1988), xxxvi.

50. "Tenacity in Diversity," *Financial Times*, Survey, 15 August 1988.

51. Robert M. Press, "Sudan Military Accused of Pilfering Food Aid," *Christian Science Monitor*, 18 July 1988.

52. Omdurman National Unity Radio broadcast, recorded in *FBIS*, Near East and South Asia edition, 27 February 1989, 13.

53. Sheila Rule, "The Rebellion Withers for a Priestess in Uganda," *New York Times*, 26 December 1987.

54. "The Struggle for Emancipation," interview with Aragesh of the TPLF Central Committee and former Chairperson of the Association of Women Fighters of Tigray, *People's Voice*, May 1988, 13.

55. This figure is from 1988. International Institute of Strategic Studies, *The Military Balance, 1988–1989* (London, 1988), 114.

56. W. Senteza-Kajubi, "Background to War and Violence in Uganda," in *War, Violence, and Children in Uganda*, ed. Cole P. Dodge and Magne Ruandalen (Oslo: Norwegian University Press, 1987), 39.

57. Deborah Scroggins and Colin Campbell, "Terror and Hunger Spread as

Sudan 'Holy War' Rages," *Atlanta Constitution,* 27 June 1988. Reprinted in U.S. Congress, House Select Committee on Hunger, *Ethiopia and Sudan: Warfare, Politics, and Famine,* Hearing, 100th Cong., 2d sess., 14 July 1988 (Washington, D.C.: U.S. Government Printing Office, 1988), 113.

58. Jane Perlez, "Ethiopia Starts to Come Unglued after String of Military Setbacks," *New York Times,* 22 March 1989.

59. Ann Mosely Lesch, "Confrontation in the Southern Sudan," *Middle East Journal* 40 (Summer 1986): 414–15.

60. On this point, see Allan Hoben, "The Origins of Famine," *New Republic,* 21 January 1985, 17.

61. "The End Is in Sight," *People's Voice,* May 1988, 3.

4 THE INTERNATIONAL FACTOR IN AFRICA'S WARS

An international factor played a role in each of Africa's wars. This factor operated at one or more of three levels: with neighboring states; with African regional actors, notably Libya or South Africa; and with powers from outside Africa choosing to become involved. Indeed, the sheer extent of international involvement and the variety of actors who chose to play a role were remarkable features of Africa's wars, and the reasons for this will be assessed in this chapter.

While many outside actors became involved in Africa's wars, all were constrained to observe certain limits on their participation. There was no African Afghanistan or Vietnam for the Soviet Union or the United States, for example, even though both were active on the continent. The sources of this constraint must also be assessed.

The role of foreign involvement as a causal factor in Africa's wars is a difficult and often controversial matter to evaluate. The thesis of this book is that the causes of every war were, at their root, internal, and that the international factor played a contributory role—helping to widen the state–society gap and raise the level of violence. Conflict and violence would almost certainly have occurred at some level in each of the afflicted countries without foreign involvement. Clearly, however, in many instances—including Angola, Ethiopia, Chad, Mozambique, Sudan, and Western Sahara—the international factor was highly significant in converting the conflict between state and society into war.

Foreign actors had initially helped to widen state–society gaps in Africa when their aid encouraged particular regimes to believe that, because of foreign backing, they were capable of imposing their will on society. The governments of Angola, Mozambique, and Ethiopia received massive Soviet military assistance which they used to wage war against their internal opponents. Meanwhile, regimes in Sudan, Somalia, Liberia, and Morocco were at some point major recipients of aid from the United States. This aid was primarily economic, but military aid was part of the aid package—and it was typically accompanied by official statements on the strategic importance of these countries to the United States. The regimes in all of these countries consequently had reason to believe that they had a superpower on their side and could proceed against the internal opposition with impunity. The eventual cutoff in U.S. aid to the regimes in Sudan, Somalia, and Liberia came too late to deter these governments from this self-destructive path.

The international factor could also work on the other side of the state–society equation, strengthening resistance forces so that they could take full advantage of the weakness of the regimes they were fighting. All around Africa, resistance forces received military aid and shelter from various external sources that was invaluable to them in their struggles. Resistance forces that lacked foreign backing had scant prospects for success.

Foreign involvement in Africa's wars unquestionably raised the level of violence. Resistance forces managed to obtain automatic weapons, ample supplies of ammunition, and anti-tank as well as anti-aircraft weapons. Government forces typically had foreign-supplied tanks and armored personnel carriers, which often fell into rebel hands, as well as First World military aircraft at their disposal. In Angola and Ethiopia, warfare became heavily mechanized as a result of outside involvement.

It would be too simple to say, however, that the international factor acted in only one direction, invariably exacerbating Africa's internal conflicts. In some instances, particularly after the mid-1980s, the actions of external powers tended to constrain participants in the fighting and encourage movement toward negotiations and conflict resolution. Regimes were being encouraged by their principal supporters and by other foreign aid donors to be more responsive to the needs and demands of resistant elements within society. As donors promoted the virtues of better governance and democratization as essential to development, they helped to push regimes around Africa toward efforts to narrow the state–society gap. Moreover, foreign actors increasingly pressured African resistance movements to look beyond entrenched views toward the possibility of negotiations and compromise.

The Angola/Namibia regional accord in 1988, the successful deployment of a UN peacekeeping force to oversee Namibia's transition to independence and democracy, the international role in the internal Angolan and Mozambican negotiations, Operation Restore Hope and the follow-up UN operation in Somalia, and the 1993 deployment of peacekeepers to Mozambique are all evidence of the changing impact of the international factor in Africa's wars. The change came about in part because of declining Cold War tensions and the reorientation of South African policy toward its domestic conflicts from 1988. But the change was also a reflection of the realization in the international community of the grave humanitarian costs of Africa's wars. The main issue with respect to international involvement in Africa's wars in the early 1990s was whether the international community would be willing to bear the costs of a substantial, long-term commitment to African peace.

Overview of External Involvement

Africa's wars would not appear to be very attractive objects for intervention by any foreign actor, whether near or far away. Their history is always complex and hard for outsiders to comprehend fully, and the course of most wars has proved difficult to predict. Resistance movements that seemed on the verge of extinction have sometimes risen from the ashes and made surprising new gains, while promising steps toward negotiated settlements have often evaporated, to the consternation of diplomats and outside peacemakers. Most wars have shown a discouraging persistence over many years. A foreign actor would seem to need an unusual degree of optimism to expect to succeed in realizing its foreign policy objectives in such situations. Nonetheless, foreign actors from Africa and around the world chose to get involved in all of Africa's wars.

Table 4.1, which identifies sources of military aid, gives some idea of the number of foreign actors that became involved. Sources of aid, including training, weapons, bases, and non-lethal equipment, have

Table 4.1

Military Aid* in Afflicted Countries

War	Military Aid to Government (donors)	Military Aid to Resistance (donors)
Angola	Soviet Union, Cuba, other Soviet bloc	South Africa, United States; UNITA claimed many other supporters
Chad	France, United States, Zaire (to Habré regime)	Libya; Sudanese complicity in giving shelter uncertain
Ethiopia	Soviet Union, other Soviet bloc, Italy, China, Libya	Sudan, Somalia, Arab states
Liberia	ECOWAS support for interim government	-
Mozambique	Soviet Union, Zimbabwe, Tanzania, Malawi, France, Britain	South Africa, private western groups
Namibia	-	Soviet Union, other Soviet bloc, Angola, Zambia
Rwanda	France, Belgium, Zaire	Resistance used Ugandan arms, Ugandan complicity uncertain
Somalia	United States, Libya, France, Italy, China	Ethiopia
Sudan	U.S., West European countries through 1985, Libya after; China, Iraq, other Arab states, Iran	Ethiopia before 1991; Libya before 1986
Uganda	Britain, Tanzania, other Commonwealth, N. Korea, Egypt before NRA takeover; Britain afterward	Libya
Western Sahara	United States, France, China	Algeria

Sources: U.S. Arms Control and Disarmament Agency, *World Military Expenditures and Arms Transfers*, 1987 and 1989 eds., as well as media reports.
*Military aid consists of troops or advisers, training, transport, equipment, or other arms aid or transfers.

been listed only when their role is fairly well established, and there were no doubt instances of covert foreign involvement that are not listed here. Allegations of such involvement are mentioned in the case-by-case discussion that follows. Military aid was not the only form of foreign assistance to the participants in Africa's wars. SWAPO, for example, received humanitarian, technical, and educational assistance from a variety of sources, including the Scandinavian countries and the United Nations Development Program, while the governments of Mozambique, Sudan, and other countries were benefiting from numerous foreign economic assistance programs. Meanwhile, of course, foreign governments, international organizations, and private agencies, acting on humanitarian grounds, were channeling relief to the victims of war.

Military assistance, however, was the form of involvement that directly helped resistance forces to wage war and governments to defend themselves; the findings in Table 4.1 make it clear that there was a remarkable range of sources for such aid. In part, this was another sign of Africa's weakness and underdevelopment. The governments of more developed countries would not have needed so much external military aid to respond to internal threats; and outsiders would have hesitated to assist internal resistance forces, since such governments would have been capable of retaliating in some manner. In part too, the range of actors listed in Table 4.1 testifies to the fact that many did have motives strong enough to propel them toward involvement in Africa's conflicts despite the unpromising prospects for success.

The absence of a few of Africa's more powerful states from the list in Table 4.1 is noteworthy. In the immediate post-independence period, it was widely expected that Algeria and Egypt would be playing a continental role on behalf of what were then seen as radical causes and in support of pan-African unity. By the 1980s, however, both countries were too absorbed in their internal problems to be playing much of an African role at all. In any event, political changes arising from these problems meant that neither was any longer a radical actor on the African stage. Algeria had given vital support to POLISARIO, and Egypt could not ignore events in Sudan, but their policies on these countries were motivated by the more compelling interests of neighbors rather than broader, pan-African concerns.

Nigeria was once thought of as an emerging middle power that would play an important role around the African continent. Its academics and statesmen had long aspired to such a role for their large and populous nation,[1] and there had been some expectation that Nigeria's oil wealth would give it the means to be a major diplomatic force in Africa generally and perhaps to help defend governments in southern Africa against South African interference. Only in 1990, however, when Nigeria spearheaded the West African response to the Liberian insurrection, did Nigeria assume a decisive role in an African war. In the 1980s, it was too absorbed by its own economic and political problems to be much involved in Africa's wars, either as peacemaker or combatant. It did attempt to mediate the Chad conflict early in the decade, and its troops led the ill-fated OAU peacekeeping force in that troubled country. At the end of the decade, Nigeria was among the countries participating in the African mediation effort in Angola; and as OAU chairman in 1991–1992, then President Ibrahim Babangida launched his unsuccessful mediation in the Sudan conflict. Otherwise, Nigeria was not a particularly significant force in the continent's wars.

Among the non-African actors, China is perhaps the most notable near-absentee from Table 4.1, appearing at all only because of a few small-volume arms transfers to African governments. China was moved in an earlier day by its world revolutionary vision and its rivalry with the Soviet Union to aid a number of African resistance movements, including Jonas Savimbi's UNITA. By the 1980s, these motivations had faded. In the early 1990s, however—as Chapter 5 will note—there was concern over new profit-motivated Chinese arms sales.

Motives for External Involvement

The motives propelling so many external actors to involve themselves in Africa's wars were diverse and are best distinguished at the three levels noted at the outset of this chapter: neighboring states, African regional actors, and external or non-African powers.

Neighboring States

Neighbors were inspired to involve themselves in wars next door because of numerous local rivalries and grievances, often going back many years. Sometimes these rivalries had as much to do with questions of local power and influence as with specific issues. Algerian aid to POLISARIO over the years, for example, was an aspect of the long-running balance-of-power contest between two neighbors that are approximately equal in population and military strength. It could also be seen as part of an Algerian desire to demonstrate Algeria's importance to a Moroccan royal elite who tended to regard its neighbor as a colonial creation without historical roots and something of an upstart. In the Horn of Africa, Somali leaders probably entertained hopes of cutting Ethiopian power down to size by aiding Ethiopian dissidents, while asserting what they saw as the rightful role of the Somali nation in the region.

Specific local issues, however, were often a factor in conflicts. In a few instances, active or latent disagreements over colonial borders played a role. Algeria's link to POLISARIO gave it a bargaining chip and a vehicle for reacting if Morocco should ever attempt to revive its claim to territory around Tindouf. Algeria's involvement in Western Sahara also had something to do with the personal mutual aversion between King Hassan and Houari Boumedienne, who was Algeria's president at the time of the Moroccan invasion.[2] Libyan leader Qadhafi, whose own tribe has an offshoot in Chad,[3] takes a particular interest in Chad's northern Aouzou strip, which has long been rumored to have uranium, phosphate, and manganese deposits. Qadhafi maintains that Chad's president made a secret agreement selling the strip to Libya in 1973, the year when Libyan troops moved in.[4] He also cites a 1935 agreement, never ratified, between France and Italy, the colonial power in Libya, in support of his claim. Sudan, meanwhile has suspected Kenya of aiding the SPLA because of a potential Kenyan claim in southern Sudan.

Aid to a resistance movement was at times motivated by the desire to counter or forestall similar aid by the neighboring state. Qadhafi probably aided Chadian dissidents not only because of the Aouzou strip but also because he feared that Chad would cooperate with Libyan dissidents, perhaps backed by outside powers, who would use Chad as a staging base to overthrow his regime.[5] Throughout the 1980s, Ethiopia and Sudan were locked in a pattern of reciprocal support for dissidents that had lasted for years, through coups and revolutions, so that it was impossible to say which should bear the greater blame. The Ethiopia/Sudan conflict nexus was also partly explained by Ethiopia's ancient fear of encirclement by Islamic forces and Sudan's quest for leverage in the country that controlled the headwaters of the Nile.

Zimbabwe's intervention in Mozambique was one of the few instances—and by far the largest—in which a state sent troops across its border to help a neighboring government. Zimbabwe was motivated in part by the self-interested desire to protect critical supply lines—in this case road, rail, and pipeline connections through Mozambique to the sea. But Mugabe's personal loyalty to FRELIMO, which had assisted him at great cost during the Zimbabwe revolution, was also an important factor, as was Zimbabwe's strong desire to frustrate South African policy designs in southern Africa.

Regional Actors

There were two African regional powers, Libya and South Africa, whose interventions had a wider scope, encompassing not only neighboring states but also more distant countries. South Africa took part on a large scale in only one conflict that was not in a neighboring state[6]— the war in Angola. Even Angola was a sort of a neighboring country from the perspective of South Africa's security planners, given the white republic's commitment in Namibia. Libya's foreign entanglements were more wide-ranging.

It would be easy to write off Colonel Qadhafi's foreign policy as wholly irrational and inexplicable because of his mercurial relations with individual heads of state and resistance leaders. His fondness for unity agreements that seemed so unrealistic also made Qadhafi's policies appear quixotic. Nonetheless, Qadhafi did have an agenda calling for the spread of Islam and social revolution in Africa,[7] and this agenda helps to explain his involvement in Africa's wars. Indeed, it is the third rationale for his involvement in Chad, which could give him a base for projecting his influence over much of western and central Africa. It was partly Qadhafi's support for social revolution that explained his aid to Museveni, a non-Moslem, during the Ugandan revolution, but Qadhafi was probably also seeking to re-establish his reputation in the area after the overthrow of Idi Amin—a Moslem who had received Libyan aid. Libyan troops had been humiliatingly defeated when Ugandan exiles and Tanzanian forces invaded Uganda in 1978. Qadhafi's aid to the SPLA in Sudan may have been inspired by his interest in social revolution and his strong personal antipathy toward President Numeiry. The pull of Islam, however, later led Qadhafi to shift his support to the government of Sadiq el-Mahdi, who had a claim to historic religious authority in Sudan, and to continue to assist the Islamic-oriented regime that later overthrew el-Mahdi. In Ethiopia, Qadhafi's interests seemed to lie more with the non-Islamic government of Mengistu Haile Mariam, perhaps because of its revolutionary origins, rather than with the Islamic elements among the resistance forces.

South Africa's involvement in southern Africa's wars was more clearly motivated by self-interest. In Angola, as in Namibia and Mozambique, the white regime was acting in a way that it thought would protect its rule and the system of apartheid within South Africa. Angola, which sheltered SWAPO and where the Soviet Union and Cuba were heavily involved, was always seen as a particular threat, and this explains South Africa's heavy commitment there. At one time, particularly in the wake of the Portuguese withdrawal from the region, the South African regime may have believed in what it said was a "total onslaught" inspired by the Soviet Union and aimed at establishing a Marxist regime in South Africa. This thesis became increasingly threadbare as the 1980s advanced, however, and by the end of the decade, the white regime had refocused its energies at home.

Regional Organizations

Over the years, many observers of African affairs have hoped that regional organizations would grow and strengthen, perhaps intervening in African wars and other conflicts in the interest of peace. Until 1990, there was little sign of progress in this direction. The ease with which Habré's forces had circumvented the OAU force in Chad in 1982 had been an embarrassment for the OAU and for Nigeria, the major element in the force. In 1990, however, the sixteen-member ECOWAS organization dispatched ECOMOG to Liberia. This force included troops from Gambia, Ghana, Guinea, and Sierra Leone, but was again dominated by Nigeria, which had by far the largest and most developed military capabilities in the region.

The members of ECOWAS probably had a mixture of motives for launching ECOMOG. Many were no doubt genuinely appalled at the deterioration of Liberia and the war's human toll—reflecting a level of suffering that had not been known in West Africa since the Nigerian civil war more than twenty years earlier. More pragmatically, there was concern that the violence in Liberia could spread to Liberia's three neighboring states and set off weapons flows throughout the region. Nor did West African leaders relish the prospect of a Liberian government under the unknown and unpredictable Charles Taylor, who was widely suspected of having ties to Libya.

While these might seem compelling reasons for regional intervention, ECOMOG was troubled by criticisms from the outset. Initially, countries unfriendly to Liberia's President Doe, notably Ivory Coast and Burkina Faso, suspected that ECOMOG represented a Nigerian scheme to prop up his regime—even though ECOMOG's mandate included the creation of an interim government. After Doe's murder, the region's small francophone states continued to suspect that ECOMOG was a device for spreading Nigeria's power and influence far beyond its borders. Nonetheless, ECOMOG was instrumental in fostering peace talks between the interim government and the NPFL, and it finally dealt a heavy blow to Taylor and in turn helped the Geneva negotiations to succeed. It may yet come to be seen as a precedent for future regional interventions.

External Powers

The motives of the non-African states involved in Africa's wars were perhaps more curious than those of the African actors. Africa, certainly, has never been perceived as a particularly vital region by the high councils of most foreign powers.[8] Why, then, did so many choose to play a role in Africa's wars?

The continent's very marginality—in the eyes of many policymakers outside the continent—may itself be part of the reason. Foreign policy designs and ambitions could be pursued more easily in Africa than in many parts of the world because the risk of dangerous reactions was small and because affordable commitments of power could have a major impact. Thus France, which could no longer exercise great power or influence over wide parts of the globe, maintained its status as a middle power in world politics partly through its military, economic, and political role in Africa.[9] Chad—not a highly consequential nation in the global scheme of things—took on special importance as a symbol of France's determination to fulfill its "Africa mission" and to stand up to Libyan perfidy.[10]

Britain, the other great colonial power in Africa, did not feel the same need to become involved in Africa's wars. It provided military training and other assistance in Uganda, where perhaps there was some sense of an obligation to try to restore the professionalism of an army that had been created in the colonial period. It was Britain, after all, that had based the Ugandan army around northerners and Moslems, setting the stage for societal breakdown of the post-colonial era. British advisers also provided training to the army of Mozambique, where Britain had once had economic interests and where there might again be investment opportunities. Some analysts speculated that Britain's role in Mozambique was intended to compensate, in African eyes, for British opposition to stronger sanctions against South Africa.

Cuba's motives more closely resembled those of France. Cuba, of course, had never enjoyed world power status, but under Castro it had ambitions. Its commitment of troops and civilian personnel in Angola furthered its reputation as a leader in the world socialist movement and among the non-aligned at a time when it was isolated and unable to act with much effect in Latin America.

The Soviet Union, with its substantial involvements in Angola, Mozambique, and Ethiopia, probably also valued Africa more for its symbolic usefulness in world politics than for its intrinsic importance. Soviet involvement in the internal affairs of these countries—which began under Brezhnev but continued through the 1980s, even under the cost-conscious Gorbachev—helped the Soviets regain some of the influence they had lost through their exclusion from the Middle East peace process and their failures generally in the global political and economic competition. According to one scholar, writing in 1987,

> The USSR has moved to the status of central actor in key crisis areas in Africa. No longer can a crisis be resolved in this area—or a significant American move be made—without taking the Soviet Union into account.[11]

Even at the end of the 1980s, as the Soviet domestic economic and political crisis deepened, the USSR continued to provide military assistance to Angola, Mozambique, and Ethiopia. Its diplomats, meanwhile, assumed a prominent role in the regional peace process in southern Africa. The views of Soviet Africanists and Africa policymakers, who had a new freedom to travel and express their views, became, for a time, a subject of great interest in Africa policy circles in the West.

Earlier, in the Brezhnev era and its aftermath, the Soviet Union may have had strategic ambitions in Africa. Ethiopia's location on the southern flank of the Middle East, the mineral wealth of southern Africa, and the petroleum shipping lanes around Africa's coasts were often mentioned as motivating factors for the Soviets in the 1970s and much of the 1980s. It seems likely, however, that strategic factors were a declining concern by the later 1980s, as it became clear that there could be no victories, and thus no strategic gains, in Ethiopia, Angola, or Mozambique.

The United States did not become as deeply involved as the USSR in Africa's wars during the 1980s, although it did aid UNITA after 1986 and rush aid to Chad in its confrontation with Libya. Journalists reported that the United States had given critical covert military assistance to Habré even before he took power in Chad.[12] The United States also continued with security assistance programs in Morocco, and for part of the decade in Sudan and Somalia, which antedated the wars those governments were pursuing.

The aid to UNITA, a subject of prolonged debate in the American government both before and after the decision was made, came about because of a combination of differing perspectives on the Angolan situation at mid-decade. It resulted partly from a unique factor: the favorable impression Savimbi had made on many members of Congress, President Reagan, and other influential Americans. Africa policymakers, meanwhile, saw aiding UNITA as a foreign policy instrument that would press what they regarded as a hitherto unresponsive Angolan government as well as Moscow and Havana, toward a regional peace settlement and internal reconciliation. Those who took a global-strategic perspective favored the program as an aspect of the "Reagan doctrine," which aimed at confronting, albeit indirectly, perceived Soviet advances under Brezhnev through aid to anti-Soviet resistance forces.[13] The presence of Cuban troops in Angola made it easier for the executive branch to win support for aid to UNITA than for the Nicaraguan *contras*.

The desire to frustrate Libyan ambitions was another strong motivation for U.S. policy in the 1980s, and it accounted for U.S. involvement in Chad—a country that otherwise would have drawn little interest. Countering Libyan influence was also a factor in U.S. aid to Morocco, Sudan, and Somalia.

The U.S. military assistance programs in these three countries, however, were explained primarily by the countries' strategic location in relation to the Middle East. Morocco and Somalia allowed access to their ports and facilities for the U.S. military;[14] and American policymakers saw this as extremely valuable, especially in connection with Persian Gulf contingencies. The wars in Morocco, Somalia, and Sudan only complicated the task of policymakers in trying to fulfill broader American objectives.

At the end of the 1980s and into the 1990s, U.S. diplomats became highly active in trying to promote negotiated settlements in Africa's wars. The Angola/Namibia accord of 1988 and the 1991 agreement between the contending parties within Angola were, in significant measure, the result of American diplomacy—and they brought significant political and strategic benefits. In these and other wars, U.S. officials were actively engaged in negotiations to open relief corridors that would allow food and emergency supplies to be channeled to the civilian victims of war. U.S. officials also tried to mediate in the Ethiopian conflict, and explored mediation prospects in Liberia and Sudan. In undertaking these more recent efforts, some U.S. policymakers may have been partly motivated by a desire to demonstrate that the United States intended to remain a force in Africa in the post–Cold War era despite the end of the U.S./Soviet African rivalry. Through 1991, moreover, policymakers wanted to assure that the Soviet pullback from positions gained under Brezhnev was consolidated and that substantial Soviet influence was not allowed to continue at some lower, less costly level with tacit American consent. This was a factor in the continuing aid to Savimbi just as it motivated U.S. aid to the Afghan resistance after the Soviet troop withdrawal. Clearly, however, U.S. motivations were also in part humanitarian—an outgrowth of the deep concern felt among many Americans over war and famine in Africa. This concern was inspired by media reports and articulated by interested individuals, church organizations, relief agencies, and lobbies for the hungry and refugees. Congressional hearings and legislative proposals aimed at promoting peace and helping the victims of war made public concern over Africa's wars and their consequences clear to policymakers.

Constraints on External Involvement

While many outside actors had motives for becoming involved in Africa's wars, most also faced constraints that tended to limit their role. Interfering African neighbors were typically weak states themselves and often could do little more than allow dissidents from next door to encamp on their territory. Most could not consider invading a neighboring state in support of resistance forces as Somalia had tried abortively in Ethiopia's Ogaden in 1977–1978. The regional actors— South Africa (in Angola) and Libya (in Chad)—did send troops across their borders in support of resistance forces, but even these comparatively powerful states learned that there were limits to what they could achieve. Each of the invaded countries presented serious obstacles to successful military operations, and the regimes in both Angola and Chad were able to bring the ancient mechanism of the balance of power to bear as they garnered countervailing support from other external sources.

The external, non-African actors faced important financial and political constraints on their African involvement. France had been able to play a combat role in Chad, but that role had to be sharply restricted lest it grow too costly or result in significant French casualties. Either eventuality could have created crippling public opposition at home.

Cuba had initially been able to deploy large numbers of troops and accept casualties in far-off Angola because the Castro regime faced only marginal constraints from domestic public opinion. Moreover, while the details of the financial arrangements that allowed it to intervene in Angola may never be known, Cuba evidently was able to obtain the funding needed to sustain its role from the Soviet Union, and perhaps at an earlier date from Angola itself.[15] Both Angola and the Soviet Union were sorely pinched at decade's end, however, and this forced an apparently reluctant Castro to acquiesce in the Angola/Namibia peace accord. Cuba's role as a significant African military power was at an end.

The Soviets, of course, had behaved for much of the 1970s and 1980s as if financial constraints were not a problem, despite the worsening difficulties of the Soviet economy. Overall, Soviet military aid to sub-Saharan Africa—which went primarily to Ethiopia, Angola, and Mozambique—totaled $18.9 billion from 1981 through 1988, as compared with just under $1 billion for the United States.[16] Even the Soviets, however, did not risk troops in Africa, although the occasional death of an adviser was reported from Angola or Ethiopia.

By the end of the 1980s, it had become clear that the Gorbachev regime was looking for ways to reduce the cost of its African role, while retaining its reputation as a major actor around the globe, a reliable ally to its Third World friends, and a player in African affairs. Financial constraints had by this time become compelling, and even public opinion was a force to be reckoned with. It was increasingly difficult for the Soviet government to justify costly commitments in Africa to an assertive Soviet public angered by empty shelves at home. High levels of Soviet arms aid to Ethiopia, Angola, and Mozambique evidently continued through the 1980s, but advisers were leaving Ethiopia and Mozambique by 1990 and a cutback in arms shipments to Ethiopia, where Soviet anger with Mengistu's inflexibility was palpable, was widely anticipated. In 1991, it may be that the Soviets could have saved Mengistu if they had been willing to launch an airlift of arms and supplies comparable to the effort that kept the Najibullah regime in power in Afghanistan for so long. But such an airlift was no longer a serious option for the afflicted Gorbachev regime. With Mengistu's ouster and the Angolan peace accord, both occurring in May 1991, the Soviet Union's ability to remain a player of any significance in African affairs was in question. The extraordinary changes in the Soviet Union beginning in August 1991 answered this question definitively. As the USSR struggled for its very existence, it was difficult to remember that it had been seen as a "central actor" that had to be taken into account in Africa just a few years before. Soviet incentives for further involvement in Africa's wars were exhausted, and the successor Russian state hoped only—and probably in vain—to secure African repayment of Soviet debt.

For the United States, through the 1980s, the question of committing combat forces to an African war could not arise because of the Vietnam experience. Military aid to one side or another in any war had to be kept in the millions of dollars, rather than the billions, because of budgetary constraints and congressional concerns over the harm that arms aid might do. Particular features of individual wars also tended to discourage Washington from playing a more active role. In Ethiopia, for example, the EPLF and the TPLF both had strong Marxist backgrounds and seemed to be aiming at the breakup of the country. Since the United States had no interest in seeing new, small, and radical Marxist states emerge in the Red Sea area, aid to the guerrillas was not an attractive option even if it might have caused problems for the Soviet Union. At the same time, Mengistu's human rights violations, Marxist economic policies, and Soviet alliance meant that there was no basis for cooperation with the Ethiopian government. In Mozambique, U.S. policymakers had grave doubts about the conduct and objectives of RENAMO, while at the same time they wanted to encourage the economic reforms undertaken by the FRELIMO regime after 1983. Thus they refused to aid the guerrillas throughout the 1980s, while giving economic assistance to the Mozambican government. Military aid to the government, which was proposed in 1985, was never provided because of opposition in Congress, where many had doubts about the conduct and objectives of FRELIMO.

The U.S. military assistance programs to the governments in Somalia and Sudan were also constrained by factors related to the fighting in those countries. In each of these impoverished states, war weakened the regimes and made the long-term political situation highly unpredictable. Thus, the value of either as a long-term strategic ally was increasingly in doubt as time passed. The wars, moreover, led to allegations of human rights violations against the two regimes. Human rights organizations, congressional committees, and others closely monitored U.S. aid programs as a result and sought restrictions to ensure that human rights violations were minimized. There was considerable impatience in the later 1980s with the failure of the governments in Sudan and Somalia to pursue negotiated settlements, and a concern that continued U.S. aid would only encourage them to persist in seeking military solutions. Moreover, in damaging the economies of these two countries, war added to the difficulties their governments experienced in repaying debts to the United States. Delinquency in repayment raised legal obstacles to further U.S. assistance. For all of these reasons—the instability of regimes, human rights problems, failure to make peace, and unpaid debts—U.S. military aid to Sudan and Somalia had virtually ended by the end of the 1980s. Decreasing Cold War tensions at the end of the 1980s were another constraining factor for the United States, at least with respect to military assistance. With the decline and eventual disappearance of the Soviet/American rivalry in Africa, the rationale for any sort of military aid to participants in African wars was severely weakened.

For external actors generally the human toll and the other damaging consequences of Africa's wars were increasingly important constraints on intervention by the end of the decade. The disastrous human consequences of Africa's wars had an impact in Moscow—as suggested by President Gorbachev's statement, at the end of 1988, that "The bell of every regional conflict tolls for all of us."[17] American observers, both in and out of government, were deeply pained by the suffering in Sudan, Ethiopia, Somalia, and other countries, and this created strong pressure in favor of policies that would promote reconciliation rather than further war.

Just as external actors were constrained in earlier years in their support for combatants in Africa's wars, however, they were also constrained in the early 1990s in their level of support for African peace. Diplomacy and various forms of pressure were brought to bear, but the forceful imposition of peace by outsiders, as happened in Somalia and was being attempted in Liberia, remained a highly unusual exception rather than the rule. Such operations were costly indeed, and in most instances international actors were not willing to bear those costs.

Case-by-Case Review

Angola

Overview

Competitive international involvement in Angola may have contributed to the outbreak of war and prolonged the fighting. Certainly it intensified the level of violence. The high levels of Soviet and Cuban aid to the MPLA in the mid-1970s probably helped to convince the regime that it could impose its will on Angolan society without taking into account the needs and demands of important elements of that society, including those elements represented by UNITA. For much of the 1980s, the MPLA continued to receive high levels of Soviet and Cuban support while South Africa heavily backed UNITA, so that neither side had a compelling reason to compromise. The effect of American aid to UNITA after 1986 is still being debated, with some arguing that it also helped to prolong the war, particularly after South African troops exited Angola in 1988. Others maintain that U.S. aid gave the United States leverage to push the two sides toward compromise. However this argument is resolved, it is at least clear that the contending parties could not have fought for so long, at such a high level of violence, if they had not had external support. Mechanized weapons, artillery, aircraft, anti-aircraft missiles, and even troops (from Cuba and South Africa) were introduced into Angola by foreign actors, making it possible for the two sides to engage in several major battles and frequent smaller clashes.

By the late 1980s, foreign involvement had reached such a high level that it began to have a reverse effect. Increased Soviet military aid, the dispatch of additional Cuban troops, large-scale direct participation by the South African army, and growing covert but publicly acknowledged U.S. aid to UNITA, evidently coming in through Zaire, provoked an alarming regional crisis. Angola, Cuba, and South Africa, under pressure from the United States and the Soviet Union, were finally persuaded to enter into the December 1988 Angola/Namibia peace accord, which provided for a phased Cuban withdrawal and an end to South African interference. Subsequently, Soviet aid began to drop as the Cuban withdrawal proceeded, and UNITA had reason to believe that U.S. assistance would not continue indefinitely. Thus, the international factor finally began to constrain the two sides and push them toward the 1991 accord. After the accord broke down, external actors again pushed for reconciliation, but—at least into September 1993—without success.

Background

In the mid-1970s, the competitive rush of supplies to the combatants in Angola by the superpowers, the intervention of Cuban troops on behalf of the MPLA, and the South African thrust toward Luanda helped widen the divisions in Angolan society and set the stage for the country's long internal war. The arrival of thousands of Cuban troops, large amounts of Soviet equipment, and Soviet advisers may well have helped convince the MPLA that it need not work toward implementation of the Alvor agreement but rather could defeat its opponents militarily—an objective it achieved with respect to the FNLA. At the same time, however, South African and American aid to the FNLA and UNITA contributed to the polarization within Angola and helped propel the crisis to the center of the Cold War stage for a time.

U.S. aid to the Angolan resistance was halted by Congress in 1976 under the "Clark amendment," passed in the wake of revelations of the covert U.S. role.[18] The amendment, which prohibited any aid to factions in Angola without the express authorization of Congress, seemed to slow competitive international involvement in Angola for a time. South Africa renewed its interventions in Angola in 1978, however, and for the next decade foreign involvement in the Angolan war remained at high levels.

For UNITA, South African support was critical. In addition to providing supplies and equipment, one South African military unit—the 32d Battalion, also known as the "Buffalo Battalion"—operated more or less continuously in Angola.[19] The battalion was reportedly manned in part by former FNLA guerrillas and commanded by South African officers as well as West European mercenaries; and elements may sometimes have posed as UNITA guerrillas.[20] In May 1985, two South African commandos were killed and one captured while attempting to blow up a Gulf Oil storage facility in Cabinda province. They were allegedly carrying UNITA leaflets that they had planned to leave at the scene,[21] and for many observers this called the provenance of UNITA's other daring raids into question.

South African aid was probably essential in destroying Soviet-supplied armor and transporting UNITA troops during the 1985 MPLA offensive[22] and in the 1986 counterattacks around Cuito Cuanavale. In September 1986, the South African defense minister openly acknowledged that his country had given moral, material, and humanitarian assistance to UNITA; and he said—rather belatedly—that military assistance was not excluded as a contingency.[23] This warning presaged the intervention of South African troops, aircraft, and artillery against the MPLA's 1987 offensive and in support of the counter-thrust at Cuito Cuanavale.

By this time, however, a number of factors were shifting the military balance against South Africa. These included Cuba's decision to rush additional troops to Angola and to introduce men and aircraft into combat roles in the south; the accumulation of years of combat experience by the Angolan army; the replenishment of that army's stocks by the Soviet Union; and the installation of a new Soviet-supplied radar system. South Africa evidently lost air superiority over southern Angola, and several aircraft were rumored to have been lost. White South Africa was shocked in June 1988 when twelve white soldiers were killed in a FAPLA–Cuban ground and air attack at the Calueque water scheme near the Angola/Namibia border. Overall, South Africa acknowledged the combat deaths of about sixty white conscripts in Angola in 1987–1988,[24] and some government critics suspected that the true figure was higher.[25]

U.S. aid to UNITA became possible in 1985, with the repeal of the Clark amendment.[26] In the first months of 1986, U.S. officials began to acknowledge that a covert program of assistance to UNITA had begun, and most press accounts estimated the value of this assistance at $15 million annually, perhaps rising to $30 million in 1988[27] and to higher levels in subsequent years. They also indicated that the assistance program included Stinger anti-aircraft missiles as well as anti-armor weapons, and that most of the aid was being channeled to Savimbi by way of facilities in neighboring Zaire.[28]

U.S. officials always insisted that the purpose of this aid was to force the MPLA to acknowledge UNITA as a legitimate political force and push the Angolan regime toward an internal reconciliation. This was true of both the Reagan and Bush administrations. Just before taking office, President-elect Bush wrote to Savimbi assuring him that "my Administration will continue all appropriate and effective assistance to UNITA"[29]—until the objective of a "process of negotiation leading to national reconciliation" was achieved. Critics, however, maintained that the covert aid program was only encouraging Savimbi to persist in an unwinnable war and delaying the peace process. They suggested that U.S. aid to UNITA was driven, at least in part, by concerns in the White House over the opinions of influential American conservatives who were sympathetic to Savimbi.

In addition to U.S. and South African aid, UNITA maintained that a number of other countries had given it support over the years. Since the movement was unpopular in Africa and much of the rest of the world because of its South African support, the number of such countries was probably small—and they had reason to cloak any involvement in secrecy. Morocco was mentioned as a UNITA backer, and some alleged that Morocco served as an indirect channel for U.S. aid even before the Clark amendment was repealed.[30] But Morocco's role, if any, has never been conclusively demonstrated. Allegations of Saudi aid, said to have been given at the urging of the United States, arose during the Iran/Contra controversy in 1987 but were not proven.[31]

In any event, external assistance to UNITA was dwarfed by Soviet and Cuban assistance to the MPLA. Western sources estimated that Soviet military aid to Angola was reaching the level of $1 billion per year by 1987, on top of $4 billion provided over the previous decade. Soviet-supplied equipment included 550 tanks, armored vehicles, artillery, anti-aircraft missiles, 55 MiG–23s, and ships and patrol boats for coastal defense.[32] An estimated 950 Soviet advisers and technicians were in the country[33]—some placed the figure higher[34]—along with 500 East German intelligence and security advisers. Cuban troop levels rose from an estimated 15,000–21,000 at the beginning of the decade to 50,000 in 1988.

By the latter part of the 1980s, however, there was growing evidence of Soviet impatience over the high cost of the long war in Angola. Reports appeared from time to time of strains between the MPLA and its foreign backers over the extent of Angola's dependence and the cost of aid. Some strains must have existed since Angola reportedly could not make payments on its accumulated $2.6 billion debt to the Soviets in the latter part of the decade and was probably unable to compensate Cuba for its help after the collapse of world oil prices in 1986.[35] Soviet pressure on Luanda to agree to the Angola/Namibia peace accord in 1988, despite the fact that UNITA remained in the field and would continue to receive U.S. aid, may have been particularly resented. Western estimates say the level of Soviet aid to the MPLA began to decline after 1988, and while the Soviets evidently lent their approval to the final offensive against UNITA at the beginning of 1990, by the end of the year, the Soviet foreign minister was taking a lead role in the push for a peace settlement.

After the 1988 accord had been concluded, the MPLA's Central Committee issued a declaration expressing "heartfelt homage to the valiant Cuban fighters who, in an exemplary and brilliant manner, participated in one of the most noble epics of mankind."[36] But however deep its gratitude, the essential point for the MPLA was that the Cubans were leaving. This reality, combined with Soviet impatience, created considerable pressure on the regime to come to terms.

UNITA, which had lost South African aid and probably did not feel that it could count on American aid indefinitely, was also under pressure after the 1988 accord. With the Cold War ending, part of the rationale for the U.S. aid program was being undercut. Sustaining support for that program in a period of budgetary constraint in the United States could be difficult, even within the executive branch. The active role of the State Department in proposing plans for a cease-fire and elections underscored the point that the administration was aiming at an early compromise rather than a further prolongation of the war. While Savimbi was aware that he had many friends in the U.S. Congress who might back him in a disagreement with the administration, there were other members who strongly opposed the UNITA aid program.

In partially classified intelligence legislation enacted at the end of 1990,[37] Congress placed half of any lethal assistance[38] to UNITA in a restricted account that could be released only with the approval of the intelligence committees of the two Houses. In addition, any lethal aid was to be suspended in the event of significant progress toward a cease-fire and free elections. President Bush vetoed this legislation, citing issues not related to Angola, but he reportedly abided by its Angola provisions.[39] Thus, congressional action put pressure on the MPLA to make firm commitments, with explicit dates attached, of the sort it had been hinting at for some time. In addition, it put Savimbi on notice of the need to reciprocate or risk losing American aid. U.S. diplomats knew that they had to intensify their efforts to find a negotiated solution before Savimbi was cut off altogether.

Clearly, then, international pressure was a critical factor in achieving the May 1991 accord. Under the accord, the MPLA and UNITA mutually pledged to refrain from acquiring "lethal material" from any source, a pledge that should have sealed an end to sixteen years of foreign military aid to combatants in the Angolan war.

Foreign responsibility for the collapse of the Angolan peace accord in September 1992 lies primarily in inattention and an unwillingness to commit the resources needed to oversee demobilization. UNITA appeared to be fighting primarily with weapons that were stockpiled and hidden during the demobilization period, although there was much suspicion that sympathetic elements in the South African military and police, as well as private groups and individuals, may have been supplying arms. The MPLA, meanwhile, was appealing for a resumption of international arms aid and was suspected of trying to use hard-currency oil earnings to purchase weapons. Diplomats from Western countries and Russia, together with UN officials, were attempting to mediate a renewal of the peace process with little hope of early success. The Clinton administration extended U.S. recognition to the MPLA in May 1993, finally giving up on the notion that Savimbi might be persuaded to compromise by a continued show of U.S. evenhandedness. In June, the United States ended its trade embargo against Angola and announced that U.S. firms would be permitted to sell non-lethal military equipment to the MPLA. Britain repealed its arms embargo against the MPLA in August, and in September the UN Security Council imposed an international embargo on the export of arms and petroleum products to UNITA. The international community, however, showed little interest in deploying a peacekeeping force to Angola, even though the death toll from the latest round of war and famine was mounting into the tens of thousands and relief workers were beginning to speak of "another Somalia." An imposed peace in such a large country, where combatants are heavily armed and experienced in combat, would be an extremely difficult proposition, particularly at a time when the United Nations has heavy peacekeeping commitments elsewhere.

Chad

Overview

Libyan intervention in Chad was the major factor determining the scale of the fighting that took place there. Chadian factions would probably have fought one another without Libyan involvement, but the fighting would have been a sort of low-level tribal warfare of no interest to the United States and of far less interest to France. While Libya must bear most of the blame for intensifying the fighting in Chad, the impact of alleged covert U.S. aid to the Habré resistance forces in the early 1980s is controversial—and difficult to determine in view of the uncertainties surrounding the aid itself and the "might-have-beens" of history. Some observers believe that it would have been better for the United States to have worked with the Goukouni government toward some sort of internal settlement in 1981, after Goukouni asked the Libyan troops to leave and they agreed to go. Long years of conflict in Chad might have been avoided, some believe, if Habré had not been encouraged to continue a covert war against Goukouni after the Libyan departure. Others maintain, however, that Goukouni was unreliable and indecisive, and that the country benefited over the long term from his departure.

French and American assistance finally helped the Habré government deal a severe blow to Qadhafi in 1987, bringing a temporary and unaccustomed peace to Chad. Unfortunately, Habré's external backers failed to dissuade him from human rights abuses and political repression that again widened the gap between state and society. Meanwhile, Libyan aid to Chad opposition forces had resumed, and in 1990, a regime more friendly to Libya took power after a new outbreak of fighting.

Background

Libyan arms and Libyan troops were critical in sustaining armed opposition forces in Chad during the 1980s. The extent of Libyan intervention is indicated by the scale of Libya's 1987 losses in terms of personnel killed or captured and equipment lost to Chadian forces. After this devastating defeat, as Habré succeeded in reconciling with some of his former enemies, Libya lacked opportunities for interfering in Chad. The growing repression within Chad, however, soon restored these opportunities, and Libya evidently played an important role in aiding the Chadian forces that took shelter in Sudan. The extent of this role, however, remains uncertain, since so little is known about events in Sudan's remote Darfur province, or in Libya itself.

Sudan's role in supporting Chad opposition elements is less clear than Libya's. Acheikh Ibn Omar, who commanded the most powerful Chadian opposition for a time in the 1980s, fled from Libya, where he had come to fear arrest, into remote Sudan with 2,000 guerrillas in July 1988.[40] His presence in Sudan led to a long period of Chad/Sudan tension, although Acheikh eventually reconciled with Habré. Chadian opposition forces again rallied in Sudan 1989, leading to further charges from Ndjamena, Chad's capital, of Sudanese interference in Chad's affairs. Since Sudan was angered by Chad's armed incursions into Darfur in pursuit of the resistance forces, and since it was forging ever closer ties to Libya throughout this period, Ndjamena's charges were probably justified. Whether the Sudanese government was actively supporting armed Chadian resistance forces, however, or simply tolerating their presence in a remote province where it exercised little control in any event, remains uncertain. Chad opposition groups also took shelter in several West African countries over the years, and it may be that they received support in one form or another from some countries, such as Benin.[41]

France was the major backer of the Habré regime, assuming the key role in fending off Libyan intervention. Operation Manta brought 3,000 French troops to Chad in 1983–1984 and stabilized the regime. This force was backed up by a contingent from Zaire, which was anxious to demonstrate its support for France since that country had become a critical prop for President Mobutu's government.

Libya's failure to implement the 1984 mutual withdrawal agreement was an embarrassment for France among its African allies, and Paris willingly dispatched another military mission in 1986, when rebels attacked across the Red Line. Operation Épervier, which included 2,000 troops at its peak as well as aircraft and air defense weapons, played an important rear-guard role as Habré consolidated his position and prepared a counter-offensive. While the French, who sought to minimize their own casualties, were probably not as aggressive as Habré would have wished, French air raids on Libyan-built airfields in northern Chad prevented the sporadic Libyan bombing runs over the capital from becoming a significant factor in the conflict. Moreover, the protection provided by French air power and air defense no doubt facilitated the Habré advance into the north. In the end, however, France may have dampened Habré's ardor for attacking into Libya proper or trying to reconquer the Aouzou strip by force. There was speculation in the press, at least, that in order to avert a wider war with Libya, France slowed arms deliveries to Habré in 1987 and pressed him to accept a diplomatic approach on Aouzou.[42] Nonetheless, France continued to protect Chad, and a reduced French contingent remained in the country at decade's end.

U.S. military assistance to Chad, which was coordinated with the French assistance program, totaled just over $34.5 million from 1983, when the program began, through 1990. This program focused on transport, including the provision and maintenance of aircraft as well as overland vehicles, and was clearly helpful to Habré in his war against internal opponents and Libya. Detailed information on the reported covert U.S. aid program to Habré before his takeover has not been published. Numerous press reports, however, have discussed the alleged American role, after 1987, in training the Libyan dissidents based in Chad.[43] Qadhafi, in supporting Deby, failed in his aim of having all of these dissidents returned to Libya, but succeeded in having them removed from Chad.

The degree to which French and American aid to the Habré regime encouraged the Chadian leader in his insensitivity to the concerns of his country's ethnic groups and clans, and in his repression of political opponents, is not known. Perhaps Habré concluded, however, that in view of his victory in 1987 and his cooperation in the Libyan "contra" program, he could do no wrong in the eyes of his foreign supporters. Yet in the end he made himself an unattractive candidate for further Western backing.

Today, the influence of Libya, which is providing financial backing to the regime, is strong, and Islamist influences from Sudan are making inroads in Chadian society. France, which provides economic aid and retains a small military presence, has exerted pressure in support of human rights and democratization, but this pressure has been limited by a concern that too active a role could lead to the loss of French influence altogether. Thus, the current balance of external forces could well encourage Deby to move in an authoritarian direction that will provoke continued societal resistance to his regime.

Ethiopia

Overview

Soviet assistance enabled Mengistu to remain inflexible and pursue the long and hopeless war in northern Ethiopia. Any leader in Addis Ababa would have had to resist secessionist attempts in vital provinces, but the carnage and destruction Ethiopia suffered must be attributed in significant measure to this outside involvement. The rebels too had outside aid, and Sudanese cooperation was very important to the Eritrean resistance. By the end of the 1980s, the Soviets were thought to be using their influence over Mengistu to push him toward a settlement, but he resisted tenaciously and was finally forced to flee the country. In 1991, external actors, led by the United States, were urging the new rulers in Addis Ababa in the direction of tolerance and rule by consent, but whether the many divisions in Ethiopian society could now be bridged, after so many years of conflict, remained to be seen.

Background

Soviet assistance to the Mengistu regime was massive and is thought to have included 600 T–54 and 100 T–62 tanks, 600 armored personnel carriers, 78 MiG–21s, and 40 MiG–23s.[44] Extrapolations from published figures suggest that the value of this assistance probably lay between $5 billion and $8 billion. Soviet advisers were estimated to number 1,400, in addition to 300 from East Germany. Even at the end of the 1980s, when many analysts thought that the Soviets were reducing their aid in order to pressure Mengistu for an end to the war,[45] Soviet transports could be seen coming and going many times a day at the civilian airport in Addis Ababa. According to a U.S. estimate, the Soviet Union provided $920 million in arms to Ethiopia even in 1989.[46] East Germany was another major backer for Mengistu. Cuban troops, meanwhile, had participated in the Ogaden war against Somalia in 1977–1978, and a remnant of 3,000 stayed in Ethiopia during most of the 1980s, evidently as a backstop to the Ethiopian army in the event of a new Somali invasion.

Resistance forces—particularly the ELF—had long alleged that Israel was assisting the Ethiopian government,[47] and press reports began to confirm these allegations after Israeli-Ethiopian diplomatic relations were restored in November 1989.[48] U.S. officials reportedly suspected that Israel had sent cluster bombs to the Ethiopian air force.[49] Israel acknowledged a payment of $35 million for Ethiopian cooperation in the evacuation of 14,000 Ethiopian Jews as the rebels approached the capital,[50] but always insisted that it had not armed the Mengistu regime. Israel's interest in Ethiopia was governed not only by its concern over the fate of Ethiopian Jews but also by geo-strategic considerations. These included the desire to support a non-Arab, non-Islamic state on the southern flank of the Middle East and to prevent the emergence of a potentially hostile, pro-Arab independent Eritrea.[51] Israel's ambassador in Addis, claimed in 1990 that an independent Eritrea would place the Red Sea under Arab control.[52]

Libya, which together with South Yemen had signed a friendship treaty with Mengistu's regime in 1981, probably began to supply the Eritreans after Israel established links with Mengistu, although some sources suggest that such aid began earlier. Various other Arab states, mostly in the Persian Gulf area, and Eritrean exiles living in Western Europe and the United States, were also thought to be important sources of aid for the Eritrean resistance forces. Sudan, however, was clearly their most important prop since it provided a secure rear area. The EPLF brought in supplies at Port Sudan for transhipment via night convoys into EPLF-held territory; and the journalists who did so much to boost the image of the movement as a self-reliant and egalitarian organization also came in by that route. Presumably, some of the supplies entering at Port Sudan were moved on to the TPLF from Eritrea. Meanwhile, a weakened ELF continued to carry out limited operations in Ethiopia from bases in eastern Sudan.[53] Some distrust was reported between the EPLF and Sudanese regimes, which tended to favor the ELF because of that organization's closer ties with the Moslem world. But the EPLF could only have been expelled with great difficulty, and Sudan needed the movement because of its usefulness as a counter to Ethiopian aid to the SPLA. At the end of the 1980s, Mengistu hosted a series of meetings between the SPLA and prominent Sudanese in an apparent effort to mediate the conflict in Sudan. This must have made the EPLF leadership anxious, since it raised the specter of a regional peace accord that would couple an end of Ethiopian support for the SPLA with the expulsion of Ethiopian dissidents from Sudan.

Sources of foreign support for other Ethiopian resistance movements can only be the subject of speculation. Somalia, which accused Ethiopia of aiding the SNM, presumably did not forego opportunities to support Somali opposition in Ethiopia. The two sides signed an agreement in April 1988 calling for troop withdrawals along their common border, a halt to "subversive activities," and the prevention of acts of destabilization, evidently because Mengistu needed to redeploy troops from the Somali border to the north. This agreement had the unintended consequence of setting off the SNM invasion of northern Somalia. A small U.S. contribution to one dissident group, the Ethiopian People's Democratic Alliance, was once reported in the press,[54] but any such aid evidently had little result. In any event, the EPDA apparently did not have guerrillas in the field.

By 1990, it should have been clear to Mengistu that his Eastern bloc aid was coming to an end and that a negotiated settlement was required. The last Cuban troops had left in September 1989, the Communist regime in East Germany had fallen, and the Soviets had reportedly warned Mengistu that their arms aid agreement would not be renewed.[55] And indeed the Ethiopian leader did give some half-hearted cooperation to a U.S.-sponsored mediation effort and sent a delegation to talks with the EPLF in Washington in January 1991.

In this case, however, the external powers were not able, as they had been in Angola, to persuade the regime to compromise on key issues, notably an independence referendum in Eritrea. The rebels themselves —making steady progress after long years of fighting with no assistance from the United States or the Soviet Union—were in no mood to back down. Finally, after Mengistu had fled, the United States may have had some success in calming the situation and beginning to heal the divisions in Ethiopia. It encouraged the EPRDF forces to move into Addis Ababa and restore law and order—a decision that was resented by the city's Amhara population. This resentment could fade if Zenawi should eventually follow through on his early promises, made with U.S. encouragement, to govern by consent and permit free elections. But questions surrounding June 1992 regional voting make this uncertain.

Liberia

Overview

As he persisted in the human rights abuses, political repression, and maladministration that did so much to help Charles Taylor win support, Liberia's President Doe was not restrained by aid donors or other international actors. In this sense, foreign actors bear some of the blame for the Liberian war, although it could be said in their defense that Doe was impervious to much well-intentioned advice offered over many years. Once the fighting broke out, many observers remained critical of the "hands off" policy of major foreign powers, particularly the United States. With the ECOWAS intervention, however, West Africa–based international forces came to play an important role in limiting conflict and promoting a negotiated settlement.

Background

Before the Liberian war, the United States was widely regarded as the paramount foreign influence in Liberia because of ties extending back to the U.S. role in founding Liberia in the nineteenth century. The U.S.-Liberian relationship was strengthened by the development of economic links in the first part of the twentieth century and by a security relationship that began in World War II. This relationship matured during the Cold War, when Liberia became the site of a Voice of America relay and other facilities. During the first half of the 1980s, before congressional pressures precipitated a decline, Liberia was among the top recipients of U.S. foreign assistance in Africa. Many observers believe, consequently, that the United States had the power to push Doe into reforms that would have averted the descent into chaos—but was reluctant to exercise that power for fear of destabilizing a Cold War ally. The Reagan administration's failure to challenge the 1985 election results, despite congressional insistence on a free and fair vote, came in for particular criticism.[56]

Those who defend U.S. policy note, however, that while Liberians and African affairs specialists may perceive the existence of a special relationship between the United States and Liberia, the fact is that Liberia never had a high priority in overall U.S. foreign policy. To have expected some sort of decisive U.S. intervention that would have altered the course of Doe's regime, from this perspective, was unrealistic —particularly since the United States would have paid a price for such an intervention in the form of criticism from those always ready to condemn "neocolonialism." Moreover, some point out, after pouring large amounts of aid into Liberia with no result, U.S. officials tended to doubt that they could have much influence over the course of events there.

Criticism of U.S. policy mounted after the war began, when a force of U.S. Navy vessels and marines arrived offshore, finally beginning evacuations of U.S. and other foreign nationals in August 1990. This force, critics believe, would have been fully capable of stabilizing Monrovia, feeding the hungry, tending the sick, and making conditions safe for international relief agencies to operate.[57] In retrospect, some observers unfavorably compared U.S. restraint in Liberia with the later interventions in northern Iraq to protect Kurds, and in Somalia. Another view, however, is that U.S. intervention would have delayed the assumption of responsibility for the situation in Liberia by Liberians themselves and by the West African states.

The ECOWAS peacekeeping operation, as noted above, has some important achievements to its credit. Yet it is expensive, and because of Nigeria's role, controversial. It is generally believed in the region, moreover, that Burkina Faso and perhaps other states sought to undermine ECOMOG's efforts by covertly aiding Taylor's forces and possibly serving as a conduit for Libyan aid. Some pundits are suggesting that ECOMOG will be remembered as "ECOBOG," but others hope that it is a harbinger of future effective regional peacekeeping efforts.

Mozambique

Overview

RENAMO was created by Rhodesian intelligence and sustained for many years by South Africa. It is possible that without this outside involvement there would have been no war in Mozambique, although as noted above there would surely have been conflict and violence. As the 1980s advanced, in any event, RENAMO grew substantially and acquired significant capabilities for sustaining itself. The FRELIMO government, meanwhile, was itself receiving significant quantities of outside military assistance, enabling it to persist in the struggle. By the end of the 1980s, the Soviets were scaling back their involvement in Mozambique and were thought to be pressing the government toward a negotiated settlement. This pressure coincided with an apparent sharp drop in South African aid to the guerrillas. The net impact of foreign involvement since the latter 1980s, consequently, was in the direction of peace rather than war. In 1993, the international community was supporting the Mozambican peace process with the deployment of a UN peacekeeping force.

Background

The role of Rhodesia and South Africa in launching and sustaining RENAMO was described in Chapter 2. The exact nature of South Africa's involvement with the movement became clouded in controversy after the March 1984 signing of the Nkomati accord by the Mozambican and South African governments. Brokered by U.S. diplomats, the accord pledged the two signatories to mutual "non-aggression and good neighborliness" and amounted to a South African promise to cut off aid to RENAMO in exchange for a pledge by Mozambique to prevent the ANC from using its territory to launch attacks into South Africa. South Africa subsequently insisted that its interference in Mozambique had ceased with Nkomati, and its officials maintained that their country's true interests lay in the closer economic and political relations they were pursuing with the Mozambican government.[58]

In September 1985, however, the FRELIMO authorities released captured RENAMO diaries that revealed extensive post-Nkomati contacts between RENAMO and South African officials as well as continuing technical assistance and supply flights. South Africa acknowledged some violations, but portrayed them as the result of excessive zeal on the part of some military elements rather than official policy. Linking indications of violations to zealots in the military, police, and intelligence service, as well as to white Mozambican exiles living in South Africa, then became a standard South African line of argument.

Mozambique as well as many other critics of South Africa maintained that despite denials, an official policy of aid to RENAMO continued. Much of the assistance was thought to be coming through

South African special forces units based in the eastern Transvaal along the Mozambique border.[59] In 1988, U.S. officials affirmed their view that RENAMO was continuing to receive communications equipment, intelligence information, sporadic shipments of small arms, and aid in conducting foreign relations from South Africa.[60] Nonetheless, at decade's end, FRELIMO—in desperate economic straits—was actively pursuing a dialogue with South Africa, and the South African government was responding warmly. South African officials were speaking out in favor of peace in Mozambique and actively encouraging a reconciliation. President Chissano himself said in July 1989 that he no longer believed the South African government was aiding RENAMO.[61] Analysts suspected, however, that private interests in South Africa, possibly including elements within the police and military, continued to do so. President de Klerk himself, asked whether wealthy Portuguese-origin exiles from Mozambique were aiding RENAMO, replied that "We do not monitor the private sector to that extent."[62]

Other sources of external support for RENAMO reportedly included private groups and individuals in West Germany, Portugal, and Brazil. Private American groups, notably the U.S.-based World Anti-Communist League, acknowledged giving non-lethal assistance to the guerrillas.[63] Malawi, a neighbor of Mozambique's and the only black African country that officially recognized South Africa, sheltered RENAMO forces at one time, but after coming under pressure from African neighbors it declared its support for FRELIMO and sent a small contingent of troops into Mozambique to try to protect a rail line.

FRELIMO benefited to an unusual degree from the military support offered by its neighbors, who added thousands of troops to the forces opposing RENAMO. Zimbabwe's well-trained and professional army, with deployments varying between 6,000 and 12,000 troops, defended the Beira corridor and attempted to open the Limpopo line leading to Maputo. The December 1990 partial accord between FRELIMO and RENAMO entrenched Zimbabwe's role as defender of these corridors. President Mugabe of Zimbabwe was determined to prevent a RENAMO takeover in Mozambique, and his country was paying a price for that determination in terms of casualties and retaliatory attacks by RENAMO inside Zimbabwe. Tanzania deployed troops against RENAMO in northern Mozambique for a time, and a Malawi contingent of 600–1,000 men represented as much as one-fifth of that country's army. A British Military Advisory and Training Team, meanwhile, was providing training to company-sized units of Mozambican soldiers at a base in Zimbabwe.[64]

Despite this aid, FRELIMO could not have remained in power without the Soviet Union, which provided more than 95 percent of the arms and equipment going to Mozambique, including tanks, armored vehicles, and military aircraft.[65] After Angola and Ethiopia, Mozambique was the third largest recipient of Soviet arms in sub-Saharan Africa, and Soviet weapons shipments were valued at $1.3 billion for 1982–1986 alone.[66] An estimated 850 Soviet military advisers were in Mozambique in 1988, together with 600 Cubans and 500 East German security advisers.[67] Some analysts suspected at the time that the Soviet advisers were displeased with the military performance of FRELIMO's army, and it was thought that the Soviet government would like to be shed of this entanglement. There were also reports that Mozambique was disappointed with Soviet aid on the grounds that it had not provided the capability for waging a mobile counter-guerrilla war. By 1990, in any event, most Soviet advisers had withdrawn, and the East German advisers were on their way as well.

With both the Soviet Union and South Africa sharply reducing their role in Mozambique, the contending parties were under considerable international pressure to bring the war to a conclusion. The pressure on Chissano was reinforced by Western donors who pointed out that while they would like to respond to Chissano's reforms, they could hardly provide major aid increases while war continued to rage. At the end of 1989, the United States put forth a seven-point statement of principles on peaceful change, reconciliation, democracy, and respect for human rights, which diplomats hoped the two sides would accept in order to move the peace process forward.[68]

The key breakthrough in peace process was achieved by the Community of St. Giles, an Italian Roman Catholic voluntary organization that had established working relations with RENAMO on humanitarian issues. Representatives of the community persuaded Dhlakama to come to Rome, launching a series of direct meetings between the combatants. The negotiations were mediated by community representatives as well as church and government officials, and lasted from July 1990 until the accord was finally signed in October 1992. By 1993, as noted in Chapter 2, the United Nations was making a major contribution to Mozambican peace by deploying UNOMOZ, mediating the disarmament process, and organizing elections expected in late 1994.

Namibia

Overview

There was resistance to South African rule in Namibia long before foreign involvement became a significant factor. However, resistance probably could not have evolved from hit-and-run attacks into a war if SWAPO had not eventually received substantial foreign support. At the same time, the international community, including the International Court of Justice, could have done more to help bridge the state–society gap in Namibia by pressing South Africa to live up to its responsibilities as a United Nations trustee. From the later 1970s, however, foreign actors brought heavy pressure to bear on South Africa to resolve the Namibian dispute, and this pressure played a major role in the eventual resolution of the conflict in 1988. The United Nations then deployed a peacekeeping force that despite initial difficulties proved effective in overseeing the transition to an independent Namibia with a democratically elected government.

Background

The responsibility for the outbreak of war in Namibia must of course lie with South Africa, but Namibia, as a League of Nations mandate and then as a United Nations Trust Territory, was always in part an international responsibility. The International Court's non-decision on Namibia in 1966 manifested the failure of the international community to act decisively against South Africa's abuse of its trust and must bear much of the blame for the outbreak of war.

Foreign support began to strengthen SWAPO significantly with Angolan independence in 1975. If it had not been able to use Angola as a base, SWAPO might not have posed a major military problem for South Africa. SWAPO returned the favor, before the implementation of the Angola/Namibia peace accord, by helping the MPLA in its war with UNITA and providing security along rail lines in central Angola. Clearly, SWAPO/MPLA relations were very close, and it seems certain that SWAPO was aided by the Soviets and Cubans in Angola. According to the International Institute of Strategic Studies, three of SWAPO's ten battalions in Angola were joint Cuban/SWAPO operations, and the movement's arms, which reportedly included SAM–7 missiles, were of Soviet origin.[69]

South Africa probably did not receive outside aid that substantially assisted its operations in Namibia. It came under a voluntary United Nations–sponsored arms embargo in 1963, and the embargo was made mandatory as a result of UN Security Council action in 1977. There have been reports of violations of these embargoes over the years, and much attention has been given to allegations of Israeli technical assistance for the South African military aircraft industry and air defense.[70] Such assistance could have been a help to South Africa in its air attacks against SWAPO targets in Angola. Nonetheless, it is clear that South Africa's Namibia-related operations were, in overwhelming proportion, self-sustained.

In the later 1970s, after many years of conflict in Namibia, international pressures assumed increasing importance as a force for peace. The U.S.-led "contact group," including Britain, France, West Germany, and Canada, managed to convene a Namibia peace conference in Geneva in January 1981—during the final days of the Carter administration. Unfortunately, this conference was aborted because of a series of obstacles raised by internal Namibian parties, which South Africa had brought to the conference as part of its delegation. These parties bitterly accused the United Nations of being partial to SWAPO and incapable of serving as a neutral referee during the peace process. The United Nations and the Western countries continued to promote negotiations on Namibia, however, and after mid-decade, these efforts won increasing support from the Soviet Union, which was seeking a solution to its Angolan entanglement. Finally, the 1988 Angola/Namibia regional peace accord was concluded and the United Nations moved into Namibia to manage the transition process.

The United Nations Transition Assistance Group in Namibia (UNTAG) was a major international contribution that served as the capstone of the peace process. UNTAG included over 4,000 troops from twenty-one countries, 1,500 civilian police, and 1,700 elections supervisors.[71] There had been some concern that the authorized military force was too small to prevent outbreaks of fighting during the transition, and indeed there was a clash on April 1, 1989, after 1,000

SWAPO guerrillas unexpectedly crossed the border before UN forces—delayed by a debate over financing the operation—were deployed. In subsequent months, however, UNTAG successfully monitored demobilization and the South African withdrawal as well as voter registration. The November balloting, closely supervised and certified by the UN, won broad international acceptance. Later, it emerged that South Africa had covertly aided some of SWAPO's rivals during the campaign, possibly reducing the size of SWAPO's majority in the assembly. These revelations, however, did not change the perception of the election as essentially free and fair, and SWAPO has not sought to revise the outcome.

Rwanda

The responsibility for failing to bridge the Hutu–Tutsi division in Rwanda must lie primarily with the Habyarimana regime. Belgium, however, as the colonial power that left Rwanda in 1962 with this division unhealed, must bear some of the blame for the outbreak of war many years later. Africa Watch, a human rights monitoring organization, has criticized Belgium and France, as well as the United States, for failing to use their aid programs in Rwanda as leverage to push for reforms.[72] Whether the Museveni regime in Uganda supported the Rwandan resistance forces is, as noted in Chapter 2, still a subject of debate. France deployed several hundred troops to Rwanda to protect French citizens, although the RPF charges that these forces have repeatedly aided the government. France denies these charges, and its main aim at present is to see international peacekeepers deployed so that it can withdraw.

Until August 1993 the international community had not seemed particularly effective in attempting to resolve the war in this small and rather remote country. The Organization of African Unity and regional leaders, as well as France, Belgium, and the United States, sought to promote negotiations and it seemed that their efforts had succeeded in July 1992, when a cease-fire was agreed to at an internationally sponsored meeting in Tanzania. However, this and subsequent cease-fires all broke down. With Western encouragement, however, the OAU sent a small military monitoring group to Rwanda, and OAU officials now claim that this force as well as OAU diplomatic efforts played a key role in the August accord.

Somalia

Overview

External support for Siad Barre's regime, including aid from the United States, Saudi Arabia, and perhaps Libya, may have convinced the Somali leader that he was strong enough to defeat his opposition by force and had no need to respond to their needs and demands. U.S. military and other security assistance to the Somali government was motivated by strategic concerns that had nothing to do with Somali politics, but support from a superpower was probably particularly encouraging to Siad. Sharp reductions in U.S. aid in the latter part of the 1980s were partly intended to persuade Siad to show greater respect for human rights and to push him toward a reconciliation in the north. Instead of responding, however, Siad looked elsewhere for help—evidently with some success. As for the resistance, the shelter and assistance given Somali rebels by Ethiopia over the years was an important asset to them in their struggle. The SNM, however, was able to carry on—and even escalate—the fighting after the Ethiopia/Somalia rapprochement of April 1988.

With the deterioration in Somalia in 1991, the international community exerted pressure for a cease-fire, or at least for the cooperation of the warring factions in the delivery of humanitarian relief. This pressure was not highly effective, and there was criticism of the United Nations, the United States, and others for not acting more decisively. Operation Restore Hope seemed to demonstrate that the international community could act effectively in Somalia, but U.S. and other forces participating in the operation did not disarm the Somali warlords, setting the stage for the difficulties UNOSOM II encountered with Aideed in southern Mogadishu. While the United Nations remains committed to promoting reconciliation the future of UNOSOM II is uncertain.

Background

The Somali army was lavishly equipped by the Soviet Union before the USSR decided to ally itself with Ethiopia in the 1977–1978 Ethiopia–Somalia war. Subsequently, the United States became the leading supplier to the Somali military, providing some $200 million in military assistance during the 1980s. In addition, economic assistance under the security-oriented Economic Support Fund (ESF) was at high levels, reaching $35 million in 1984. U.S. military assistance, which was always described as primarily non-lethal or defensive, dropped sharply in 1987—from $20.2 million to $8.2 million—in the face of the mounting condemnation of human rights abuses in Somalia. Military assistance fell again to $6.5 million in 1988,[73] while ESF aid fell to $4 million as the United States urged the regime toward a reconciliation in the north. By 1990, apart from $800,000 spent on military education and training, U.S. security assistance to Somalia was at an end, and the aid program had come to consist almost entirely of emergency relief.

The U.S. security assistance program was never intended as a sign of approval of the conduct of the Siad regime. Instead, it was motivated by the Cold War and U.S. strategic interests in the Indian Ocean, the Persian Gulf, and the approaches to the Suez Canal. During the Ethiopia–Somalia war in 1977–1978, the Carter administration came under intense pressure from "globalists" to respond to Somalia's apparent vulnerability in the face of a Soviet/Cuban–backed regime in Ethiopia. This concern, which of course remained important during the Reagan administration, combined with U.S. anxieties over stability in the Persian Gulf during the Iran–Iraq war to drive U.S. aid to Somalia to its peak levels. Later, in part because of the growing violence within Somalia, the country came to seem less useful in strategic terms, and human rights issues became paramount in U.S. policy.

According to a U.S. General Accounting Office report, however, a U.S. shipment of 1,200 automatic rifles together with 2.8 million rounds of ammunition did reach northern Somalia in June 1988 and was used by government troops in the fighting.[74] Subsequently, deliveries of scheduled assistance were delayed[75] and limited to non-lethal items in order to increase the pressure on the regime.[76]

With human rights violations making it increasingly difficult for Somalia to obtain help in the West, the Siad Barre government began to cultivate better relations with the Soviet Union in 1986. By that date, however, it was too late to persuade Moscow to take on another expensive African client. Somalia also reportedly recruited mercenary fighter-bomber pilots of white Rhodesian and South African origin.[77] In addition, Saudi Arabia appears to have become an important source of funds. Siad, who had particularly close relations with the Saudi regime over many years, evidently won a new Saudi aid pledge just before his ouster by offering to send Somali troops to join in the confrontation with Iraq.[78] Libya was also believed to be supplying arms to Somalia after U.S. assistance ended. In 1989, while on a visit to the United States, Somali prime minister Ali Samantar denied SNM allegations that Libya had provided chemical weapons, but gave conflicting responses on whether Libya had given conventional arms.[79]

The armed Somali resistance historically found shelter in Ethiopia, where it was given arms and broadcast facilities. Somali officials maintain that Cuba had trained SNM cadres at Ethiopian bases.[80] The relationship between Ethiopia and the Somali guerrillas became unclear after the April 1988 border stabilization agreement. Rebel activity may have been carried on, at least for a time, independently of Ethiopia. However, some observers, as well as Somali officials, suspected that some form of Ethiopian aid continued.[81]

As southern Somalia and the capital fell into chaos in 1991, international concern over the escalating humanitarian crisis deepened. The United Nations and its agencies, together with private and voluntary organizations, struggled to assist the hundreds of thousands of refugees that spilled across Somalia's borders, and there were brave efforts to fly relief supplies into Mogadishu airport despite the shooting there. After the November 1991 outbreak in Mogadishu, the Organization of African Unity and the Arab League joined the United Nations in pressing for an end to the violence. Top UN officials went into Mogadishu to try to arrange a cease-fire, and in February 1992 the warring factions, meeting in New York, agreed to halt the fighting. On March 5, a UN ship bringing relief supplies was shelled, but in subsequent weeks it appeared that the United Nations had succeeded in achieving some reduction in the violence. UN and Red Cross relief efforts, under the protection of locally hired armed guards, began to make some headway—amid concern that factional fighting could intensify at any time.

Despite this progress, the United Nations came in for criticism for doing too little, too late.[82] U.S. policymakers were criticized for indifference to the suffering in Somalia, and for allegedly undermining UN efforts to respond.[83] Many Africans maintained that the Western nations and the UN were more concerned about suffering in the former Yugoslavia than in Somalia. Those who defended the international response, however, maintained that the United Nations and others were doing about as well as could be expected in relieving suffering Somalia in view of the harsh conditions there and the recalcitrance of the warring factions.

The remarkable U.S. decision to deploy armed forces to Somalia in December 1992 brought an imposed peace to Somalia and served as a catalyst for UNOSOM II, the largest peacekeeping operation Africa has seen to date. Operation Restore Hope came about for a number of reasons, including compelling media coverage of the suffering in Somalia, congressional pressure for action following a number of visits to Somalia by members of Congress, and the impact of reports of deaths among Somali children on President Bush.[84] After his defeat in the November 1992 election, President Bush may have felt freer to act than earlier, when any setbacks in Somalia might have exacted a toll in votes. Perhaps, too, some speculated, there was also some sense that humanitarian intervention in Somalia would help to restore the administration's reputation after the election and affirm President Bush's reputation as an effective leader in world affairs.

The combination of circumstances that led to Operation Restore Hope, in short, was highly unusual, and a similar combination may not soon recur. The operation itself cost the United States alone $750 million, far above initial estimates of $200 million to $300 million, and the follow-on UN effort will cost far more.[85] But whether or not Operation Restore Hope is a precedent, the people of Somalia have benefited immeasurably from the restoration of order and the influx of international famine relief. However, the decision of the U.S.-led forces not to try to disarm the contending Somali factions, despite appeals from UN Secretary General Boutros Boutros-Ghali that they do so, later confronted UNOSOM II with an immense problem. U.S. decision-makers calculated that efforts to disarm the factions would lead to violence, perhaps undermining public support for the U.S. deployment, and hoped that the arms issue could be dealt with later as UN-sponsored reconciliation efforts moved forward. Aideed's armed uprising in southern Mogadishu, which soon claimed the attention of most of the UN peacekeepers in Somalia, began to threaten the rehabilitation and reconciliation program just a month after Operation Restore Hope came to an end. Dissent broke out within the UN operation, as the Italian commander, backed by Rome, sharply questioned the policy of confrontation with Aideed. UN officials, backed by the Clinton administration, remained firm in their commitment to the success of UNOSOM II and pointed out that the Aideed problem was affecting only one part of one city while the rest of the country was beginning a slow recovery. The crisis of early October 1993, however, brought Clinton's insistence on a March 31, 1994 U.S. withdrawal from Somalia. Whether the international community will remain committed to Somali reconciliation and recovery after March 31 is not yet clear.

Sudan

Overview

There would have probably been a war in Sudan, though at lower levels of violence, without any foreign involvement. Numeiry, when he provoked the war, was pursuing an agenda that reflected deeply held views in the north. The SPLA, in responding, launched its resistance without foreign help using stockpiled and captured weapons. Nonetheless, high levels of U.S. military aid in the 1970s and the first half of the 1980s may have encouraged Numeiry in the mistaken belief that he had firm American backing and could persist in trying to achieve a military solution in the south. Cuts in aid came only after the regime was firmly committed to a course of war. Ethiopian military aid, as well as other forms of assistance, were very important to the SPLA and certainly contributed to the resistance. There were repeated international efforts to mediate an end to the fighting in Sudan in the later 1980s and early 1990s, but none met with success.

Background

U.S. military assistance to Sudan totaled $296 million for the years 1980 through 1985, making the country the largest recipient of such aid, after Morocco (and Egypt), on the African continent. ESF aid came to $506 million during the same years. U.S. security assistance was given, not as a sign of approval of Numeiry's policies, but because Sudan—as Africa's largest country, with a Red Sea coast and near to Saudi Arabia—seemed to be strategically important. Nonetheless, it could hardly help but suggest to Numeiry that he was an important U.S. ally who could be certain of continuing support no matter what his policies or conduct. In this he was wrong, and aid was already falling when he was overthrown—largely because of congressional insistence that security aid be conditioned on progress toward peace. Numeiry's successors also failed to move toward peace, and aid fell sharply in 1986. There was no new security assistance for Sudan in 1988 or 1989, apart from a small military education program valued at less than $1 million annually, and the overall aid program, as in the case of Somalia, came to focus on food aid and humanitarian relief.

The U.S. aid reductions in the second half of the 1980s were a reflection of concerns not only over the lack of progress toward peace, but also over Sudan's growing ties with Libya and its inability to deal effectively with major economic problems. Human rights violations under the Bashir regime added an additional complication in relations with the United States, and Bashir's suspension of Sudanese democracy meant that U.S. assistance, apart from relief aid, could not, by law, be resumed. U.S. economic pressures and other expressions of American disapproval, however, failed to change Sudanese policy.

Libya, a bitter enemy of the Numeiry regime, was once a supporter of the SPLA, but after a period of some uncertainty following Numeiry's overthrow—when it was suspected of aiding both sides—it shifted its support to the central government of Sadiq el-Mahdi. Information is sketchy, but Libyan fighter planes and bombers are believed to have supported Sudanese army operations against the SPLA. It is believed that Sadiq concluded a major arms deal with Libya during a visit to Qadhafi in March 1989. Bashir's ties to Libya have been even closer, and in March 1990 he signed an accord on the phased unification of the two countries.

The Sudanese government and people were strongly sympathetic to Iraq during the Persian Gulf crisis, and for this they paid a price. Iraq had probably been supplying arms to Khartoum before the war, while Saudi Arabia, Kuwait, and other Persian Gulf states were a major source of funds. With Iraq under sanctions and the Persian Gulf states deeply angry, none of this aid is likely to be restored for a long time to come. Iran, however, is attempting to gain influence over Sudan, and Iranian president Rafsanjani visited Khartoum in December 1991. This visit was followed by numerous reports that Iran was providing arms, advisers, and even troops to Sudan. The degree of Iran's actual involvement, however, was highly uncertain; although the regime's energetic offensive in the south in 1992 suggested that Iranian aid might indeed be compensating for the loss of assistance from Iraq and the Persian Gulf.

The SPLA became heavily dependent over the years on Ethiopia for shelter, arms, and training. Ethiopia also provided political offices in Addis Ababa and a powerful clandestine radio station. The SPLA was thought to be based primarily in Ethiopia's western Illubabor province, where, according to some unverifiable Sudanese allegations, it received training from Cuban advisers. The dialogue between Sudan and Ethiopia, which began after Sadiq took office, posed something of a threat to the SPLA, and Garang must have been concerned over the possibility a mutual non-interference pact that would lead to his movement's expulsion from Ethiopia. Nonetheless, the Ethiopian regime remained highly considerate of Garang's interests. Aid continued, and Garang was allowed to meet and negotiate with Sudanese leaders as well as representatives of international relief agencies in the Ethiopian capital.

The new regime that took power in Ethiopia in 1991 expelled the SPLA as a demonstration of gratitude for the support Sudan had given the Ethiopian resistance over the years. This might have made the SPLA more open to negotiations—but indications are that Garang remains determined to continue the struggle with captured supplies and weapons, perhaps supplemented by covert supplies from other friends. In 1992, there were reports that Persian Gulf states might be aiding the SPLA in order to counter Iranian influence in Khartoum.

The identity of the SPLA's other friends has been a subject of controversy. The Bashir regime, as well as Sudanese politicians prior to Bashir's takeover, charged that Israel was aiding the SPLA[86] as it had aided the Anya-Nya in the first southern war.[87] Sadiq, however, had reserved his strongest condemnations for neighboring Kenya, which he accused of aiding the rebels and—evidently because it was a predominantly black African state with a large Christian population—of "complete agreement with the idea of the rebellion itself."[88] Kenya allowed the SPLA to maintain an office in Nairobi, and it cooperated in international relief efforts for southern Sudan, but there was no independent confirmation of a Kenyan role in providing arms aid to the resistance. Uganda, another predominantly black, Christian neighbor to the south, has also come under Sudanese suspicion from time to time.

Foreign mediators have repeatedly tried to foster negotiations in Sudan, but always without success. After Operation Restore Hope was launched in Somalia, there was some concern in Khartoum that an internationally imposed peace would be attempted in the south. There was little real interest among external actors, however, in becoming entangled in a costly armed humanitarian operation in landlocked southern Sudan, particularly in view of possible armed opposition by the Sudanese army. The possibility of creating zones of safety in the south, where civilians would be protected from attack by all parties, drew greater interest. Prospects for setting up such zones were poor, however, since the simultaneous consent of Khartoum and the contending factions of the SPLA seemed unlikely, and because even with such consent, the zones would still have to be protected by foreign troops.

Uganda

Responsibility for the gap between state and society in Uganda prior to the outbreak of war lies with Uganda's leaders and not with any outside power. As in the case of Rwanda, the colonial power could be faulted for leaving structures in place—in this case, a northern-dominated army—that contributed to post-independence conflict. Perhaps Britain and other external actors could have done more to constrain the leaders of independent Uganda as their errors of policy and conduct deepened. Tanzania, when it intervened with Ugandan exiles to oust Amin in 1979, initially appeared to be helping to heal the divisions in Uganda, but in the end it only set the stage for Obote's return to power and more long years of violence.

The Ugandan revolution under Yoweri Museveni was largely autonomous and would have gone ahead with captured weapons and the arms freely available in Uganda. Nonetheless, Museveni took care to acknowledge Libyan support, which must have been important. Libya, indeed, welcomed the NRA's victory as a "great triumph of the Libyan people and of all popular revolutionary forces throughout the world."[89] Despite this hyperbole, however, Museveni turned out to be a wholly independent actor once the revolution was won, showing no sign of subservience to Qadhafi or of the Libyan leader's extremism in domestic and foreign policy. Resistance forces operating after 1986 also made use of arms and supplies easily obtained locally, but they may have been marginally helped by Kenya's willingness to host refugees.

The NRA regarded Kenya, which consistently tried to portray Uganda as an outpost of Libyan subversion, as its principal nemesis after the revolution. Ostensible safety checks in Kenya that delayed trucks bringing vital supplies from the Kenyan port at Mombasa, for example, were seen as attempts to subvert the revolution. Kenya was also generally suspected of funding Ugandan dissidents who took shelter on its territory, and of facilitating their movement back into Uganda as guerrillas. Many Ugandans believed that Kenya's President Moi was hostile to the new regime because he feared that it would stabilize Uganda and eventually enable it to displace Kenya as the dominant nation in East Africa. They also felt that Moi was hostile to Museveni in particular because, like Moi's major domestic rivals, he was of Bantu origin, while Moi's ethnic background was closer to the Nilotic groups in Uganda. Kenya has a long tradition, however, of allowing exiles from other African countries to reside there, and its sporadic clamp-downs on transport from Mombasa to landlocked neighbors were nothing new. Consequently, it was difficult to determine whether or not—or to what degree—Kenya was indeed attempting to subvert Museveni.

Western Sahara

Overview

King Hassan acted on the basis of his own imperatives and what he perceived to be the imperatives of the Moroccan nation when he annexed Western Sahara. At the same time, however, the king may well have been encouraged to pursue a military rather than a diplomatic solution because of the ready availability of foreign-supplied weapons and the knowledge that the United States—though it wanted no part of the Saharan war—was, for strategic reasons, his ally. The war in Western Sahara was also sustained by the willingness of one country, Algeria, to shelter and assist the resistance. Without Algerian help, the movement would have had only a limited ability to carry on the struggle from remote regions of Mauritania or as terrorists.

By the end of the 1980s, the Saharan war seemed headed toward resolution, in part because of international pressures, as preparations began for a UN-supervised referendum. King Hassan, however, subsequently raised a number of obstacles to the UN effort, and pressure from the international community, where Hassan had important friends and allies, was not sufficient to persuade him to allow the peace process to move forward.

Background

Morocco's King Hassan has always had powerful friends abroad, and he kept those friends throughout the Saharan war. His country is a substantial recipient of French assistance, while U.S. arms aid totaled more than $525 million during the decade of the 1980s. U.S. military aid declined after a peak of $101 million in 1983, but remained substantial. High levels of assistance have been motivated by Morocco's strategic location in relation to sea lanes, Europe, and the Middle East, and by its value as a balance to Libyan influence.

The United States never recognized Morocco's annexation of Western Sahara, but close U.S. ties to the Moroccan regime made effective opposition to that annexation impossible. While there was concern, particularly in Congress, over the possible use of U.S.-supplied arms in the Saharan war,[90] it seems certain that some U.S. weapons did find their way into the disputed territory. Saudi Arabia was another major supporter of King Hassan, and South African equipment also reached Morocco.

The arms and shelter given POLISARIO by Algeria were critical to the movement's survival as a guerrilla force. Military aid from Libya was also important early in POLISARIO's history, but this assistance was evidently cut off in a series of Qadhafi–Hassan rapprochements beginning in 1981 and culminating in the unexpected Libya–Morocco Treaty of Union in August 1984. Improved relations between the two countries appeared to be based on Moroccan acquiescence to Libya's intervention in Chad in exchange for an end to Libyan support for the guerrillas.[91] While King Hassan canceled the unity agreement in 1986 following U.S. criticism and disagreements with Qadhafi over Morocco's moderate stance on the Middle East conflict,[92] further rapprochements ensued and Libya probably did not renew its interference on any significant scale.

Visitors to POLISARIO camps were often impressed by the large stores of heavy Soviet weaponry on display, and some concluded that the Soviets were major backers of the guerrillas. Regional analysts generally believe, however, that Soviet arms were given to the movement by Algeria and Libya—major purchasers of Soviet weapons—and were not supplied directly. The USSR, in fact, attempted to cultivate good relations with Morocco throughout the conflict period because of an interest in Morocco's strategic location and regional influence, as well as its phosphate and fishing resources. However, it seems doubtful that Soviet weapons could have been given to POLISARIO if Moscow specifically objected, and it could be argued that the USSR was keeping a hand in by consenting to these supplies in case events began to develop favorably for the guerrillas.

By the end of the 1980s, Algeria was confronting major economic and social problems and was anxious to heal past wounds with Morocco. Indeed, it wished to join with the Moroccan regime in preparing the region for the problems and opportunities that could arise from European economic integration in 1992. Its long-standing ties to POLISARIO kept Algeria from abandoning the movement altogether, and there is no indication that it tried to prevent the incidents that took place in late 1989. Nonetheless, Algeria clearly preferred that the movement—which was entirely dependent on Algerian goodwill—end its conflict with Morocco as soon as possible. The king, for his part, knew that his foreign friends would prefer that he bring the Western Sahara matter to a close as well. In their view, it had complicated Morocco's relations with other countries and limited Hassan's credibility as a regional leader for far too long. Thus, when the United Nations began to deploy MINURSO in 1991, after overcoming numerous objections raised by Hassan, many hoped that a resolution was at hand. Yet Hassan hesitated and continued to place obstacles in the path of MINURSO, and it was far from certain that the UN-backed referendum would ever be held. Perhaps Hassan's allies will one day insist that he cooperate with the United Nations, but as they contemplate the Islamic resurgence now threatening the Algerian regime, they may hesitate to take any step that could weaken Hassan.

Conclusion

At the beginning of the 1980s, the international factor often tended to deepen social tensions in Africa and add fuel, in the form of arms and money, to the flames of conflict. In contrast, by the end of the decade, the international dimension was more a source of mediation and pressure for restraint, making substantial contributions toward conflict resolution. UNTAG, UNOSOM II, and UNOMOZ demonstrated that the international community was willing to bear significant risks and costs in pursuit of African peace. Yet external actors were reluctant to risk peacekeeping in Angola and Sudan, and the entanglement faced by the

United Nations in southern Mogadishu in 1993 raised questions about future international contributions in support of peace efforts. The next chapter assesses likely short-term trends in both the international and domestic dimensions of African war.

Notes

1. According to one scholar, "peace in the African continent without a direct Nigerian contribution has become almost inconceivable"; George A. Obiozor, "National Capability: Focus on Nigeria," *Nigerian Forum* (November–December 1987): 311. An external affairs minister once stated that the "promotion of peace and stability" in Africa was a fundamental principle of Nigerian foreign policy, but went on to lament the failure of African states to show due respect for Nigeria's role; A. Bolaji Akinyemi, "Reciprocity in Nigerian Foreign Policy (The Akinyemi Doctrine)," *Nigerian Forum* (May–June, 1987): 151–56.

2. John Damis, "The Western Sahara Dispute as a Source of Regional Conflict in North Africa," in *Contemporary North Africa: Issues of Development and Integration*, ed. Halim Barakat (Washington, D.C.: Center for Contemporary Arab Studies, 1985), 139–43.

3. René Lemarchand, "Chad: The Misadventures of the North–South Dialectic," *African Studies Review* 29 (September 1986): 37.

4. Franiziska James, "Habré's Hour of Glory," *Africa Report,* September–October 1987, 20. On 31 August 1989, Habré signed an accord providing for the eventual submission of the Aouzou dispute to the International Court of Justice. The fate of the Aouzou issue, however, is highly uncertain in view of the December 1990 ouster of Habré and the takeover of Chad by a regime that has received substantial Libyan support.

5. René Lemarchand, "The Case of Chad," in *The Green and The Black: Qadhafi's Policies in Africa,* ed. René Lemarchand (Bloomington and Indianapolis: Indiana University Press, 1988), 109–10. Lemarchand's observation proved prescient as a partial explanation of Qadhafi's aid to the forces that ousted Habré in 1990. By that time, a substantial force of Libyan "contras" had been assembled in Chad. For further information, see below.

6. As will be noted, there were reports of South African pilots flying fighter-bombers in the Somali war, but it was difficult to ascertain whether they were acting with official backing or as private individuals. If there was an official role, it probably had something to do with South African concern over protecting routes used for "sanctions-busting" flights.

7. Sulayman Nyang, "The Islamic Factor in Libya's Africa Policy," *Africa and the World* 1 (January 1988): 13–23.

8. For a discussion of disinterest in Africa at top U.S. policymaking levels, as distinct from the mid-level, see Michael Clough, *Free at Last? U.S. Policy Toward Africa and the End of the Cold War* (New York: Council on Foreign Relations, 1992), 40–53.

9. John Chipman, *French Military Policy and African Security,* Adelphi Papers, no. 201 (London: International Institute for Strategic Studies, 1985).

10. Ibid., 29–30.

11. Helen Desfosses, "The USSR and Africa," *Issue: A Journal of Opinion* 16, no. 1 (1987): 4.

12. Bob Woodward, *Veil: The Secret Wars of the CIA, 1981–1987* (New York: Simon and Schuster, 1987), 96–97, 157–58, 310; David B. Ottaway and Joanne Omang, "History of Aid to Rebels Is Checkered," *Washington Post,* 27 May 1985.

13. Raymond W. Copson and Richard P. Cronin, "The 'Reagan Doctrine' and its Prospects," *Survival* 29 (January–February 1987): 40–55.

14. U.S. Department of Defense, *Congressional Presentation for Security Assistance Program, Fiscal Year 1990* (Washington, D.C., 1989), 207, 250.

15. Western sources reportedly believed that Angola compensated Cuba for foreign exchange costs connected with its operations until the Angolan economic crisis worsened in 1984. Payments for non-military advisers may have then been halted, but the situation with respect to payments for military aid was unclear. Gillian Gunn, "The Angolan Economy: A Status Report," *CSIS Africa Notes* (Washington, D.C., 30 May 1986). As noted below, all payments for such aid may have been halted after 1986 as world oil prices declined.

16. U.S. Library of Congress, Congressional Research Service, *Trends in Conventional Arms Transfers to the Third World by Major Supplier, 1981–1988,* CRS Report no. 89–434 F by Richard F. Grimmett (Washington, D.C., 9 May 1988), 36. These are data on arms transfer agreements based on U.S. government sources.

17. Gorbachev added that "those conflicts are taking place in the Third World, which already faces many ills and problems of such magnitude that it has to be a matter of concern to us all." Statement by Mikhail S. Gorbachev at the Plenary Meeting of the United Nations General Assembly, 7 December 1988.

18. The Clark amendment was initially part of the 1976 Security Assistance authorization (Public Law 94–329, Section 404). A slightly modified version appeared in the International Security Assistance and Development Cooperation Act of 1980 (Public Law 96–533, Section 118). The Clark amendment had been preceded in December 1975 by the "Tunney amendment," a one-year cutoff appearing in the defense appropriations legislation.

19. Helmoed-Romer Heitman, *The South African War Machine* (Novato, Calif.: Presidio Press, 1985), 107. Heitman portrays the battalion as an anti-SWAPO unit rather than a prop for UNITA.

20. Robert Jaster, "A Regional Security Role for Africa's Front-Line States," in *Southern Africa: Regional Security Problems and Prospects,* ed. Robert Jaster (New York: St. Martin's Press, 1985), 110.

21. *Africa Research Bulletin,* Political Series, May 1985, 7635.

22. Patrick A. Tyler, "Rebel Success Turns on South African Aid," *Washington Post,* 30 July 1986.

23. *Beeld* (South Africa), 23 September 1986, reprinted in U.S. Foreign Broadcast and Information Service, *Daily Report, Sub-Saharan Africa* (hereinafter, *FBIS),* 25 September 1986.

24. John Battersby, "Pretoria Finishes Its Angola Pullout," *New York Times,* 31 August 1988.

25. Bernard E. Trainor, "Stream of Victims Tests Pretoria's War Hospital," *New York Times,* 8 August 1988.

26. Section 118 of the International Security Assistance Act of 1980 (Public Law 96–533) was repealed. This was a somewhat modified version of the original amendment.

27. David Ottaway, "Angolan Rebels Ask Rise in U.S. Aid," *Washington Post,* 25 April 1989.

28. David Ottaway, "Senators Seek Agreement on Angola Policy," *Washington Post,* 29 January 1989; Christopher Wren, "Angolan Rebels Look to Life after South Africans," *New York Times,* 30 October 1988; James Brooke, "U.S. Arms Airlift to Angola Rebels Is Said to Go On," *New York Times,* 27 July 1987.

29. Letter dated 6 January 1989, reprinted in *Washington Post,* 12 January 1989.

30. Fred Bridgland, *Jonas Savimbi: A Key to Africa* (London: Holder and Stoughton, Coronet edition, 1988), 326; Claudia Wright, "Journey to Marrakesh: U.S. Moroccan Security Relations," *International Security* 7 (Spring 1983): 173–74.

31. "Yet Another Saudi Connection. Did Illegal Support Go to Angolan Rebels as Well as Contras?" *Time,* 29 June 1987, 16.

32. International Institute for Strategic Studies (IISS), *The Military Balance, 1988–1989* (London: IISS, 1988), 122.

33. Ibid., 123.

34. One reporter, questioning the IISS figure, noted that "truckloads of uniformed Russians can be seen in various parts of the country. There are, in addition to pilots, officers and Soviet commandos that guard airport tarmacs where sophisticated equipment is in use." Jill Joliffe, "Rising Tension in Angola Heightens Nation's Reliance on Soviets," *Christian Science Monitor,* 4 May 1987.

35. Gunn, "A Guide to the Intricacies of the Angola–Namibia Negotiations," *CSIS Africa Notes* (8 September 1988): 5.

36. Luanda Domestic Service broadcast, 9 January 1989, recorded in *FBIS,* 10 January 1989, 11.

37. U.S. Congress, House, *Intelligence Authorization Act for Fiscal Year 1991, Conference Report to Accompany S. 2834,* Report 101–928 (Washington, D.C.: U.S. Government Printing Office, 23 October 1990), 34–36.

38. According to a press report, the total amount of assistance approved for UNITA was $60 million; *Washington Post,* 24 October 1990.

39. The chairmen of the House and Senate intelligence committees informed the executive branch that they expected the intelligence agencies to adhere to the limitations and conditions in the bill. Letter from Representative Anthony Beilenson and Senator David Boren to William Webster, director of Central Intelligence, 4 December 1990.

40. See "How Qadhafi Betrayed Acheik," *New African,* December 1988; and "Chad: Opposition in Tatters," *New African,* February 1989.

41. British Broadcasting Service, BBC World Service, Network Africa, 5 April 1988, recorded in *FBIS,* Near East and South Asia edition, 6 April 1988, 8.

42. James Brooke, "Armed Truce Divides Chad and Libyans," *New York Times,* 27 March 1988.

43. François Soudan, "Objectif Kaddafi: L'histoire secrète des 'contras' Libyen," *Jeune Afrique,* 19 December 1990–1 January 1991, 10–13; Clifford Kraus, "Failed Anti-Qadhafi Effort Leaves U.S. Picking Up the Pieces," *New York Times,* 12 March 1991.

44. IISS, *The Military Balance, 1988–1989*, 128.

45. See, for example, Mary Battiata, "Soviets Press Ethiopia to End War, Envoys Say," *Washington Post*, 21 April 1989.

46. Library of Congress, *Trends in Conventional Arms Transfers, 1982–1989*, CRS Report No. 90–298 F, 19 June 1990, 61.

47. See, for example, the allegation reported by the Qatar News Agency and recorded in *FBIS*, 20 March 1989, 5.

48. In 1990, military attaches at embassies in Addis Ababa were reportedly noting arrivals of cluster bombs, Uzi submachine guns and other small arms, and several military advisers from Israel. Julian Ozanne, "Embattled Horn of Africa Is Centre of Fresh Power Struggle," *Financial Times*, 3 April 1990.

49. *New York Times*, 21 January 1990.

50. Joel Brinkley, "Ethiopia Officials Flown into Israel," *New York Times*, 30 May 1991.

51. For discussions, see W. Andrew Terrill, "The Arab–Israeli Rivalry for Africa—Aftermath of Camp David," *Conflict* 6 (1986): 355–369; and Olusola Ojo, *Africa and Israel: Relations in Perspective* (Boulder, Colo.: Westview Press, 1988).

52. *New York Times*, 7 February 1990.

53. "Ethiopia: Eritrea Takes Stock," *Africa Confidential*, 29 April 1987, 6.

54. *Washington Post*, 25 April 1986.

55. Ozanne, "Embattled Horn of Africa," *Financial Times*, 3 April 1991.

56. Africa Watch, *Liberia: A Human Rights Disaster; Violations of the Laws of War by All Parties to the Conflict*, Washington, D.C., 26 October 1990, 22.

57. Neil Henry, "Doctor's Group Criticizes U.S. for Not Intervening in Liberia," *Washington Post*, 16 August 1990; "Some Liberians Accuse the U.S. of Betrayal," *New York Times*, 21 August 1990.

58. See, for example, South African radio commentary, 19 January 1988, recorded in *FBIS*, 20 January 1988.

59. "Mozambique/South Africa: The Special Forces Behind RENAMO," *Africa Confidential*, 2 December 1987, 1–3.

60. Caryle Murphy, "Mozambican Refugees Detail Reign of Terror by RENAMO," *Washington Post*, 20 April 1988. On this issue, see also William Minter, *The Mozambican National Resistance (RENAMO) as Described by Ex-Participants*, research report submitted to Ford Foundation and Swedish International Development Agency (Washington, D.C., March 1989).

61. Chissano added, however, that he thought that elements in South Africa were still assisting the guerrillas. Karl Maier, "Mozambican President Offers Talks with Rebels," *Washington Post*, 18 July 1989.

62. Christopher Wren, "No Aid to Mozambique Rebels, de Klerk Says," *New York Times*, 17 December 1989.

63. See Robert Pear and James Brooke, "Rightists in U.S. Aid Mozambique Rebels," *New York Times*, 22 May 1988; Richard Harwood, "Contras' Private Pipeline Pumps at U.S. Behest," *Washington Post*, 16 October 1986; Robert Reinhold, "Ex-General Hints at Big Role as U.S. Champion of Contras," *New York Times*, 14 October 1986.

64. See Allen Isaacman, "Mozambique," *Survival* 30 (January–February 1988): 33.

65. Kurt M. Campbell, *Southern Africa in Soviet Foreign Policy,* Adelphi Papers no. 227 (London: International Institute for Strategic Studies, 1987), 15.

66. U.S. Arms Control and Disarmament Agency, *World Military Expenditures and Arms Transfers, 1987* (Washington, D.C., 1988), 127.

67. IISS, *The Military Balance, 1988–1989,* 135.

68. "Mozambique: Moving with the Times," *Africa Confidential,* 9 February 1990, 1.

69. IISS, *The Military Balance, 1988–1989,* 141.

70. Glenn Frankel, "Israeli Economy Depends on Nation's Role as Arms Exporter," *Washington Post,* 12 December 1986; Gary Van Staden, "SAAF Puts Half of Africa within Its Striking Range," *Star* (Johannesburg), overseas airmail edition, 19 November 1986.

71. National Democratic Institute for International Affairs, *Nation Building: The UN and Namibia* (Washington, D.C., 1990), 65–73.

72. Africa Watch, *Rwanda: Talking and Waging War, Human Rights since the October 1990 Invasion* (Washington, D.C., 27 February 1992), 30.

73. Department of Defense, *Congressional Presentation for Security Assistance Programs, Fiscal Year 1990,* 251.

74. U.S. General Accounting Office, *Somalia: Observations Regarding the Northern Conflict and Resulting Conditions,* report to Congressional Requesters (Washington, D.C., May 1989), 8.

75. George Gedda, "U.S. Secretly Cut Off Some Military Aid to Ally Last Summer," Associated Press, 6 February 1989; Ruth Sinai, "Report: U.S. Supplied Weapons, Then Sent Help for Victims," Associated Press, 25 May 1989.

76. General Accounting Office, *Somalia: Observations Regarding the Northern Conflict,* 7–8.

77. "Somalia: Showdown in the North," *Africa Confidential,* 29 July 1988. See also Richard D. Greenfield, "The Somali–South African Connection," *African Events,* April 1989, 32–35.

78. "Saudis Offer Fuel, $70 Million to Siad Barre," *Le Monde,* 27 December 1990, translated and reprinted in *FBIS,* 24 January 1991, 7.

79. Ruth Sinai, "Somali Premier Heckled as He Accuses Ethiopia of Arming Rebels," Associated Press, 3 February 1989.

80. Interview with Somali foreign minister in *Al-Majallah* (London), 19–25 October 1988, translated and reprinted in *FBIS,* 21 October 1988, 11.

81. U.S. Library of Congress, Congressional Research Service, *Somalia: Current Conditions and U.S. Policy,* CRS Report no. 90–252 by Theodros S. Dagne (Washington, D.C., 12 May 1990), 12.

82. U.S. Library of Congress, Congressional Research Service, *Somalia: A Country at War—Prospects for Peace,* CRS Report no. 92–522 F by Theodros S. Dagne (Washington, D.C., 15 June 1992), 5.

83. Africa Watch and Physicians for Human Rights, *Somalia: No Mercy in Mogadishu* (Washington, D.C., and London, 26 March 1992), 24–25.

84. U.S. Library of Congress, Congressional Research Service, *Somalia: Operation Restore Hope,* CRS Issue Brief 92131 by Raymond W. Copson (Washington, D.C., continuously updated).

85. Ibid. The first year of UNOSOM II is expected to cost $1.6 billion.

86. These allegations came primarily from the National Islamic Front, headed

by Hassan al-Turabi. See Middle East News Agency (Cairo) broadcast, 2 February 1989, recorded in *FBIS,* Near East edition, 3 February 1989. Prime Minister Sadiq himself, in charging "church circles" and "capitalist companies such as Lonrho" with aiding Garang, alleged that "Israel also exerts every effort to strengthen instability in the Arab area." Sudanese broadcast, 14 October 1988, recorded in *FBIS,* Near East edition, 18 October 1988, 15.

87. See, for example, Tim Niblock, *Class and Power in Sudan: The Dynamics of Sudanese Politics, 1898–1985* (Albany: State University of New York Press, 1987), 274–77.

88. Sudanese radio broadcast, 18 October 1988, recorded in *FBIS,* Near East edition, 20 October 1988, 23.

89. Blaine Harden, "New Ugandan Leader Got Arms from Libya," *Washington Post,* 1 January 1986.

90. In 1985, Congress added a policy statement to the foreign assistance legislation:

> The policy of the United States shall be to support a negotiated solution to the conflict in the Western Sahara taking into account the principle of self-determination. . . . As part of this policy, the United States . . . should seek to ensure that the furnishing of . . . military assistance is consistent with United States policy which seeks a negotiated settlement.

International Security and Development Cooperation Act of 1985 (Public Law 99–83), approved 8 August 1985.

91. John Damis, "The Impact of the Saharan Dispute on Moroccan Foreign and Domestic Policy," in *The Political Economy of Morocco,* ed. I. William Zartman (New York: Praeger, 1987), 195.

92. Ibid.

5 AFRICA'S WARS IN THE 1990s: A CHANGING AFRICA IN A CHANGING WORLD

War and its attendant suffering continue in Africa in the first years of the 1990s. Since the later 1980s, however, there have been a number of encouraging developments that have brought some of Africa's most destructive wars to a end and raised expectations for early peace in others. Trends affecting the African state—where the roots of Africa's wars lie—and the international state system, which once exacerbated African conflicts, give grounds for hoping that Africa's burden of war will ease considerably in the years ahead. This chapter attempts both to assess the forces that appear to be helping to ease this burden and to weigh those forces against others that could allow war to remain a major African problem. Clearly it is unlikely, in view of Africa's continuing social, economic, and political problems, that war will disappear altogether. Indeed, if, as many fear, Africa's economic situation continues to deteriorate, with accompanying increases in social tensions and political strife, the burden of war could soon begin to increase once again.

Future wars might differ from those seen in the past in Angola and Ethiopia, since heavy weapons and modern equipment supplied by external powers will not be readily available. But the bitter struggles in Liberia and Somalia at the beginning of the 1990s demonstrated that even in the absence of new supplies of First World weapons, arms can be found—and that these arms can continue to make war highly destructive of African peoples and societies. The next chapter discusses ways in which the international community might contribute to reducing this destruction and easing the burden that war has imposed on Africa.

Overview

Around Africa, governments are under intense domestic pressure, reinforced by pressures from key international actors, for political reforms. Where these pressures will lead the continent is as yet highly uncertain. There is deep concern that in many countries political change will unleash pent-up social, political, and ethnic resentments leading to a period of profound instability. Nonetheless, some outside observers and many participants in Africa's current political struggle hope and expect that in a large number of countries multi-party democracies, including systems of checks and balances based on the Western model, will eventually emerge. Others are doubtful about the appropriateness of multi-party democracy in Africa's troubled situation, but nonetheless believe that new and uniquely African forms of government are now developing—and that in contrast to past forms of government, these will have a firm popular base.[1] Still others are less concerned about the forms of government that may now be emerging than about the quality of "governance." They are hoping that the change and uncertainty of the present will eventually result in more effective political institutions, and in regimes that are less corrupt and more responsive to the needs and demands of their societies.[2] Such regimes will govern, not for the benefit of individual leaders and their ethnic groups, but on behalf of the nation as a whole, as the "civic public realm" regains legitimacy.[3]

A concern amidst all of the change now occurring in Africa is that central government authority will be weakened, allowing more countries to fall into chaos and war along ethnic or regional lines, as happened in Liberia in 1990 or Somalia in 1991. This is clearly a possibility, and there are instances of potential chaos or breakup all around the continent. But at the same time, there is reason to hope that political change in Africa will not inevitably lead to disaster. Many countries with deep social divisions, such as Nigeria and South Africa, are holding together, at least to date, through fundamental transitions. Ethiopia and Eritrea, on the other hand, appear to have found a formula—by peaceful means—that will permit an orderly separation. Moreover, it is surely a hopeful sign that many of those participating in the struggle for political change in Africa appear not to be interested in revenge or in power for its own sake, but in a better life for themselves and their children, the right to be heard, and political systems more firmly based on the consent of the governed and more responsive to their needs. Where their struggle succeeds, war will be far less likely. Perhaps some countries will break apart, but the successor states—as in Eritrea, perhaps Somaliland, and potentially southern Sudan—could have social coherence that will tend to reduce conflict and generate popular support for their regimes. Nonetheless, even in new and smaller countries, should any emerge, governments will need to show tolerance for diversity, since almost any conceivable African territorial unit will have potential social fault lines that could widen in the face of repression.

A second set of encouraging developments is in the international state system, where the incentives for involvement in Africa's wars have sharply declined. The contest for influence in Africa between the United States and other Western powers on the one hand, and the Soviet Union and eastern bloc countries on the other, has come to an end. As a result, the quantity of arms reaching Africa is dropping; and African leaders, whether in government or in the armed opposition, are finding that they can no longer exploit the tensions of the Cold War in order to win foreign backing. Instead of tolerating repressive and corrupt regimes on strategic grounds, major external actors have become a force in pushing for political reforms. Moreover, they have actively promoted negotiations aimed at ending some of Africa's most destructive wars, and have lent their support to an increased role for the United Nations in maintaining peace once settlements have been achieved. Western foreign assistance levels, though not rising significantly, have at least held steady into the early 1990s, despite the easing of Cold War competition. A concern, however, is that with the complete collapse of Soviet power in 1991 and the disappearance of any strategic rationale for involvement in Africa, Western policymakers may eventually lose interest in the continent, its wars, and its forms of government. To date, nonetheless, the Western nations remain engaged in African affairs.

Rivalry between Israel on the one hand, and the Arab countries and Iran on the other, may remain a factor tending to promote conflict in the Horn of Africa, as may the rivalries involving Iran, Iraq, and other states around the Persian Gulf. It is worth noting, however, that the departure of most Ethiopian Jews from Ethiopia has largely removed one motive for Israeli involvement. France still sees itself as a force in Africa, but its intention to distance itself from Africa's most repressive regimes—regimes of the sort most likely to drag France into wars— will probably continue despite the change in government in 1993. These trends in the international system are backed up, though still weakly, by changes in the African state system, including the reduction in South African intervention in southern Africa and some assertion of a peacekeeping and mediation role on the part of African regional organizations.

Despite these favorable trends, a number of African countries will probably continue to suffer war for years to come, and new wars may occur. Some regimes are stoutly resisting pressure for greater tolerance and respect for political freedoms, and their resistance will be a source of conflict. Moreover, ethnic and regional cleavages remain throughout the continent, and Africa's poverty threatens to deepen in view of the foreign debt accumulated by many regimes, stagnant levels of foreign assistance, the impact of AIDS on the most productive age groups in society, and a host of other problems. Indeed, poverty and the social tensions it causes have the potential to undermine all of Africa's progress toward better governance and a more peaceful future. Finally, while the international political environment may have improved, combatants and potential combatants will still find it possible to obtain arms from external sources and stockpiles. Consequently, war is far from being eliminated as a central obstacle to human welfare and progress in Africa.

Background

The first important sign of hope in Africa's ongoing wars appeared with the Museveni victory in Uganda in 1986. The regime Museveni established had many shortcomings, including repeated human rights violations by troops in the north, but it was a populist regime that established a hierarchy of "resistance councils" reaching down to the local level. These "RCs" brought a new measure of consent and participation to government in Uganda and helped to relieve social tensions. The next major step forward was the December 1988 southwestern

Africa peace accord, which opened the way to Namibian independence in 1990 and set the stage for the Angolan peace accord of May 1991. Just as the Angolan war was drawing to a close, Mengistu fled Ethiopia, the EPRDF swept into Addis Ababa, and the EPLF defeated the last elements of the Ethiopian army in Eritrea. Ethiopia was at peace, albeit a tenuous peace, for the first time in over twenty years. Other developments, including the ECOMOG deployment in Liberia, the arrival of MINURSO in Western Sahara, the 1992 Mozambique peace accord, the deployment of Operation Restore Hope, and progress toward a UN-supervised referendum in Western Sahara, tended to strengthen hopes for an African future that would not be so deeply scarred by war.

Despite the favorable developments in many of Africa's wars, war and the threat of war remain a major problem around the continent. The resumption of fighting in Angola and the problems faced by MINURSO in Western Sahara showed that the hopes raised in 1990 and 1991 would not in every case be easily fulfilled. Meanwhile, fighting continues in Sudan and Liberia, while there is lingering resistance in northern Uganda. The new regime in Ethiopia has taken some steps to win the consent of the country's diverse ethnic and regionally based armed resistance movements, but the Oromo and the Amhara are wary, and new outbreaks of conflict seem possible. Famine has been suppressed in Somalia, but clan, subclan, and factional tensions remain; arms are still widely available; southern Mogadishu is in rebellion; and the Somaliland secession issue has yet to be resolved. Finally, several of Africa's conflict situations that have yet to develop into war, as in Senegal and Zaire, seem to be worsening. Consequently, Africa's future with respect to peace and war is very much in the balance.

Changes in the African State

The true nature and likely future course of the changes now under way in the African state are subjects of great uncertainty and debate. What is certain is that since 1989, governments around the continent have faced mounting popular protest and defiance. From Mali to Madagascar, from Cameroon to Zambia, protesters have demanded political freedoms, national political conferences, new constitutions, and free elections. By late 1991, a leading expert counted twenty-five African countries, or about half the continent's total, that were "democratic or moderately to strongly committed to democratic change."[4] Some regimes, as in Cameroon, resisted change and attempted to suppress the dissent; but elsewhere, as in Zambia, regimes made major concessions and eventually gave way—though after prolonged delay. Analysts generally expected that most regimes still resisting reforms, as in Kenya and Zaire, would eventually be forced into concessions by domestic and international pressures, or sooner or later face upheaval.

The political changes now under way in Africa are often regarded as part of a global movement toward "democratization," and it may indeed be that Africa is headed in this direction. Certainly, demonstrators and opposition leaders around the continent are demanding fully democratic, multi-party political systems. Typically, these opposition forces have to a significant degree united across ethnic and class divisions, creating movements with a broader social base than the regimes in power.[5]

Africa had numerous elected regimes in the first years of independence, but these regimes failed on many counts, including their ability to promote social peace and progress. Often, they proved to be inept and corrupt, and like later regimes they were tempted to manipulate and even inflame ethnic and other divisions in society in order to hold on to power.[6] When they were overthrown by the armed forces, there was little popular protest—indeed, there was often celebration and a strong sense relief.

Certain factors operative today, however, suggest that newly created elected regimes will be more responsive, tolerant, and principled than those Africa has known in the past. The sheer depth of popular frustration with the old ways—corruption, ethnic favoritism, and repression of dissent—will tend to create strong popular expectations of better conduct on the part of elected regimes. These new regimes, moreover, will be created largely by emerging African political leaders, with a powerful popular base, and not—as was the case with Africa's first democracies—by colonial powers acting in conjunction with a local elite they had helped to create. Thus, new democratic regimes are likely to be more genuinely oriented toward responding, from the outset, to the needs of society.

Elites will of course dominate the elected and appointive positions in these governments, as in any other, but it is important to note that Africa's elites are themselves undergoing a profound generational change. With the spread of university education in Africa, and the ability of tens of thousands of Africans to seek educations abroad, Africa's elites are vastly larger in number than at independence. Many members of these elites are tempted to live abroad permanently, taking work in their host countries or accepting positions in the international political and financial bureaucracies.[7] But many are remaining in Africa or returning to it—often to become founders or active members of the human rights organizations, nascent political parties, newspapers, and journals that are leading the democracy movement.[8] Lawyers, economists, journalists, and businessmen have been joined by leaders of religious organizations,[9] including clergymen of their own generation, in the struggle for democracy. These emerging elites are familiar with Western political practices, democratic systems incorporating checks and balances, good governance, and the importance of protecting civil liberties. They are also well aware of the failures of authoritarian models not only in Africa but also in the former communist world. Once in power, they may be less likely, in general, to succumb to the ethnic and venal temptations that seduced the old. Thus it could be that new regimes will emerge in Africa over the next few years that will be more closely based in African societies, and more responsive to the needs and demands arising in those societies.[10] In each country where such a transition occurs, there should be little reason for armed internal resistance to occur.

As noted above, some observers of Africa believe—or hope—that the continent is moving not toward Western-style, multi-party democracy, which in their view would weaken central authority and deepen ethnic tensions, but toward uniquely African democratic forms or simply toward improved governance, even if under authoritarian regimes. Such regimes would fall short of the expectations of the emerging democratic forces in Africa itself, but should they emerge, they too would be far less likely to provoke war than the regimes Africa has known in the past.

Just how widespread the transition to more democratic systems, or to better governance, may prove to be is the great unknown at present. This uncertainty arises largely from the grave economic difficulties that Africa continues to confront, and from the interdependence of political and economic change. Scholars are agreed that prospects for a political transformation are greatest if political change is accompanied by economic transformation, and some would argue that political transformation must ultimately fail in the face of economic stagnation or decline. Only with economic growth can emerging democratic regimes begin to meet some of the popular expectations inspired by democratization, or by reforms in the direction of better governance. Meanwhile, many analysts believe that economic progress depends on democratization or at least on substantial reform—including "greater openness, transparency, and accountability"[11] in government. If the processes of economic and political change are indeed dependent on one another, then a setback in either could damage both. The depth and complexity of Africa's economic problems are particularly worrisome, suggesting that African economies will not readily respond to initial political changes. In the absence of a response, democratization and reform may falter as popular anger and frustration lead to ethnic clashes, the emergence of demagogues, and military takeovers.

A troubling paradox is that some of the energy in the democracy movement in Zambia, Madagascar, and many other countries derives from anger over economic reform programs intended to spark growth. Such reforms include austerity in government spending, reductions in food subsidies, and a loosening of exchange controls with the aim of boosting exports and curbing imports. Undertaken with the prodding of Western donors and the international financial institutions, these measures are intended to free the private sector from government controls, strengthen market forces, and allow economic growth to resume.

Analysts have hoped that a stronger market in Africa would reinforce national unity and coherence not only by promoting growth but also by giving people a stake in society and building common interests across ethnic divisions.[12] Market-oriented reform programs, however, may not survive democratization unless per capita economic growth can get under way. In the absence of rising incomes, marketization may only deepen popular anger and intensify competition for scarce resources along ethnic and religious fault lines.

As the 1990s advance, in the midst of a global recession, there are few signs of an economic upturn in Africa, despite efforts at economic reform. The World Bank continues to predict a 0.3 percent real per capita increase in income in sub-Saharan Africa for the decade as a whole, but acknowledges per capita income declines of 2 percent in 1990 and an estimated 1 percent in 1991.[13] Moreover, according to the World Bank, some 304 million Africans will be living below the poverty line in the year 2000, as against 216 million in 1990.[14] Nonetheless, some economic analysts continue to take heart from the positive growth recorded in a few countries undertaking reforms, such as Ghana and Kenya, and improved prospects for economic cooperation within Africa as regimes adopt pragmatic, reform-oriented policies. Interest in strengthening Africa's regional economic groupings has revived, and the Organization of African Unity voted in June 1991 to begin to move very slowly toward an African economic union. Hopes for a political settlement in South Africa, combined with progress toward peace in the southern Africa region, have raised expectations for a southern Africa regional expansion centered on the South African economy. Meanwhile, observers continue to note the strength of the non-formal economy in Africa and to hope that with the relaxation of government economic controls growth in this sector will accelerate.

Yet reform programs and prospects for growth will continue to be threatened by underlying economic problems, including low prices for Africa's commodity exports and an unattractive investment climate compared to that found in Asia and other parts of the world. The sub-Saharan region's still-mounting foreign debt was estimated at $161 billion for 1990, requiring an annual debt service of $11 billion.[15] Even the hopes for southern Africa had to be deferred as the region confronted a devastating drought in 1992.

These at least are familiar problems, but Africa faces a new threat— AIDS—with potential consequences that are as yet only dimly understood. An estimated 6 million Africans, including 500,000 infants, are thought to be infected by the HIV virus,[16] while 800,000 have come down with symptoms of the disease. With between 24 percent and 37 percent infected in some eastern and southern African countries, scientists are now beginning to write of the possibility of an eventual population decline in the worst-afflicted states.[17] Young adults, from whose ranks the leaders and producers of the immediate future will be drawn, are most gravely affected, and their deaths will have maximum economic impact. In addition, millions of their children will grow up as orphans, deprived of normal parenting.

The African state, in short, is poised at a critical moment at the beginning of the 1990s. Political forces that could lead to a profound transformation—and reduce the risk of war—are present, but they are only weakly supported, at best, by economic forces. Poverty remains an overwhelming reality and could grow worse, undermining political change and exacerbating social tensions. In a deteriorating economic environment, even leaders drawn from a new and wiser generation may be unable to cope with ethnic, religious, regional, and class divisions in society. In such a situation, new outbreaks of armed violence, attempts at regional secession, and war could well occur.

Changes in the Afflicted States

Where there has been progress toward political reform among Africa's war-torn countries, toward increased tolerance and greater respect for diverse elements in society, war has been brought to a conclusion or a possible conclusion has come into view. As in the rest of Africa, however, the trend of events in the afflicted states is not yet clearly established. Some regimes have not undertaken reforms, and in some of those that have, tentative steps forward could be reversed.

In Namibia, however, there seems to be little prospect of a renewed repression or of violent armed conflict. Namibia's independence constitution has a built-in system of checks and balances, including an entrenched bill of rights, a limit of two five-year presidential terms for any individual, and a parliamentary review of declarations of emergency that should help to prevent any drift toward authoritarianism and intolerance—even though the country remains marked by diversities of income and ethnic origin.

The Mozambique peace accord called for elections in 1993, but the processes of demobilization, registration, and balloting will not be completed until 1994. Dhlakama has raised numerous objections to the implementation of the peace plan, but with UNOMOZ present and acting with the model of UNTAG before it, there is reason to hope that peace and democracy can indeed be achieved.

Uganda, as noted above, had achieved a measure of consent in the rural areas through the system of resistance councils—although Museveni is wary of multi-party systems and has postponed national elections until 1994.

In Africa's other afflicted countries, democratic reforms have been either absent or highly tentative at best. The situation in Ethiopia is perhaps the most hopeful, in part because the government maintains that it is committed to democratic reforms and national elections, scheduled for January 1994. Moreover, many highly educated exiles, committed to political and economic reform, have returned from the

Western nations where they took shelter and are working to ensure that the democratization process succeeds. Nonetheless, doubts about the conduct of the 1992 regional elections and tensions among the Tigray, Amhara, and Oromo pose questions for the future of democracy in Ethiopia. Eritrea's referendum on independence was conducted fairly, according to international observers, but whether the EPLF will now permit a fully functioning, multi-party system in Eritrea is far from certain. Sudan had a partially democratic system from 1986 to 1989, but this was a democracy for the northern Islamic majority. The elected government remained adamant in refusing to accommodate basic demands of the southern rebels. After the 1989 coup, Sudan's remarkably free press, which had allowed the expression of opposing views—including southern ones—was abolished. Today, the prospect of democracy in Sudan is remote.

In Liberia, the peace accord calls for elections once demobilization is completed, but whether free elections can be held in this highly factionalized situation, and a responsible government established, is questionable. The same question arises in Rwanda, where elections are part of the internationally mediated peace accord. In the Western Sahara territory, finally, it must be assumed that any referendum conducted under United Nations auspices will be largely free and fair —but it is far from clear whether elections will soon be held.

The breakdown of the Angolan peace process, it must be noted, demonstrates a key difficulty in promoting peace and establishing democracy in countries that have long been at war. The resistance forces in Angola, Mozambique, Sudan, and elsewhere have developed a stake in their way of life and may perceive only modest incentives either for coming to terms in the first place or for abiding by any agreement they may sign. As noted in Chapter 3, their leaders may have attained a certain international stature, while the resistance fighters—ill-suited to urban life and uninterested or untrained in peasant farming—may have found in war a means of surviving in difficult economic times. To convince leaders and followers that they must lay down their arms in these circumstances and try to fit themselves into civilian society, even a reformed civilian society, can be problematic indeed. Where fighting does come to an end, long-term social stresses can be expected as the soldiers of both the government and the resistance attempt to resume normal lives and find work in impoverished societies.

Developments in the International System

The changes in the African state were accompanied by—and to some degree encouraged by—profound changes taking place in the international system beginning in the later 1980s. The favorable impact of declining superpower tensions on African conflict was assessed in the preceding chapter. The collapse of the Eastern European regimes in 1989 was another major development that had a noticeable impact in Africa. The rise of African democratic forces reflected deep currents of African thought and feeling, but African democrats unquestionably drew inspiration from the fall of authoritarian regimes in Eastern Europe. Moreover, Africa's authoritarian leaders, as they loosened controls and acceded to multi-party demands or national political conferences, were fully conscious of the fates of Ceausescu, Hoenecker, and other Eastern European leaders when they tried to resist popular democratic forces. Nor was it possible any longer for these leaders to turn to Eastern Europe or the Soviet Union to bolster their failing regimes—or to threaten to do so in order to win Western backing.

The easing of global tensions was reflected in a reduction in arms transfers to Africa as the decade turned (Table 5.1), and the impact of this development could only be favorable. The data, which reflect the dollar value of agreements for future transfers, indicate that billions of dollars in arms will continue to flow to Africa, and large quantities of these arms will no doubt remain available for years to come. However, the trend in Soviet arms transfers is clear. The value of transfer agreements by most other suppliers, including the United States, has also declined. However, the increase in arms agreements by China; continuing sales by Russia, though at a much lower level than in past years; and substantial agreements by "all others" are discouraging and suggest that arms will probably continue to be available from external suppliers seeking profits or pursuing some political or ideological agenda in Africa. The numerous reports of growing Iranian arms supplies to Sudan underline this danger. The arms provided by these other suppliers, however, will almost certainly not be sufficient to alter the overall downward trend.

Another encouraging development in the international system at the end of the 1980s was a revival of interest in the United Nations peacekeeping system as a means of reducing regional tensions. The Soviet Union's turnaround on the United Nations and its advocacy of

Table 5.1

Arms Transfer Agreements, Africa, 1985–1992 (millions of current U.S. dollars)

Supplier	1985 - 1988	1989-1992
United States	421	139
Soviet Union/Russia	9,800	2,700
France	600	100
United Kingdom	0	100
China	100	400
Germany	100	0
Italy	200	100
Other European	700	300
All others	1,200	900
TOTALS	13,121	4,739

Source: U.S. Library of Congress, Congressional Research Service, *Conventional Arms Transfers to the Third World, 1985–1992,* CRS Report no. 93-656 F by Richard F. Grimmett, 52. Grimmett's data are taken from U.S. government sources.

UN peacekeeping as an instrument of international security was one of the most remarkable policy reversals under Gorbachev.[18] The Soviets had nearly destroyed the United Nations over issues related to the Congo (now Zaire) operation in the 1960s. In the United States, by the 1980s, many had come to doubt that the United Nations could play a constructive role in bringing Third World conflicts to an end.

The dispatch of the highly successful UNTAG to Namibia in 1989 was one of the first manifestations of the revival of UN peacekeeping. After Namibia's independence, observers were uncertain about a United Nations peacekeeping role in other African wars, apart from the Western Sahara situation. Western Sahara, like Namibia, was a colonial legacy in which the United Nations had a good claim to be involved. Other wars were more clearly domestic matters from which the United Nations was excluded from intervening by Article 2, paragraph 7 of its Charter. The 1991 Angolan settlement saw the two internal parties invite a small United Nations force to monitor both the cease-fire and the elections, but the subsequent breakdown showed that such a force was powerless to deal with a former combatant determined to sabotage the peace process. UNOSOM I, sent to the Somali capital after prolonged negotiations with the contending factions, proved highly ineffective. The deployment of the planned 3,500 troops was repeatedly delayed, and Aideed would not allow the 500 Pakistanis who did arrive to move beyond the airport.

The UN experience in Angola, and with UNOSOM I, led to the realization that UN forces, when deployed, must have a credible capability for dealing with violent opposition to the peace process, should such opposition arise. This realization was reflected in the 28,000 troops deployed for the military component of UNOSOM II and in the 7,500 for UNOMOZ. Operation Restore Hope, which was authorized by a United Nations Security Council resolution, and UNOSOM II also demonstrated that in certain situations of extreme civilian suffering and breakdown of governing authority, the international community was willing to accept that the Charter restrictions against intervening in domestic affairs do not apply. UNOSOM II, however, may prove to be a limited or even a negative precedent with respect to the deployment of peacekeeping operations in Africa. In part, this has to do with the uniqueness of the Somali situation. Members may still hesitate to authorize operations in situations where civilian suffering may be great but a government remains in power and objects to a UN role. The size and the cost of the force that had to be sent to Somalia could also tend to be a deterrent to future peacekeeping deployments. Expected to cost $1.6 billion in its first year alone, UNOSOM II has clearly strained UN resources for planning and management, particularly in view of Aideed's resistance and heavy UN peacekeeping commitments elsewhere. Moreover, the U.S. withdrawal decision suggests that governments in Western developed countries, subject to intense scrutiny from the press and their legislatures, may not be willing to risk significant casualties in such operations in the future. If they do not participate, peacekeeping forces will be deprived of the most advanced military capabilities and could suffer serious consequences.

Apart from peacekeeping, the United Nations and its agencies, particularly UNICEF, were active in coordinating humanitarian relief operations conducted in the midst of African wars. These relief operations have unquestionably saved lives, but they have been hamstrung by limited funding, concerns over showing due respect for the sovereignty of the host country, and constraints imposed by suspicious contending armies.[19] Some have hoped that in focusing attention on the suffering of innocent civilians and in building experience in cooperation for humanitarian purposes, relief operations would help to promote the cause of peace. To date, however, there is no clear evidence that relief efforts have had this effect.

As Cold War tensions eased, many African observers became concerned that an important rationale for development assistance to Africa was being removed and that aid flows would soon begin a sharp decline. Such a decline would surely deepen Africa's poverty and the social cleavages that contribute to outbreaks of war; but as the decade turned, development assistance flows were somewhat higher than they had been at mid-decade and appeared to be holding steady. According to the Organization for Economic Cooperation and Development (OECD), net official development assistance grew from $16 billion in 1985 to $17 billion in 1989 (constant 1989 dollars) and maintained the same level in 1990. Aid from the Western countries, Japan, the Arab states, and international agencies was $15.1 billion in 1985 (constant 1989 dollars) and $15.8 billion in 1990.[20] By 1989/90, sub-Saharan Africa was receiving over 34 percent of all development aid from the Western donors and Japan, a proportion that was higher than the 29 percent given in 1979/80.[21] Moreover, major individual donors were continuing to devote a major portion of their aid programs to Africa. Nearly 65 percent of all development assistance from the European Community organization was going to Africa, as was 95 percent of Irish aid, 59 percent of Nordic aid, 54 percent of French aid, and 15 percent of Japanese aid.[22] Meanwhile, the developed nations were moving toward debt forgiveness for the poorest African nations, which would be a boon for countries that each year owed five times more than they earned from exports.[23]

In the United States, Congress boosted U.S. development aid to Africa by 25 percent for fiscal 1991, reflecting concerns over Africa's future articulated by anti-hunger organizations, church-sponsored humanitarian groups, and African American leaders and movements. Congress had been expected to vote a comparable increase for 1992, putting development aid for Africa at the $1 billion level for the first time.[24] The overall foreign aid authorization for fiscal 1992 failed to pass the Congress, however, because many members of the Democratic Party felt that President Bush had failed to speak out forcefully on the need for a strong foreign assistance program. Concerned that their support for foreign assistance might be used against them in upcoming elections, many of these Democrats in the House of Representatives joined with Republican opponents of foreign aid to vote down the legislation—killing the second anticipated African aid increase.

The failure of this increase demonstrated an underlying reality of Western aid flows to Africa. While these flows have increased slightly, large-scale boosts have not occurred because of domestic political and economic factors within the developed nations—even though Africa is passing through a time of critical need. Moreover, facing recession at home and limited prospects for trade and investment in Africa, the developed nations did not increase their economic contribution to African development outside development assistance channels. In August 1991, then UN secretary general Pérez de Cuellar called for a substantial increase in international support for African economic growth in order to "ensure the sustainable development of a continent faced with an unrelenting crisis of tragic proportions." [25] The occasion of his appeal—the conclusion of a failed special five-year UN Program of Action for Africa—was not an auspicious one. The secretary general pointed out that during this five-year period, despite the slight increase in official development assistance, other transfers, including export credits and private flows, had fallen, resulting in an overall drop in real net resource transfers. [26]

The Western countries were, however, using their assistance programs to try to promote the favorable political changes taking place in many African states. This trend was in part related to the end of the Cold War since, with the disappearance of the Soviet threat, Western leaders felt less need to cultivate authoritarian African allies. They could more freely insist that regimes receiving Western aid respect human rights and the democratic values generally endorsed by Western publics. Indeed, policymakers were aware that public opinion in the West could probably not be persuaded to endorse any significant aid to repressive regimes in Africa now that the Cold War had come to an end.

In June 1990, at the Franco-African summit held at La Baule, France, President François Mitterrand surprised and discomfited African leaders when he urged them to create multi-party systems and hold free elections. Moreover, French refusal to prop up Mobutu in the Zairean crisis that began in September 1991 marked a firm break with the past. French cooperation minister Edwige Avice affirmed at the time that what was happening between France and Zaire was a "very important signal," adding that "our foreign policy on these matters is represented by our support of democracy."[27] Subsequently, skeptics came to question the depth of this French commitment, and many were concerned that the more conservative French government, which came into power in March 1993, would be less active on democratization issues. Nonetheless, France has kept its distance from Mobutu, despite a brief meeting between Mitterand and Mobutu the 1993 Francophone summit in Mauritius and it seems likely that French public opinion will push the new government to show a continued preference for democratic regimes generally.

The United States, meanwhile, has undertaken special programs aimed at promoting democratic reforms in Africa, and the Bush administration's assistant secretary of state for Africa, Herman Cohen, once suggested that U.S. economic assistance might soon be linked to "political pluralism."[28] During the Zaire crisis in late 1991, Cohen affirmed that African governments emerging from dictatorship must "immediately go into a democratic system if they expect assistance from the Western world," or, more bluntly, "no democracy, no cooperation."[29] The outlines of the Clinton administration's Africa policy are still emerging, but support for democracy has already been declared to be a fundamental objective of its foreign aid program. Moreover, officials of the new administration have said that they expect Africa to be an important foreign policy priority. While events elsewhere in the world may make it difficult to live up to this expectation, clearly U.S. pressure for democratization in Africa will continue.

The United States has given some of its support for political reform in Africa through the National Endowment for Democracy (NED). Created by Congress in 1983, the NED is a private, non-profit organization (as distinct from a government agency) intended to encourage democratic institutions around the world. In 1992, the Endowment, which is supported by U.S. government funds, gave about $4.4 million in support of projects by democratic institutions in African countries.[30] Critics of the NED, noting the sweeping changes taking place around Africa, argue that this amount is far too small, and they compare it unfavorably with the $8.3 million going to Eastern Europe and Soviet successor states. The NED's defenders, on the other hand, note that the amount of funding for Africa is increasing steadily, despite the sensitivity of many African governments to any outside aid for internal democratic forces.

The World Bank has refrained from explicitly endorsing democracy on the grounds that its mandate lies in economics rather than politics. Nonetheless, the Bank is increasingly forthright in pointing out that political reform is widely needed in Africa in order to create conditions required for economic development. It insists that it is necessary for regimes to "rethink the state" in order to strengthen institutions, reduce corruption, and obtain the social consensus needed for political stability and legitimacy. Moreover, the Bank acknowledges that political freedoms and civil liberties are not an obstacle to development, and that they "seem to be associated with progress in health and education."[31] In advocating reduced corruption, investment in education, and a relatively equitable distribution of income,[32] the Bank is supporting reforms that will tend to make war less likely.[33]

Changes in the African State System

The changes in the African state and in the international system, which together are creating a somewhat more favorable outlook with respect to war, are being reinforced, to some degree, by changes in the African state system. One major development affecting the southern part of the continent is the inward re-orientation of South African policy. In West Africa, the ECOWAS intervention in Liberia—despite certain initial errors and problems—provided the first sign in years that African regional organizations might become effective in peacekeeping. Meanwhile, the movement toward greater democracy within African states could also have an impact on the state system, since it should, if it continues to move forward, reduce the number of mutually suspicious authoritarian regimes tempted to interfere against one another. Moreover, there should be fewer dissident groups seeking external support. Unfortunately, there is as yet little indication that the Organization of African Unity is emerging as an effective mediator or peacekeeper, even though its secretary general wishes it to do so. Nor has any African state or African leader developed a genuine capability to mediate between combatants in Africa's wars.

South Africa's decision at the end of the 1980s to extricate itself from Angola and Namibia, and to try to forge stronger economic ties with Mozambique, was a major force for reduced conflict in the southern African region. A number of factors lay behind the change in South Africa's regional policy. South African decision makers gradually came to the realization in the latter part of the decade that the international system was changing and that the concept of a threat to

South Africa from the Soviet Union and its allies was no longer credible. Die-hard adherents to the "total onslaught" view were late in coming to this realization, but the successful implementation of the December 1988 regional accord finally convinced even Defense Minister Magnus Malan that neither the Soviet Union nor the African states to the north posed a danger to South African security.[34]

Meanwhile, President F.W. de Klerk and his closest advisers had become convinced that the solution to South Africa's international problems, including its political isolation and economic sanctions, lay in resolving the internal conflict over apartheid. The country's severe economic depression at the end of the 1980s made it clear that if South Africa, including its white population, was to have any hope of prosperity in the future, good relations with the world at large and with its neighbors were essential. Economic growth and employment for South Africa's burgeoning population were clearly going to require a rapid expansion of foreign trade and an upsurge in foreign investment—neither of which were possible while apartheid continued. Even bare survival might be at stake, since South Africa's supplies of surplus water are dwindling. Vast water projects requiring the cooperation of neighboring states will need to be completed early in the next century if South Africa's population is not to exceed the carrying capacity of the environment.

With free elections to a transitional assembly now scheduled for April 27, 1994, prospects for continued democratization in South Africa are fairly high. Nonetheless, opposition from militants on the white right and the African left, and from Zulu leader Chief Mangosuthu Buthelezi, continue to jeopardize prospects for transition. Should the initiative ultimately fail, and South Africa begin to move toward race war and partition, both of which remain possibilities,[35] the region could be plunged into a prolonged crisis.

Presumably, some of South Africa's neighbors to the north would resume their support for violent overthrow of any white regime, which would in turn resume armed counter-measures. Such a regime would be under the control of extreme rightist elements, who would be in a vengeful mood and insensitive to international criticism. With powerful advanced weapons at their disposal, and vast stores of small arms, they could wreak immense harm in the region.

A successful South African resolution, however, combined with other favorable developments in the region, could bring about an era of regional economic growth that will make further war less likely.[36] The economic and political reforms now under way in Zambia should enable that country to reap the benefits of a South African accord, and both Zimbabwe and Mozambique should benefit as well. If peace could come to Angola, the entire southern Africa region would be set for a period of economic growth driven by the pent-up energies of the South African dynamo.

Far to the north, as the new decade began, Qadhafi's Libya—at least according to some observers—was chastened by U.S. sanctions and, like South Africa, far less likely to try to destabilize its neighbors. Whether this was true or not was highly uncertain, particularly in view of reports that Libya was involved in events in Liberia and Chad, and perhaps in Somalia and Sudan as well, in 1989 and 1990. But Libya was cultivating a relationship with Egypt and seeking a return of U.S. oil companies.[37] In February 1989, Qadhafi sought acceptance by his neighbors in northwestern Africa by entering into a five-nation "Union of the Arab Great Maghreb." Troubled by problems in Libya's oil industry and moderate world oil prices, as well as international sanctions arising from his refusal, to date, to extradite two suspects in the Lockerbie plane disaster, it may well be that the Libyan leader has drawn in his horns in the region for a time. Even if he should try to strike out against his enemies once again his capabilities are quite limited today.

Since its founding in 1963, observers have hoped that the Organization of African Unity could become a major force for peace in Africa. Unfortunately, however, the OAU has yet to demonstrate a convincing capability to contribute to the resolution of Africa's wars. As one writer noted in 1987,

> Committed to the preservation of the status quo and the principle of the territorial integrity of member states (guaranteed under Article III of the charter), the OAU has not generally been effective either in regulating or bringing to a peaceful solution conflicts within member states, particularly those concerning secessionist claims.... The organization has had no involvement in the long, highly intense Sudanese civil war or in the continued problem in Burundi. It had very little to do with the civil war in Angola.... The current vexed issues of Chad and Western Sahara have effectively exposed the virtual impotence of the OAU.[38]

There is as yet little reason to alter this assessment, although OAU contributions to the 1993 settlements in Rwanda and Liberia give grounds for hope. Prominent African leaders, including OAU secretary general Salim Ahmed Salim, have written and spoken eloquently of the need for the organization to resolve Africa's conflicts as a prerequisite to the continent's development.[39] At their February 1993 meeting, OAU foreign ministers endorsed Salim's proposal to establish a pan-African peacekeeping force, but skeptics were quick to point out that such a force could hardly be financed in view of the organization's chronic financial difficulties. At the June 1993 OAU summit in Cairo, heads of state approved many of Salim's proposed conflict-resolution structures but not the peacekeeping force.

In fairness, it must be said that the OAU did help to arrange a cease-fire in Chad in 1987 and that African diplomats believe that their role in easing tensions in the Angolan war and other conflicts has been underestimated. Nonetheless, it is striking that the principal mediators in Angola, Mozambique, and Western Sahara are external to Africa and that the OAU has had so little to contribute to solving conflicts in Somalia, Sudan, and elsewhere. For a time in 1991, it seemed that the OAU would itself became a refugee, when Addis Ababa, site of its headquarters, was swept up in a war that the OAU had been powerless to end.[40] Overall, member states owe about $70 million to the OAU,[41] and the organization has little hope of becoming an effective actor until it establishes a sound financial base.

Part of the problem may be that the OAU, at its highest level, continues to be largely a club of authoritarian national leaders who are lukewarm to the idea of a regional body involving itself in internal conflicts. This reticence may change if a new generation of African leaders, largely chosen by more democratic means than their predecessors, should come to power. Certainly many observers are hoping that a new pan-African consciousness will soon emerge—one that will see African leaders taking responsibility for the well-being of Africa's people as a whole.[42] Another disappointment in the African state system has been the very limited success of individual African governments and African leaders in mediating African conflicts. It might be thought that African leaders would be particularly successful in this area, in part because of a common worldview they might share with the participants and in part because of influence they might have acquired, by virtue of proximity, over those participants. Neighboring states in particular often have considerable apparent leverage because they may have some control over trade flows and may be providing assistance to one of the combatants. UNITA had to listen to President Mobutu in 1989 when he decided to play a mediating role in the Angolan conflict, because, according to numerous reports, Zaire had been helping to channel aid to the guerrillas. But the MPLA also had to listen because Zaire was capable of doing much worse to destabilize Angola if it chose to do so. At the same time, through trade and the use of Angola's ports, Zaire could make a substantial contribution to Angola's prosperity if peace could be achieved.

In the end, however, these and other African mediation efforts failed. This failure may have been a reflection of the unwillingness of the combatants to come to terms at a particular moment, but in some instances it probably also reflected doubts over the disinterestedness of the mediator. The MPLA could never bring itself to trust Mobutu with his long history of supporting MPLA opponents, and would not willingly cooperate in Mobutu's efforts to cultivate a reputation as a distinguished leader in African diplomacy. Similarly, Kenya was gradually discredited as a mediator in the Mozambican conflict as it came under growing suspicion of sympathy and support for RENAMO.

This is not to say, however, that more clearly disinterested mediators will succeed. Nigeria's President Ibrahim Babangida began a major mediation effort in the Sudan conflict in 1991, but made no real headway before he left office in 1993. Babangida was serving as chairman of the Organization of African Unity when he undertook the Sudan effort, but his office did not seem to give him leverage over the combatants.

Conclusion

Africa at the beginning of the 1990s stands at a crossroads with respect to war. Several factors are now at work that could help to ease this costly affliction. These include the progress toward more responsive regimes within African states; the end of the Cold War, which had divided the international system throughout the era of African independence; the first signs of an emerging peacekeeping capability on the part of regional organizations; and the inward reorientation of South African policy. Yet at the same time, major obstacles to the advent of a more peaceful era remain—among them, the continued existence of many repressive regimes, very limited prospects for economic growth or for increased development aid to promote growth, the persistent availability of arms, and serious ethnic tensions. The swift descent of

Liberia and Somalia into chaos as the 1990s opened showed how easily these factors can bring about war and immense human suffering.

Whether the forces tending toward peace will predominate remains to be seen. Perhaps the most realistic assessment is that there will be some improvement in the near term, even as war remains a major problem. In view of the many uncertainties surrounding Africa's future, however, the long-term picture is clouded indeed. If economic growth does not soon get under way, progress toward greater participation, consent, and democracy in government may falter, and social tensions will rise in the midst of deepening impoverishment. In such circumstances, urban unrest, coups, secessionism, and new outbreaks of war seem inevitable. Only with continued political change and growth will further progress toward a more peaceful era be possible.

Notes

1. Basil Davidson and Barry Munslow, "The Crisis of the Nation-State in Africa," *Review of African Political Economy* (Winter 1990); see the comments by Davidson on pp. 20–21.

2. This appears to be the position of the World Bank, which can find no basis for favoring democratic over authoritarian regimes on economic performance grounds. Institutional development and reduced corruption, which can occur under either type of regime, are the key factors in economic development, according to the Bank. World Bank, *World Development Report, 1991* (Washington, D.C., 1991), 128–47.

3. Goran Hyden, "Governance and the Study of Politics," in *Governance and Politics in Africa,* ed. Goran Hyden and Michael Bratton (Boulder, Colo.: Lynne Rienner, 1992), 1–26.

4. Richard Joseph, "Africa: The Rebirth of Political Freedom," *Journal of Democracy* 2 (Fall 1991): 11.

5. Ibid., 20.

6. Jon Kraus, "Building Democracy in Africa," *Current History* (May 1991): 209–12.

7. Millard Arnold, "Africa in the 1990s," *Fletcher Forum* 15 (Winter 1991): 11. This entire edition of the *Fletcher Forum* is devoted to sub-Saharan Africa in the 1990s.

8. Henry Neil, "New Breed of African Patriots Emerges to Press for Democracy," *Washington Post,* 4 July 1991; Donatella Lorch, "Ethiopians Return, Glad to Help Build a New Land," *New York Times,* 13 May 1993.

9. Bratton and Nicolas van de Walle, "Toward Governance in Africa: Popular Demands and State Responses," in *Governance and Politics in Africa,* ed. Hyden and Bratton, 49–50.

10. Frank A. Kunz, "Liberalization in Africa—Some Preliminary Reflections," *African Affairs* 90 (April 1991): 231–35.

11. Richard Joseph, "Partnership, not Patronship," *Africa Report,* September–October 1990, 30.

12. Goran Hyden, "Problems and Prospects of State Coherence," in *State Versus Ethnic Claims,* ed. Donald Rothchild and Victor A. Olurunsola (Boulder, Colo.: Westview Press, 1983), 78.

13. World Bank, *World Development Report, 1992* (Washington, D.C., 1992), 32.

14. Ibid., 30. The Bank places the poverty line at $370 in annual per capita income in 1985 purchasing power parity dollars.

15. World Bank, *World Debt Tables,* 1990–1991 ed., vol. 1 (Washington, D.C., 1991), 130.

16. "The Sobering Geography of AIDS," *Science,* 19 April 1991, 373.

17. R.M. Anderson, R.M. May, M.C. Boily, G.P. Garnett, and J.T. Rowley, "The Spread of HIV–1 in Africa: Sexual Contact Patterns and the Predicted Demographic Impact of AIDS," *Nature* 352 (15 August 1991): 581–89.

18. Some analysts observed, however, that Gorbachev's enthusiasm for the United Nations may have cooled with time. His December 1988 speech to the United Nations General Assembly praised the world body, but did not repeat his clarion calls for a new international security system within the United Nations framework. See U.S. Library of Congress, Congressional Research Service, *The Gorbachev Speech to the United Nations, New York, December 7, 1988,* CRS Report no. 88–776 coordinated by Francis Miko (Washington, D.C., 28 December 1988).

19. On these issues, see Larry Minear, *Humanitarianism under Seige* (Trenton, N.J.: Red Sea Press, 1991).

20. Organization for Economic Cooperation and Development (OECD), *Development Co-Operation, 1991 Report* (Paris, December 1991), 186 and 212.

21. Ibid., 180.

22. Ibid.

23. World Bank, *World Debt Tables,* 1988–1989 ed., vol. 1, xv.

24. U.S. Library of Congress, Congressional Research Service, *Africa: U.S. Foreign Assistance Issues,* CRS Issue Brief no. 91097 by Raymond W. Copson, Ted S. Dagne, and Brenda Branaman (Washington, D.C., continuously updated). In constant-dollar terms, however, total non-food economic aid is not yet returning to levels seen in the first half of the 1980s. At that time, large amounts of economic aid went to Liberia, Sudan, and Somalia from security assistance programs.

25. United Nations, *Economic Crisis in Africa, Final Review and Appraisal of the Implementation of the United Nations Programme of Action for African Economic Recovery and Development 1986–1990 (UNPAAERD),* Report of the UN Secretary General prepared for the session of the Ad Hoc Committee of the Whole of the UN General Assembly (New York, 3–13 September 1991), foreword.

26. Ibid., 14.

27. Paris, Antenne–2 Television Network, 26 October 1991, recorded and translated by FBIS wire service.

28. Congressional Research Service, *Africa: U.S. Foreign Assistance Issues.*

29. U.S. Congress, Senate, Committee on Foreign Relations, Subcommittee on African Affairs, *The Situation in Zaire,* Hearing, 102d Cong., 1st sess., 6 November 1991 (Washington, D.C.: U.S. Government Printing Office, 1992), 7.

30. U.S. Library of Congress, Congressional Research Service, *National Endowment for Democracy,* CRS Issue Brief no. 90093 by Ellen Collier (Washington, D.C., continuously updated). Of Africa's $4.4 million, $1.6 million went to South African projects.

31. Ibid., 10.

32. World Bank, *World Development Report, 1991,* 9–10; 128–47.

33. In a text box, *World Development Report, 1991,* notes that "Inevitably, war retards development," 141.

34. David E. Albright, "South Africa's Changing Threat Perceptions and Strategic Response," *In Depth* 1 (Spring 1991): 168–77.

35. Pauline Baker, "South Africa on the Move," *Current History* (May 1990): 233.

36. Millard Arnold, "Southern Africa in the Year 2000: An Optimistic Scenario," *CSIS Africa Notes* (28 March 1991).

37. Come Back America, We Need You," *The Middle East,* June 1991, 25–28; "Qaddhafi Aims for Respectability," *Middle East Economic Digest,* 28 June 1991, 4–5.

38. S.K.B. Asante, "The Role of the Organization of African Unity in Promoting Peace, Development, and Regional Security in Africa," in *Africa: Perspectives on Peace and Development,* ed. Emmanuel Hansen (London and New Jersey: United Nations University and Zed Books, 1987), 127.

39. "Summit of Deep Concerns," *West Africa,* 10–16 June 1991, 953. Just before the summit, a four-day African Leadership Forum held in Uganda concluded that security, stability, and development in Africa are inextricably linked and that the erosion of stability is a major factor in Africa's continuing crisis. Radio Uganda broadcast, 23 May 1991, recorded in U.S. Foreign Broadcast Information Service, *Daily Report, Sub-Saharan Africa (FBIS),* 28 May 1991, 2.

40. See Sennen Andriamirado, "L'OUA en quête d'avenir," *Jeune Afrique,* 5 June 1991, 16–17.

41. Tsegaye Tadesse, "Pay Up, Ethiopian Leader Tells OAU Late Payers," Reuters, 15 February 1993.

42. Davidson and Munslow, "The Crisis of the Nation-State in Africa."

6 EASING AFRICA'S BURDEN OF WAR: THE ROLE OF THE INTERNATIONAL COMMUNITY

At this critical moment in African history, when recent progress toward a more peaceful future is under threat, the potential role of the international community in assuring that the right course is taken becomes highly relevant. Of course, war in Africa is primarily a problem for Africa itself to resolve. It is a problem not only for Africa's political leaders, but also for its teachers and students, philosophers, writers, and local authorities. It should be at the top of the agenda for Africa's development and financial institutions, and for its international organizations.

Nonetheless, as Chapter 4 made clear, actors from outside Africa have long played a role in Africa's wars—exacerbating some conflicts in the past and more recently helping to steer some wars toward settlement. The previous chapter showed that the level of future external interest in Africa is in question, and the resources likely to be made available to help Africa resolve its myriad problems seem certain to be constrained. Conceivably, publics outside Africa, afflicted by "compassion fatigue," will lose interest in Africa's problems. Perhaps their governments will increasingly neglect Africa as they focus on domestic issues, or on foreign problems nearer at hand.

Despite these dangers, this chapter makes the optimistic assumption that many external actors will remain interested in Africa to some significant degree in the years ahead, and that they will want to influence the continent in the direction of peace. Clearly, the United Nations and its agencies, as well as humanitarian and relief organizations generally, must remain active in Africa if they are to retain legitimacy as central actors in the cause of peace and humanitarian affairs. The Western developed nations and Japan will probably also be active at some level, since the humanitarian concerns that inspire individuals and groups within their societies are based on lasting values. Humanitarian concern over hunger in Africa, over suffering among African children, and over the fate of Africa's refugees and displaced people will not soon disappear. Economic concerns will probably also play some part in fostering interest in African peace. Despite Africa's current poverty, many African countries, including South Africa, Sudan, Zaire, Angola, Mozambique, and Nigeria, can make a significant contribution to global prosperity—but only if they are at peace. Business interests, bankers, and finance officials active in Africa or seeking a role there will press this reality on governments and international organizations as they seek help in improving the climate for trade and investment.

If, then, there is to be continued external interest in promoting peace in Africa, what policy options are available to governments and international organizations? In particular, in view of likely future constraints on funding for African programs, what options are potentially most effective, most affordable, and most likely to win public support?

Efforts Directed at the African State

African wars have their roots in the problems of the African state, and international efforts aimed at influencing the continent in the direction of peace should continue to be directed at those problems. Action at the level of the state could have political, economic, and diplomatic dimensions.

Additional Support for African Political Reform

Africa's movement toward regimes that are more responsive to the needs and demands of diverse groups and interests in society is a development of profound importance that could greatly ease the social tensions that lead to war. Additional support for reform in Africa need not be highly expensive, since that support can be expressed in part through diplomatic gestures and symbols. The recent American ambassador to Kenya, Smith Hempstone, explored the possibilities in this area for several years. In March 1991, he ran afoul of Kenyan president Daniel arap Moi simply for handing out books on American democracy at Kenyan schools. Critics in the Kenyan parliament tried to outdo one another in condemning Hempstone, and when his support for democracy did not waver, his position became extremely uncomfortable—even potentially unsafe. Nonetheless, democratic elements in Kenya took great encouragement from Hempstone's stance, which made the position of the United States, once Kenya's main source foreign backing, crystal clear to the Moi regime. As a result, the regime was constrained in its ability to suppress opposition forces, however much it might have wished to do so.

Kenya, Zaire, and Malawi have also been subjected to cutoffs in Western economic aid on political grounds—a form of pressure that has no negative impact on foreign aid budgets and can indeed temporarily free up funds for use elsewhere. Cutoffs can be costly if a regime should retaliate in some way, perhaps by seizing assets of foreign-owned firms, but African regimes are generally reluctant to take such action for fear of further isolating themselves from the international economy. South Africa came under extreme international economic pressure for reform over many years, including sanctions and lending cutoffs, but retaliation was minimal. While some South Africans still downplay the importance of these sanctions in the opening of negotiations on democracy,[1] the critical impact of sanctions is undeniable.

Insofar as support for democratization does cost money, expenditures are likely to be modest in comparison with other forms of aid. Support for parliamentary exchanges; speakers' programs; elections monitoring; and assistance to political parties for printing, transportation, and the like need not require large financial commitments. Moreover, this type of aid is attractive to publics in the democratic nations of the world since it is in accord with their own widely shared beliefs in human rights and democratic freedoms.

In post-conflict situations, the international community could support democratization by assisting in the demobilization and reintegration of government and resistance soldiers. Foreign aid programs designed to house and train ex-combatants would be a significant contribution. In addition, the smaller, combined armies that typically emerge from the peace process are usually in urgent need of instruction on the role and responsibilities of peacetime armed forces in democratic political systems. The armed forces of the Western democracies could make a unique contribution in providing this sort of military education and training.

In short, there is considerable scope for effective and affordable action by external actors in support of further democratization in Africa. It is for this reason that congressional pressure for making U.S. non-food economic aid conditional on progress in democratization is mounting.[2] Other donors, including the World Bank, may soon move in the same direction.

Economic Aid Focus on Reducing Social Tensions

It is by now clear that there will not be large aid increases for Africa, and surely no "Marshall Plan for Africa," in the foreseeable future. Advocates of aid to promote African peace and development in the years ahead will do well if they are able to maintain the current pattern of incremental growth in assistance levels. As far as peace is concerned, aid is likely to be most effective if the objective of easing tensions between groups within African societies is made paramount. Aid programs should seek to reduce regional and ethnic tensions, and care should be taken to assure that aid projects do nothing to widen those divisions. Foreign aid should be perceived within African countries as something that benefits society as a whole, rather than a ruling clique or a privileged group or region.

Aid that is focused on creating opportunities for productive employment throughout society could help to reduce incentives for the creation of armed resistance forces. Efforts to ease rural poverty, reduce the isolation of rural areas, and integrate rural people into national life would make it more difficult for grievances to fester in remote areas. Poor rural people, given hope, would have far less reason to become soldiers in resistance armies.

Aid directed at enhancing the knowledge and capabilities of Africa's emerging leadership generation could also help to promote the cause of peace. Support for higher education, including programs to ease overcrowding and provide books and equipment at African universities, would not only reduce tensions within African student populations but also help to deepen knowledge and enhance problem-solving capabilities among young leaders. Student exchange programs, as well as programs for external travel for young professionals and civil servants, could help to promote skills and values that could contribute to national integration and growth. Foreign assistance in support of programs in African peace studies, conflict resolution, and conflict management could help to focus some of Africa's emerging leaders directly on the problem of easing Africa's burden of war.

Many foreign assistance programs, of course, are already aiming at job creation, easing rural poverty, and promoting higher education. This is not the place for a review of those programs or for detailed proposals for new programs. It is the place to suggest, however, that since peace is essential to the future well-being of Africa's people, aid programs be should carefully examined, and if necessary reformulated, to maximize their contribution to peace.

An International Program of Pressure on Combatants

In today's world of economic interdependence, instantaneous communications, rapid transportation, and the free flow of information across borders, no African government is immune to international pressure for changes in conduct. As South Africa learned, to be regarded as a "pariah state" because of domestic policies can have severe international consequences, which in turn can intensify domestic problems in a sort of "feedback loop." Resistance movements operating in remote areas and less in the public eye are not as vulnerable to international pressures, but they too must maintain a certain standard of acceptability to be taken seriously on the world stage. If they come to be regarded as mere bandit gangs, they will lack sympathizers and support among foreign interest groups, and they will not be thought of as suitable candidates for a seat at the table should internationally sponsored negotiations get under way. Moreover, their negative image abroad will tend to damage their reputation with potential supporters at home. Apart from these practical considerations, most government and resistance leaders are to some degree susceptible to moral suasion on behalf of peace—although, as Idi Amin demonstrated, there are exceptions.

The vulnerability of most combatants to foreign pressures gives the international community options for trying to persuade combatants to better protect civilian non-combatants, to enter into peace talks, and to agree to reasonable proposals for negotiated settlements. Like measures in support of political reforms, this pressure could take the form of public statements, diplomatic action, and inducements through aid and trade that could win public support and need not be prohibitively expensive. International pressures for peace, of course, have already been brought to bear on numerous occasions—and with some success, as in the opening of food corridors in Sudan or the conclusion of the Angolan peace accord. To date, however, the international community has taken a case-by-case approach, focusing on particular wars at certain moments, rather than launching a broad and consistent program of pressure for peace.

The Western nations, notably the United States, France, and Britain —and for some African countries, Italy and Portugal—are in a particularly good position to lead an international program of pressure on the combatants in Africa's wars because of their past role and continuing influence around the continent. Their statements and policies on Africa always receive attention; their radio broadcasts are widely heard; and their libraries, cultural centers, and speakers' programs in Africa are typically filled to capacity by avid seekers after information and new perspectives. Clearly some sort of Western statement that solving the problem of war is critical to Africa's future, and that the Western nations had decided to give this problem top priority, would be bound to have an impact. Such a statement might be issued at a meeting of the Group of 7 industrial powers, for example, and backed by other Western-dominated institutions, such as the European Community and the World Bank. The institutions and officials of the United Nations have a key role to play, particularly in terms of general statements and behind-the-scenes discussions that would not infringe on the principle of non-interference in the internal affairs of member states. When states collapse under the pressure of internal violence, as in the cases of Liberia or Somalia, the non-interference issue becomes less relevant, and this should allow the UN to assume a more direct and outspoken role.

Western reminders that democratic and responsive governments have the best chance of avoiding internal war might be a part of the international campaign on behalf of peace in Africa. Certainly such reminders would be heard by Africa's people, even if they were not immediately heeded by governments. Pointed allusions to the prospects for increased aid, trade, and investment if peace should come might strengthen the incentives for negotiation, even if aid on the scale of the Marshall Plan cannot be offered. Repeated reminders of the availability of Western good offices could also tend to intensify pressures for negotiated settlements. It is true of course, that some governments would resent these pressures and that some Western peace initiatives would inevitably fail. Nonetheless, over the long term, an outspoken Western-led movement in favor of African peace would almost certainly make a major contribution.

Persuading African States to Accept Legal Norms

International pressure for peace in Africa might include pressures to persuade African governments to accept existing international legal norms affecting internal war.[3] While these norms do not affect the underlying causes of war, nor require states to end abuses that can lead to war, they at least bind the signatories to certain standards of conduct.

The development of international law with respect to internal wars has lagged behind the law of international conflicts.[4] This is because of the persistent sensitivity among modern states over international involvement in domestic affairs. Nonetheless, there exists today a considerable body of law that is relevant to Africa's internal wars. Common Article 3 of the Geneva Conventions of 1949 requires the humane treatment in wars not of an international character of persons not taking an active part in hostilities—although it does not specifically refer to some of the evils found in modern African wars, such as the disruption of humanitarian relief efforts. Protocol II to the 1949 conventions, which was negotiated in 1977, is more to the point. Also applying to non-international conflicts, the protocol provides that the civilian population shall be protected against the dangers of military operations and shall not be the object of attack. The protocol bans "starvation of civilians as a method of combat" and authorizes international relief actions—though only with the consent of the host nation. Enslavement and the forced removal of civilian populations are also prohibited, and special provisions on the protection of children are included.

Some international agreements not specifically related to war, such as the Universal Declaration of Human Rights or the new Convention on the Rights of the Child, are also highly relevant to the problems faced by Africa's civilians in times of war. The African Charter on Human and People's Rights, agreed to at the 1979 Organization of African Unity summit, specifies that "every human being shall be entitled to respect for his life and the integrity of his person." The African Charter also includes general statements on rights to physical health and education, as well as the protection of the family—rights that are typically not respected in times of war in Africa. There is also an OAU convention on the humanitarian treatment of refugees, concluded in 1969.

The principal obstacle to the emergence of a stronger regime with respect to the treatment of civilians is the continuing reluctance of African governments, like governments elsewhere,[5] to be bound by restrictions over their conduct of domestic affairs. It may also be that African countries to some degree distrust international humanitarian law as essentially a European-inspired institution—and one that gave Africans little protection during the colonial era.[6] The reservations of African governments are reflected in the limited support of African countries (and other countries) for Protocol II, to which only twenty-five African states have become party. Most of the war-torn states, including Ethiopia and Sudan, have failed to accede. Angola and Mozambique have accepted Protocol I, which applies to international conflicts, but refuse to accept Protocol II.[7]

Government reluctance to become entangled in conventions that could restrict government conduct with respect to civilians is also reflected in the weakness of existing agreements. None has effective enforcement mechanisms, and all can be violated with little immediate penalty. Liberia, for example, is a party to Protocol II, but its government was widely criticized for violating the rights of civilians as internal war burgeoned in the first months of 1990. In a sense, the Liberian government eventually paid a price for these actions, since its conduct deepened the rebellion, precipitating a breakdown in law and order that eventually brought ECOWAS intervention. Nonetheless, one suspects that Protocol II and its restrictions were very far from the minds of the late President Doe and his commanders as they launched their initial response to the uprising. This was so at least in part because there was little prospect that they would be punished for violations of the protocol.

Another problem with existing conventions is that resistance movements, by their very nature as non-state actors, cannot formally subscribe to them. This does not deprive existing conventions that have obtained the necessary ratifications of the force of law. But it does mean that resistance movements and their leaders may not see such conventions as relevant to them. Since they play no role in drafting, debating, or ratifying the conventions, they are not likely to be well informed as to their contents. Thus, special efforts may need to be made in order to persuade resistance leaders that it is in their interest to respect conventions governing civil war.

The international community might try to win support for—and compliance with—existing conventions affecting internal war by several means.[8] Concerned governments, international organizations, and humanitarian organizations may wish to increase the political pressure on this issue in order to nudge African governments toward signing existing conventions and respecting those they have signed. To some degree, this has already happened through the International Committee of the Red Cross (ICRC), which launched a Campaign for the Protection of War Victims in 1987. This campaign included an appeal to all states to consider becoming parties to the Geneva protocols and recommended a universal campaign to make the rights of civilians known to armies and civilians alike. It must be said, however, that the ICRC campaign received minimal attention in the journals and magazines most often read by African policymakers, intellectuals, and students. Nor was it featured in the African media. Any future effort along these lines would benefit from high-level endorsements by world leaders, UN support, and the participation of the foreign ministries of major powers—and of their embassies in Africa.

Programs for training diplomats, other officials, and soldiers in humanitarian law might be strengthened as part of an international effort to secure greater protection for civilians in Africa's wars. Some training of this sort already occurs through international organizations and military assistance programs. Nonetheless, it seems clear that international organizations, foundations, African universities, military exchange programs, and other programs and institutions could do a great deal more to disseminate information on humanitarian law.

Efforts Directed at African Regional Actors

Apart from the ECOWAS operation in Liberia, Africa's regional organizations have demonstrated only limited capabilities for responding to Africa's wars. Yet they have significant potential as peacekeepers and mediators. As associations of neighboring states, they have a keen interest in preventing the disruptions to trade and the spillover violence that can result from war, and they have a special legitimacy, which non-African actors lack, in addressing African government and resistance leaders on behalf of peace. To date, as noted in an earlier chapter, African regional organizations have been reluctant to involve themselves in the internal affairs of member states, but the creation of ECOMOG shows an emerging awareness that such restraint may be dysfunctional for a region and for Africa as a whole.

The international community can help to strengthen Africa's regional organizations, although, again, the effort must be undertaken primarily by Africans themselves. Africa's regional organizations could be strengthened to some degree simply by wider recognition and encouragement on the part of the international community. The Organization of African Unity has won a role within the United Nations system, but it is rare indeed for leaders and officials of the world's more powerful nations to speak about, pay visits to, or otherwise deal with the OAU. Of course, if the OAU had shown itself to be effective in dealing with Africa's wars and the continent's other problems, it would have achieved greater international recognition. But at the same time, its effectiveness and the effectiveness of other African regional organizations might be enhanced if they were given more encouragement by key external actors.

This encouragement could at times take the form of technical support, a type of aid that need not be costly for donors. Training could be made available for OAU personnel in mediation techniques, for example; or aid might be given to various regional organizations for the acquisition of books, journals, and documents relevant to the problem of African war. During the 1980s, the Southern African Development Coordination Conference (SADCC) won growing recognition as an effective agency in regional development coordination, but its success was partly due to the encouragement and technical support it received from the international community from its inception. SADCC, now the Southern African Development Community, won this support because external actors sympathized with the plight of its members resulting from their confrontation with South Africa. Surely African peace is a cause equally worthy of international sympathy and support.

International aid for African peacekeeping operations might be helpful to Africa in dealing with particular conflicts. The ECOMOG intervention in Liberia points to an emerging African capability for responding to crises with African intervention forces. In the future, such interventions could emerge as a means of responding to those African conflicts that have difficulty in achieving a place on the global agenda.

Yet ECOMOG put a severe financial strain on the participating states from the outset. Had they been less strapped, the operation might have been larger, briefer, and more successful. Support for peacekeeping, always an expensive proposition, could tend to be more costly than other forms of support for African regional organizations. But budgetary support of only a few million dollars would have been extremely helpful to ECOMOG.[9] If such support had been undertaken through the United Nations, the expense could have been shared among many countries. Other forms of aid could be less costly. Sharing satellite intelligence with the peacekeepers, for example, would not involve added expense, and providing limited transportation might be counted as a training expense by the air forces of the donor nations. Training for African peacekeepers in the removal of mines would be somewhat more expensive but would help Africa deal with a bitter legacy of war that continues to kill children and farmers.

The possibility of generating international support for African organizations working on behalf of peace was suggested by a July 1991 U.S. congressional hearing on prospects for a "CSCE for Africa," modeled on the Conference on Security and Cooperation in Europe (CSCE), created at Helsinki in 1975 to deal with European problems in international security affairs, human rights, economic cooperation, and other matters. This is an idea being championed by retired General Olusegun Obasanjo, former president of Nigeria and founder of the African Leadership Conference. The CSCE is given considerable credit for easing East–West tensions and promoting human rights and political reforms in Eastern Europe and the Soviet Union in the years subsequent to its founding. The "Charter of Paris for a New Europe," signed at the November 1990 CSCE meeting, created a number of new institutions, including a permanent secretariat, a conflict prevention center,[10] and an office of free elections. The CSCE also adopted a proposal on establishing a parliamentary assembly.

With its regular heads-of-state meetings and its new council of foreign ministers, the CSCE in some ways resembles the OAU. But its growing influence, its activism, and its clear human rights agenda are in sharp contrast to today's OAU. The African leaders who have dominated the OAU over the years would surely not have allowed it to evolve along CSCE lines despite initial enthusiasm over "pan-Africanism." As a new generation comes to power in Africa, however, this may change—and international encouragement for such a change could well prove beneficial.

Efforts at the International System Level

While the international community can act in part by attempting to influence African states and African regional organizations, cooperative actions taken among external actors can also contribute to easing Africa's burden of war.

A Wider Scope for Humanitarian Diplomacy and Humanitarian Intervention

Operation Restore Hope, coming in the wake of the UN-sanctioned international relief operation on behalf of the Kurdish population of northern Iraq, has revived interest in international intervention as a means of dealing with war and its humanitarian consequences in the Third World. Many hope that First World armies, with their tremendous combat and logistical capabilities, will find a growing role in Africa's wars—maintaining peace, protecting displaced people, and delivering food to the hungry.

International *deus ex machina* solutions to Africa's wars and the suffering they cause, however, remain unlikely in most situations. First World governments, facing domestic political and economic constraints on foreign deployments, will rarely want to send forces to Africa, either unilaterally or as part of an international peacekeeping effort. The difficulties faced by UNOSOM II in Somalia, as noted in the previous chapter, will only heighten their reluctance. Nonetheless, while large-scale international intervention to impose and enforce peace will remain the exception, smaller, less costly peacekeeping and humanitarian deployments could play a constructive role. Success for UNOMOZ in Mozambique, though still uncertain, would improve prospects for small operations with the consent of the contending parties. The United Nations undertook major reforms in 1991 in order to strengthen its capabilities in humanitarian relief and peacekeeping, and Secretary General Boutros Boutros-Ghali has shown a keen interest in issues of war and peace in Africa, taking a lead role on Somalia and Mozambique. Thus it may be that limited international humanitarian responses to Africa's wars have a wider scope in the post–Cold War world, where the fear that any strong international action might lead to a paralyzing superpower confrontation has disappeared.

If the possibilities for humanitarian intervention are to develop, humanitarian diplomacy will have to be exercised at the highest levels by external governments and international organizations. Ideally, governments and resistance movements within afflicted countries could be persuaded to accept such interventions willingly and to refrain from interfering with humanitarian operations. Such cooperation is not to be expected, however. Winning it will require utmost efforts on the part of the United Nations and its agencies, backed up by the international community at large. The UN secretary general will also, no doubt, have to exercise humanitarian diplomacy to win financial backing for operations from UN members, particularly the wealthier members who are best able to contribute.[11] He will be able to point out, however, that in working through the United Nations they will be visibly responding to a humanitarian emergency but at the same time sharing the costs with others. Should the operation fail or run into difficulties, public criticism will be directed, at least in part, at the United Nations, rather than at donor governments.

It will be difficult nonetheless, for the Secretary General or anyone else to win international support for humanitarian operations in the wake of the setbacks suffered by UNOSOM II in 1993. Aideed, whatever his eventual fate, has already done untold damage to the prospects for humanitarian intervention in Africa's wars. However, should events in southern Mogadishu eventually take a favorable turn, it may be that Operation Restore Hope and UNOSOM II will come to be seen as successful humanitarian interventions that opened the way to decisive international action, in rare but urgent situations, in other African conflicts—even against the will of the contending parties.

Continued Efforts to Restrain Arms Supplies

Arms sales to Africa have already declined, and in July 1991, major arms suppliers met in Paris in the wake of the Persian Gulf conflict to impose new restraints on the arms trade generally. The United States, Britain, France, the Soviet Union, and China agreed to an initiative which, though primarily directed toward the Middle East, would promote restraint and "increased transparency" in arms sales worldwide. The initiative faces the usual international difficulties in enforcement, and there are already charges that some signatories are evading it in the Middle East. Nonetheless, it seems clear that the major Western powers are well aware of the need to sharply restrict arms exports to Africa.

China, however, is suspected of continuing to seek arms sales in Africa, and some Middle Eastern countries, including Iran, appear to be competing to supply arms in the Horn of Africa for strategic or ideological reasons. There may be other channels of clandestine and private arms supplies. Surely the international community can find more effective means to expose, publicize, and reduce this traffic in arms.

Conclusion

The survey of African war and its causes and costs presented in this volume should leave no illusions as to the gravity of the problem or its intractability. Nonetheless, there are steps that can be taken by the international community to strengthen the forces of peace in the African state, the African state system, and the international system itself. Despite the end of the Cold War, the international community remains engaged with Africa, reflecting a continued international concern for the fate of the continent and its people. Whether this concern will now lead to an intensified and coordinated international effort to ease Africa's burden of war remains to be seen, but the foundations of such an effort are already being laid in this era of unprecedented change in international relations.

Notes

1. Herman Giliomee, "The Last Trek? Afrikaners in Transition to Democracy," *South Africa International* 22 (January 1992): 112–13.

2. The failed FY 1992 and FY 1993 foreign assistance authorization, as approved by House and Senate conference, urged the president to increase U.S. support for democratization in Africa. H.R. 2508, International Cooperation Act of 1991, Title X.

3. This section is drawn from a paper presented by the author at the 1990 meeting of the African Studies Association, held in Baltimore.

4. Keith Suter, *An International Law of Guerrilla Warfare: The Global Politics of Law-Making* (New York: St. Martin's Press, 1984), 11–14.

5. The United States has itself not ratified Protocol II to the Geneva Conventions.

6. Mutoy Mubiala, "African States and the Promotion of Humanitarian Principles," *International Review of the Red Cross* (March–April 1989): 101.

7. International Committee of the Red Cross, *Dissemination,* May 1990, 20.

8. On these points, see the very thorough survey in Mubiala, "African States and the Promotion of Humanitarian Principles," 103–9.

9. The U.S. Congress, recognizing the progress made by ECOMOG in promoting peace in Liberia, attempted to set aside funds to support the operation in its failed foreign assistance authorization for fiscal years 1992 and 1993.

10. The failed foreign assistance authorization considered by Congress in 1991 would have directed the Agency for International Development to take steps toward the creation of an African Center for Conflict Resolution. The center would have assisted in resolving regional, sub-national, and national conflicts in Africa. This provision originated in the House Foreign Affairs Committee's Subcommittee on Africa, chaired by Representative Mervyn Dymally, who retired from Congress in 1992.

11. Debate on these issues is likely to center for some time on a recent report issued by the secretary general himself; United Nations, General Assembly and Security Council, *An Agenda for Peace: Preventive Diplomacy, Peacemaking and Peace-keeping,* Report of the Secretary General pursuant to the statement adopted by the Summit Meeting of the Security Council on 31 January 1992, UN document A/47/266,E/24111 (New York, 17 June 1992).

SUGGESTED READINGS

Angola

Bender, Gerald J. *Angola under the Portuguese: The Myth and the Reality.* London: Heinemann Educational Books, 1978.

Bridgland, Fred. *Jonas Savimbi: A Key to Africa.* New York: Paragon House, 1987.

Crocker, Chester. *High Noon in Southern Africa: Making Peace in a Rough Neighborhood.* New York: W.W. Norton, 1992.

Kitchen, Helen, ed. *Angola, Mozambique, and the West.* Washington Papers no. 130. New York: Praeger, 1987.

Marcum, John A. *The Angolan Revolution.* Cambridge, Mass.: M.I.T. Press, 1969–78.

————. "Angola: Twenty-five Years of War. *Current History* 85 (May 1986): 193–96, 229–31.

Chad

Castillon, Michel. "Low-Intensity Conflict in the 1980s: The French Experience. *Military Review* 66 (January 1986): 68–77.

Lemarchand, René. "Chad: The Misadventures of the North–South Dialectic." *African Studies Review* 29 (September 1986): 27–41.

Whiteman, Kaye. *Chad.* London: The Minority Rights Group, 1988.

Ethiopia

Clapham, Christopher S. *Transformation and Continuity in Revolutionary Ethiopia.* Cambridge: Cambridge University Press, 1988.

Doornbus, Martin, Lionel Cliffe, Abdel Ghaffar, M. Ahmed, and John Markakis, eds. *Beyond Conflict in the Horn: Prospects for Peace, Recovery, and Development in Ethiopia, Somalia, Eritrea, and Sudan.* The Hague: Institute of Social Studies, 1992.

Henze, Paul. "Ethnic Strains and Regional Conflict in Ethiopia." *Conflict* 8 (1988): 111–40.

Keller, Edmond J. "Revolution and State Power in Ethiopia." *Current History* 87 (May 1988): 217–20, 230–32.

————. *Revolutionary Ethiopia.* Bloomington: Indiana University Press, 1988.

Markakis, John. *Class and Revolution in Ethiopia.* Trenton, N.J.: Red Sea Press, 1986.

Schwab, Peter. *Ethiopia: Politics, Economics, and Society.* Boulder, Colo.: Lynne Rienner, 1985.

Mozambique

Finnegan, William. *A Complicated War: The Harrowing of Mozambique.* Berkeley and Los Angeles: University of California Press, 1992.

Hanlon, Joseph. *Mozambique.* London: Zed Books, 1984.

Henriksen, Thomas H. *Revolution and Counterrevolution.* Westport, Conn.: Greenwood Press, 1983.

Isaacman, Allen F. *Mozambique.* Boulder, Colo.: Westview Press, 1983.

Moorcraft, Paul. "Mozambique's Long Civil War: Renamo—Puppets or Patriots?" *International Defense Review* 20 (1987): 1313–16.

Munslow, Barry. "Mozambique and the Death of Machel." *Third World Quarterly* (January 1988): 23–36.

Vines, Alex. *RENAMO: Terrorism in Mozambique.* London: James Currey, Ltd.; and Bloomington: Indiana University Press, 1991.

Namibia

Du Pisani, Andre. *SWA/Namibia: The Politics of Continuity and Change.* Johannesburg: J. Ball Publishers, 1986.

Katjavivi, Peter H. *A History of Resistance in Namibia.* London: James Currey; Addis Ababa: OAU; Paris: Unesco Press, 1988.

National Democratic Institute for International Affairs. *Nation Building: The U.N. and Namibia.* Washington, D.C.: 1988.

Soggot, David. *Namibia.* New York: St. Martin's Press, 1986.

Somalia

Laitin, David D. *Somalia.* Boulder, Colo.: Westview Press, 1987.

Lewis, I.M. "The Ogaden and the Fragility of Somali Segmentary Nationalism." *African Affairs* 88 (October 1989): 573–79.

———. *A Modern History of Somalia.* Boulder, Colo.: Westview Press, 1988.

Metz, Helen, ed. *Somalia: A Country Study*, 4th ed. Washington, D.C.: Library of Congress, Federal Research Division, 1993.

Samatar, Ahmed I. "Somalia Impasse: State Power and Dissent Politics." *Third World Quarterly* 9 (July 1987): 871–90.

Sudan

Abd Al-Rahim, Muddathir, ed. *Sudan since Independence: Studies of the Political Development since 1956.* Aldershot, Hants, England: Gower, 1986.

Deng, Francis M., and Prosser Gifford, eds. *The Search for Peace and Unity in the Sudan.* Washington, D.C.: Wilson Center Press, 1987.

Khalid, Mansour, ed. *John Garang Speaks.* London, New York: KPI, 1987.

Markakis, John. *National and Class Conflict in the Horn of Africa.* Cambridge: Cambridge University Press, 1987.

Niblock, Tim. *Class and Power in Sudan.* Albany: State University of New York Press, 1987.

Uganda

Gertzel, Cherry. "Uganda's Continuing Search for Peace." *Current History* (May 1990): 205–8, 231–32.

Hansen, Holger Bernt, and Michael Twaddle, eds. *Uganda Now: Between Decay and Development*. Athens: Ohio University Press, 1988.

Kasfir, Nelson. "Uganda's Uncertain Quest for Recovery." *Current History* 84 (April 1985): 169–73, 187.

Mamdani, Mahmood. "Uganda in Transition: Two Years of the NRA/NRM." *Third World Quarterly* 10 (July 1988): 1155–81.

Western Sahara

Hodges, Tony. *Western Sahara*. Westport, Conn.: L. Hill, 1983.

Lawless, Richard, and Laila Monahan, eds. *War and Refugees: The Western Sahara Conflict*. London: Pinter, 1987.

Lewis, William H. "Morocco and the Western Sahara." *Current History* 84 (May 1985): 213–16.

Zartman, I. William, ed. *The Political Economy of Morocco*. New York: Praeger, 1987.

INDEX

UNOSOM II, 53–54, 139, 142–43, 150, 169, 192, 193
UNTAG (United Nations Transition Group), 137–38, 150, 165, 168
UPA (Ugandan People's Army), 48
USC (United Somali Congress), 52, 83, 89
USSR. *See* Soviet Union

Voice of America, 131

Weapons, access to, 95–97, 193–94
Western Sahara, 54, 59–62, 77, 78, 160, 166. *See also* Popular Front for the Liberation of Saguia el-Hamra and Rio de Oro (POLISARIO)
Algeria and, 109
ethnic/regional factors in, 80, 83
foreign involvement in, 147–49
foreign military aid, 106
human rights violations in, 13
political stances of resistance movements in, 90
refugees and displaced persons in, 7, 8

Western Somali Liberation Front (WSLF), 36
Wildlife, effect of war on, 16–17
Women in resistance groups, 94
World Bank, 18, 40, 163, 172–73, 184
WSLF (Western Somali Liberation Front), 36

Zaghawa (ethnic group), 64
Zaire, 15, 68, 75, 161, 183
and Chad, 126
and France, 171–72
and MPLA, 177
Zambia, 15, 75, 161, 163, 175
ZANU (Zimbabwe African National Union), 38, 40
Zenawi, Meles, 22, 38, 86, 94, 130
Zimbabwe, 15, 68, 175
and Mozambique, 40–41, 109–10, 134
poaching in, 17
Zimbabwe African National Union (ZANU), 38, 40

Raymond W. Copson holds a Ph.D. in international studies from The Johns Hopkins University. He has been a lecturer at the University of Nairobi, Kenya, and at the University of Ibadan, Nigeria. Since 1978, he has specialized in African affairs with the Congressional Research Service (CRS) of the Library of Congress. Currently, he is head of the Europe, Middle East, and Africa section of CRS.

DATE DUE

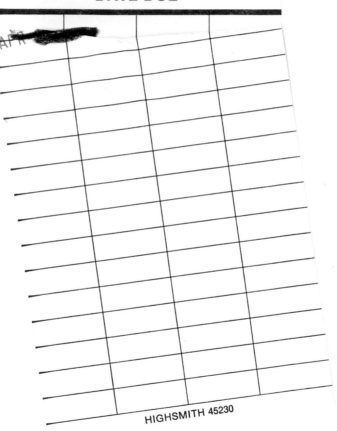

HIGHSMITH 45230